D1479055

TWISTING THE LION'S TAIL

Twisting the Lion's Tail

American Anglophobia between the World Wars

John E. Moser

NEW YORK UNIVERSITY PRESS
Washington Square, New York

© John E. Moser 1999

First published in the U.S.A. in 1999 by
NEW YORK UNIVERSITY PRESS
Washington Square
New York, N.Y. 10003

This book is printed on paper suitable for recycling and
made from fully managed and sustained forest sources.

Library of Congress Cataloging-in-Publication Data
Moser, John E., 1966–
Twisting the lion's tail : American Anglophobia between the
World Wars / John E. Moser.
p. cm.
Includes bibliographical references.
ISBN 0–8147–5615–8
1. Great Britain—Foreign public opinion, American. 2. Public
opinion—United States—History—20th century. 3. United States–
–Relations—Great Britain. 4. Great Britain—Relations—United
States. 5. United States—Politics and government—1901–1953.
I. Title.
E183.8.G7M74   1998
303.48'273041—dc21   98–13175
                                                           CIP

Printed in Great Britain

For my parents
Frank and Judy Moser

Contents

Acknowledgements

This project has its origins in a paper written for a graduate seminar at the University of Illinois at Urbana-Champaign. The director of the seminar was Professor William C. Widenor, and it was he who first suggested the topic of American anglophobia. Soon afterward Bill became my major advisor, my mentor, and finally my friend, and so I'd like to thank him first and foremost. The other two members of my committee, Professors Paul W. Schroeder and Walter Arnstein, also provided invaluable assistance in helping me to turn a seminar paper into a dissertation, and then into a book.

In the process of gathering source material, I am indebted to the kind and capable staffs of all the manuscript collections I visited. Particularly helpful were Sandy Slater and Dean Yates at the Elwyn B. Robinson Department of Special Collections at the University of North Dakota, and Dwight Miller and Dale Mayer of the Herbert Hoover Presidential Library. Finally, Dorothy Brenoel at Thiel College in Greenville, Pennsylvania helped me to locate and obtain some crucial works that came out while I was at the writing stage, even though I had no official affiliation with the college.

Funding for my research came mainly from a Claude R. Lambe Fellowship from the Institute for Humane Studies at George Mason University, as well as an award from the Department of History at the University of Illinois. My work at the Herbert Hoover Presidential Library was supported by a generous grant from the Robert R. McCormick Tribune Foundation. Much of the actual writing took place while I was employed at a Jockey retail outlet at the Grove City Factory Shops, and I would like to thank the manager, Tracy Bonetti, for understanding my occasional need to interrupt my work in order to jot down a sudden thought on a yellow Post-It note.

Finally I wish to thank my dear wife, Monica, for her willingness to live on a graduate student's salary far longer than she deserved, and for her parents, George and Brenda Henry, for their much-needed moral support.

John E. Moser
December 1997

Introduction

In his famous Farewell Address of 1796, George Washington admonished his countrymen to avoid 'excessive dislike' of any particular country. Though he mentioned no specific nation or nations, there is little doubt that Washington had England in mind. Indeed, the first president had some cause for concern that sentimental animosities and attachments might get in the way of a realistic foreign policy. Already by this time a two-party system had begun to develop, and one of the issues which set them apart was their attitude toward Great Britain. On the one hand, the Federalists, with Alexander Hamilton as their leader and New England their main base of support, were inclined, despite the experience of the Revolution, to view the British as potential allies against the radicalism of revolutionary France. Their opponents, the Democratic Republicans, led by Thomas Jefferson and strongest in the South and West, were far less willing to forgive and forget the role of Great Britain as the enemy of American liberty. For them, England was still the hated realm of monarchy, aristocracy, and empire, with whom no long-term accommodation was possible. Washington sided with the former; to his mind, it was far more important that the young Republic establish a rational foreign policy based on a recognition of the national interest. A future alignment with Great Britain might be indicated, but only if it proved in the best interest of the United States, and neither sentimental cultural attachments nor historic prejudices should cloud any such decision.[1]

Yet this was far easier said than done, and the battle between anglophiles and anglophobes would continue well into the twentieth century. Much of this stemmed from the way in which Americans identified their country. In his 1963 book *The American Image of the Old World*, historian Cushing Strout discussed how Americans have traditionally defined themselves by pointing toward Europe and claiming that this is what they were not.[2] Indeed, throughout much of their history Americans have looked upon

1

European politics (if not always European culture) as hope-
lessly backward and inferior, mired in ceaseless conflict
among classes and races, its leaders bent on oppressing their
subjects and making war on their neighbors. The United
States was, by contrast, a land of equality and opportunity,
and, for the most part, of peace. Unlike Europeans, who
waged war for conquest, Americans supposedly eschewed
territorial gains, and when they did claim new lands, they
did so only to bestow on their inhabitants the blessings of
liberty and equality.

Great Britain occupied a unique position within this attractive myth. Unlike, say, the French or the Germans,
Britons and Americans shared a linguistic and cultural heritage. Moreover, until fairly recently a majority of the
American population was of British (including Scottish and
Irish) descent. And though Britain undoubtedly had ties to
the rest of Europe, it was separated by the English Channel
from the warring states of the Continent. Perhaps ironically,
this is part of the reason why Americans were so prone to
judge the British especially harshly – despite the ready
example of America, Great Britain's leaders had steadfastly
refused to abandon their class-based social structure or their
shopworn monarchy. Then there was the Empire, which
rivaled that of ancient Rome in size and certainly exceeded it
in power; if colonialism and wars of conquest were institutions which Americans claimed to despise, the British were
unquestionably closely wedded to both.

It is fairly easy to explain why Americans were anti-British
during the first century of American independence. Great
Britain, after all, had been the nation of George III and Lord
North, the archenemy in every Fourth of July pageant and
school textbook. Until the First World War, the United States
was perpetually in debt to the British, and this, coupled with
the fact that British concerns owned vast stretches of
American land, goes a long way in explaining the economic
resentment felt toward the Mother Country. Furthermore,
Great Britain was the only European power with which the
young nation had to contend on a regular basis, especially
since Canada remained a British possession. French and
Spanish colonialism might have been viewed as just as repre-
hensible as that of the British, but the imperialism of

'perfidious Albion' was the one variety which for Americans hit closest to home.

Yet nineteenth-century anglophobia is not the subject of this study; far more difficult to account for (and thus more interesting) is its persistence into the first half of the twentieth century. The fact is that until the late 1940s American politicians (in certain parts of the country more than others, to be sure) continued to find 'twisting the lion's tail' to be an effective method of being elected to public office, and once in office, of garnering support for or rallying opposition to a wide variety of foreign and domestic initiatives. Students of American foreign relations may find this puzzling, given that Anglo-American relations during the same era (with the exception of a brief period of tension in 1928–1929) had never been better. With the exception of a brief moment of tension over a Venezuelan boundary dispute in the 1890s there had not been a serious crisis between the two English-speaking powers since the Civil War, and from the 1890s onward both sides were pursuing policies designed to bring the U.S. and Britain closer to some sort of understanding. Of the European powers, Britain was the only one not to protest America's war against Spain; and, returning the favor, America was alone among the Great Powers in not condemning Britain's campaign against the Boers of South Africa. Underlying all this was a growing belief in the importance of race and ethnicity; authors as diverse as naval theorist Alfred Thayer Mahan and Congregational minister Josiah Strong spoke not merely of an American mission but of an *Anglo-Saxon* destiny to dominate and uplift the globe.[3] Institutions such as the Rhodes Scholarships and the Pilgrims Trust were set up at the turn of the century to nurture closer relations between the English-speaking nations. For the first time, American elites were abandoning their traditional hostility to Britain and embracing the idea of Anglo-American partnership.

The coming of the World War only strengthened this development. While still hoping for neutrality, Americans overwhelmingly came to support the British cause in the war against Germany. Though they certainly did not approve of the British policy of search and seizure of American ships, they were far more outraged by the sinking of passenger

liners by German submarines. When President Wilson put
his decision to declare war before the Congress, there was
overwhelming support from Democrats and Republicans
alike. Even men like Senators Hiram Johnson (R-CA),
William Borah (R-ID) and Henry Cabot Lodge (R-MA), all of
whom had reputations as serious anglophobes, voted to go to
war alongside Great Britain.[4] Even those who voted against
the war resolution tended to do so more on pacifistic
grounds than on the basis of anti-British sentiment.

U.S. entry into the war naturally brought England and
America even closer. School history textbooks deemed
hostile to Great Britain were revised or removed from the
curriculum; the American Revolution was to be blamed on
George III, a German monarch under the sway of a 'junker
aristocracy.' Robert Underwood Johnson's poem *The Sword
of Lafayette* told readers that 'we girded up to fight not
England, but her Prussian King.' A Federal judge even went
so far as to jail one filmmaker producing a documentary entitled *The Spirit of '76* on the grounds that it portrayed the
British in too negative a light.[5]

Nevertheless, with the end of the war anglophobia made
its return, and did so with a vengeance. But while this new
wave of anti-British feeling appealed to many of the same
themes as the old – to traditional Americanism, to the evils of
monarchy and aristocracy, to the threat of the Royal Navy
and the dangers of British imperialism – it sprang from different origins. In 1921 Henry Seidel Canby addressed the
issue in a perceptive article in *Harper's*. According to Canby,
the main source of American anglophobia was no longer the
upper classes; it now arose from certain ethnic groups in the
U.S. who resented these very elites. These Americans, especially of German and Irish descent, refused to accept the idea
of Anglo-Saxon unity, and saw efforts toward this as an
attempt to marginalize their role in society. Furthermore, by
striking out at the British, the traditional enemy of the U.S.,
they were attempting to assert their own brand of
Americanism. Canby concluded that their anglophobia could
not be cured by any actions on Britain's part, but would
subside only when these more recent immigrants felt they
had reached a position of social equality with the Anglo-
Saxon elite.[6]

Yet while the Irish- and German-American communities constituted a strong political voice in certain sections of the country (parts of the midwest, and some northeastern cities) they did not amount to a particularly potent force in terms of the entire nation. If theirs had been the only voices denouncing the British, their impact would have amounted to little more than an interesting historical footnote, but because this relatively small (though vocal) movement intersected with much broader issues of national concern in the years 1919–1921, the country itself turned decidedly anti-British. As the editors of the liberal *New Republic* pointed out a few years later, 'the pugnacious American is gravely in need of some…tangible and accessible stone on which to whet its patriotic sword.' And since the defeat of Germany, they reminded their readers, 'The British Empire is the only great power…which is in a position seriously to damage or threaten the United States.'[7]

Though the reemergence of anglophobia in American political discourse was certainly noticed by contemporaries, it has been for the most part overlooked by historians, despite the recent growth of scholarly interest in U.S. foreign policy during the interwar period. What little discussion has been made of it has placed it in the context of the general 'isolationism' felt by Americans during these years. Samuel Lubell, for instance, in *The Future of American Politics* (1948) claimed that hatred of England based on ethnicity provided the entire motive force for the isolationist movement. Manfred Jonas, however, in his important 1966 work *Isolationism in America, 1935–1941*, challenges this idea – 'The key to isolationist thinking was not liking or dislike for particular foreign powers,' he wrote, 'but studied indifference to all of them.'[8] Neither gives a completely accurate picture of the relationship between anglophobia and isolationism; the former assumes that all 'isolationists' were anti-British, which is demonstrably untrue. And Jonas, while nearer to the truth than Lubell, never deals with anglophobia as a force independent of isolationism, and at times wholly opposed to it. This merely serves to illustrate the slippery nature of terms such as 'internationalist' and 'isolationist.' Senator Kenneth D. McKellar (D-TN), for example, though a self-styled internationalist who supported Woodrow Wilson's League of

Nations, the World Court, and later Lend-Lease to Great
Britain, was one of the staunchest critics of the British government during the 1920s. On the other hand, Sen.
Gerald Prentiss Nye (R-ND), an ardent anti-interventionist whose
denunciations of British policy during the years 1939–1941
were among the most vehement ever heard on the Senate
floor, had been a bitter opponent of the Anglo-American
arms race which developed in the late 1920s.

It is the thesis of this work that anglophobia not only made
a dramatic reappearance in America at the end of the First
World War, but that a loosely organized coalition of anti-
British forces remained a potent political force until roughly
1948, by which time anglophobia had been almost completely overshadowed by fear of Soviet expansionism. This
coalition originally had at its core a number of groups organized along ethnic lines, such as the Friends of Irish Freedom
and the Steuben Society, but over the years the role of
the foreign-born declined significantly. At the same time,
however, various other factions – progressive Republicans,
mainstream Republicans, southern Democrats, liberals, the
Navy League, Zionists, etc. – entered or abandoned the coalition as determined by their ideological positions, or as
political winds changed direction. Occasionally the coalition
scored a great victory, such as the defeat of the Versailles
Treaty, the election of 'Big Bill' Thompson as mayor of
Chicago in 1927, or the Cruiser Bill of 1928; more commonly, however, the anglophobes found themselves fighting a
losing battle as relations between the United States and Great
Britain grew increasingly close. Nevertheless the accusation
of 'Anglophile' was still viewed as a powerful political weapon
as late as the 1940s. Even during the Second World War,
when the two countries were cooperating to an extent unprecedented in history, there remained among most
Americans a visceral distrust of British motives. U.S. politicians would have to be careful always to safeguard the
interests of the United States, even at the expense of those of
its allies, or face the wrath of the voters in the next election.

Finally, and perhaps most importantly, although anglophobia was not strong enough to prevent the development
of the so-called 'special relationship' between Great Britain
and the U.S., it did have some effect on it. The publicists

who advocated Anglo-Saxon unity in the late 19th century spoke and wrote of a partnership between equals. Moreover, they argued as though the need for such an alignment was self-evident; both England and America were destined to come together in a great racial struggle for control of (and the improvement of) the world. Yet most Americans remained suspicious enough of England that the need for an alliance was anything but self-evident. They had to be convinced, first of all, that Britain was not the chief enemy of the United States, and even then there was the widespread belief that America would be tricked into supporting British imperialism. Indeed, it was only when England appeared weak enough that the U.S. would be the dominant power in any Anglo-American alliance that such an alliance became politically feasible. This, then, is a story of changing attitudes. The signing of the NATO pact in 1949 would have been utterly unthinkable in 1921; Americans at that time could not imagine how any alliance with Great Britain (or any other foreign nation, for that matter) might benefit the United States. How they came to change their mind about the British is the subject of this account.

Our story begins in 1918, when Woodrow Wilson took a serious political risk. After more than a year and a half of war, Americans were increasingly fed up with high taxes, rationing, and other features of the wartime economy. Moreover, the Progressive coalition which had controlled Congress since 1912, and had helped to reelect Wilson in 1916, was rapidly coming apart. Republicans were confidently predicting victory in the 1918 midterm elections, and so to divert national attention away from domestic affairs, Wilson made a fateful announcement. Long an admirer of the English Parliamentary system (it had been the subject of his doctoral dissertation), he proclaimed that the congressional elections would amount to a referendum on his foreign policy – Americans could show their support for Wilson's foreign policy by voting for Democrats. Wilson's strategy backfired badly. Voters still cast their ballots on the basis of local and domestic national issues (particularly Prohibition), and Republicans gained control of both houses of Congress. The president had only succeeded in making himself appear ridiculous on the eve of the scheduled peace conference, to be held in Paris.

Wilson then compounded this with a second major miscalculation; in putting together a delegation to go to Paris (a delegation which he himself would lead) he ignored the Republican-dominated Congress altogether, preferring to appoint career diplomats and reliable members of his administration. For members of the G.O.P., who were not inclined to see eye-to-eye with the president on his foreign policy in any case, this amounted to a direct challenge.

The diplomatic wrangling at the peace conference has been recounted far too often to warrant a great deal of attention here. The story is familiar to most students of the period – Wilson, undercut by the proven unpopularity of his party at home, fighting for his Fourteen Points (especially the League of Nations) against the more experienced European practitioners of power politics, being forced to compromise on his basic principles time and again, but holding firm on, and eventually getting, his League of Nations. But what the president did not realize until it was too late was that his vision of the League was at variance with that of much of the American public, and certainly with that imagined by many Republicans. The new chairman of the Senate Foreign Relations Committee, Henry Cabot Lodge, had a number of reasons for opposing Wilson's League, even though he had been an early advocate of an international peacekeeping organization. First of all, there was an undeniable partisan aspect – as a leader of the opposition party he was in some sense bound to take issue with a treaty introduced by a Democratic president, especially when no congressional input had been invited in the making of the treaty. Secondly, Lodge feared that the League as formulated at Versailles would commit the United States to military intervention in remote areas of the world where there was no clear American interest. On the one hand, this would take power over foreign policy away from Congress, which reserved the sole constitutional right to declare war. On the other hand, the American people themselves might balk at the idea of such foreign interventions, and their support for the League might soon wane. For Lodge, it was better to abandon the League altogether than to make commitments now that might not be kept in the future. Wilson, however, felt that Lodge was acting on purely partisan grounds, and denied both that the League would amount to any diminution of congressional authority or that it obligated the U.S. in advance to any particular course of action. Lodge nevertheless remained unconvinced, and the Treaty of Versailles gained a powerful enemy in the Senate.[9]

Yet defeating the treaty would be far from easy. As Lodge pointed out on the Senate floor in late 1918, Wilson was proceeding on the assumption that 'the Senate…would not and could not dare to reject a treaty of peace.' War-weary Americans were likely to back any effort made toward a final conclusion – they would therefore have to be convinced.[10]

Fortunately for the Massachusetts Republican, there were numerous sources of opposition to Versailles from outside Lodge's own conservative ranks. The most vocal were Irish-Americans, who, though loyal Democrats, demanded that Wilson's call for self-determination of peoples be applied to Ireland as well. In 1917 they formed an effective pressure group, the Friends of Irish Freedom, under the leadership of a Tammany judge, Daniel F. Cohalan. But when the group sent a delegation to Paris to appeal their cause to the president, they were rebuffed, thus turning the organization irrevocably against Versailles. Lodge himself had long sought to cultivate the support of Irish-Americans as a means of luring them away from the Democrats; as early as 1883 his friend George Frisbie Hoar had warned him that '[u]nless we can break this compact foreign vote, we are gone….'[11]

German-Americans were likewise opposed to the treaty, but unlike their Irish counterparts had to be aroused to action. Most had supported the American war effort, and had especially liked Wilson's rhetoric about a generous peace for their Fatherland. Many Germans, however, were targeted for harassment during the war, and were outraged by the harsh terms of Versailles. Yet though they were reluctant to speak out in protest (they were concerned lest opponents of the treaty might be labeled 'Hun sympathizers' if they received overt German support), Senators from areas heavily populated by German-Americans knew exactly what their constituents thought about the treaty. In May 1919 a small group formed the Steuben Society of America, which promised to 'get' those who had 'gotten' German-Americans during the war, and furthermore guaranteed three million votes to any opponent of the League who would run for president in 1920.[12]

Then there were the western progressives, most of whom were nominally Republican but far more populist in their political leanings. Senators such as William Borah (R-ID), Robert La Follette (R-WI), Hiram Johnson (R-CA) and George Norris (R-NE) rejected Wilson's notion that the Old World could be redeemed by the New. Europe was unreformable, and would remain forever mired in its 'balance of power' politics and the wars which they produced. Joined by populist Democrats such as Tom Watson of Georgia and James A. Reed of Missouri, they formed the core of a group which came to be known as 'Irreconcilables,' those who (unlike Lodge) vowed their opposition to *any* sort of League of Nations.

Finally, and perhaps most wounding to Wilson, there was the defection of many American liberals, those whom Thomas J. Knock calls the 'progressive internationalists.' Prominent journalists and intellectuals such as Herbert S. Croly, Oswald Garrison Villard, Amos Pinchot, and Upton Sinclair had played an important role in the so-called 'Coalition of 1916,' which had ensured the reelection of Wilson. They had welcomed U.S. entry into the war as an attempt to replace European-style power politics with a new, progressive world order, and to this end they had been enthusiastic supporters of the League of Nations. By 1919, however, the relationship between the progressive internationalists and Wilson had cooled considerably. The liberals deeply resented wartime violations of civil liberties such as the Espionage Act of 1917, as well as the increasing intolerance directed toward German-Americans. Their sense of disillusionment deepened when Wilson agreed to send U.S. forces to intervene in revolutionary Russia, but the final break came over Versailles, which they believed was a surrender of the ideals for which America had fought. In the liberal journal the *Nation*, for instance, J. A. Hobson referred to the League as provided for in the treaty as 'A New Holy Alliance,' while Oswald Garrison Villard called it a peace of 'intrigue, selfish aggression, and naked imperialism.' Like the Irish-Americans, they believed an independent Ireland ought to be part of any peace settlement, while like German-Americans they felt the terms of Versailles were far too harsh for Germany.[13]

Lodge, therefore, had the building blocks of an anti-Versailles coalition practically laid out before him; all he needed was some kind of mortar to bring them together. While all the above-mentioned groups had grievances against the treaty, each one emphasized different aspects, and while most wanted some kind of League of Nations, others rejected the concept out of hand. Moreover, Republicans had to find some kind of rationale for their opposition that could be put before the public. After all, Lodge could hardly tell his constituents the real reason why he objected to the League; namely, that it was a bad idea because Americans could not be counted upon to live up to their obligations. What was required was a common ground of attack which would also have some popular appeal. An anti-British strategy could do just that. Each of the groups opposed to Versailles had some grievance against Great Britain as well; Irish- and German-Americans saw England as the prime enemy of their respective homelands; progressives and populists distrusted the 'balance of power' policies that Great Britain represented, and furthermore they associated the British with 'the interests,' international bankers and businessmen from the Northeast; liberals tended to focus on the British Empire, not only in Ireland but in India and Egypt as well.

Indeed, it seemed that the only part of the coalition without any particular antipathy toward the British were the Republicans themselves. After all, it had been under the Republican administrations of McKinley, Roosevelt and Taft that Anglo-American relations had moved from barely-restrained mutual hostility to something approaching friendship. Indeed, in 1900 the Democratic party platform had included a plank attacking 'the ill-concealed Republican alliance with England.' From 1915 to 1917 many members of the G.O.P. (including Lodge and Roosevelt) had been far more eager even than Wilson to enter the war on Great Britain's side.[14] But while Lodge and his allies in the Senate

were initially reluctant to participate in a new orgy of
Britain-baiting, it soon became obvious that it was by far the
most successful strategy for rallying the anti-Versailles
forces.[15]

Therefore the Senate battle against the Treaty of
Versailles soon became a battle against Great Britain. Peter
Gerry (D-RI) and David I. Walsh (D-MA) demanded self-
determination and independence for Ireland, while Albert
B. Fall (R-NM) claimed that under the League the United
States would be obliged to send troops to help quell unrest
on the Emerald Isle. Robert La Follette displayed maps
showing the colonial gains which the British would make
under the treaty, and chided Wilson for wanting the United
States to associate with such an imperialist power. Borah announced that membership in the League of Nations would
force America 'to give back to George V what it took away
from George III.' But the most compelling argument was
that the League itself was stacked in Britain's favor, since in
the League assembly not only would Great Britain have a
vote, but Canada, Australia, New Zealand, South Africa, and
India would have votes as well. Since all five were dominions
in the British Empire, Lodge maintained, Great Britain
would not command one vote but six. This led Borah to call
the League 'the greatest triumph for English diplomacy in
three centuries of English diplomatic life,' a sentiment
echoed by many others in the Senate and in the press.[16]

Against this formidable anti-British coalition the Treaty of
Versailles stood no chance. Wilson, however, refused any
compromise with his opponents, and instructed those
Democrats still loyal to him not to support any amendments
or reservations to the treaty – for the president, a watered-
down league was worse than no league at all. Instead he
embarked on a nationwide speaking tour of the country,
making a direct popular appeal; yet this ended in disaster
when he was overcome by a debilitating stroke during a stop
in Pueblo, Colorado. When it came time for the Senate to act
on the treaty, the vote to ratify fell well short of the required
two-thirds, thus leaving the United States out of the League
of Nations for which Wilson had fought at Paris. Many historians have seen this as the triumph of 'isolationism' over
'internationalism,' but the terms of the debate were not

nearly so simple. Of the forces aligned against Versailles, only a relative few – the so-called 'irreconcilables' – were opposed to any sort of League.[17] The Irish would most likely have stuck by Wilson had he chosen to speak up for their cause, while Lodge and many of his fellow Republicans wanted nothing more than a means by which the U.S. might opt out of actions mandated by the League. The Germans and the liberals, meanwhile, were far more outraged over Germany's fate at the peace table than they were by the terms of the League Covenant.[18] Most of these groups supported an international role for the United States; what they rejected was the notion that the only way this role could be performed was through membership in a league dominated by Great Britain. In short, it was anglophobia, and not isolationism, that ultimately defeated the Treaty of Versailles.

The ashes of the treaty fight were still smoldering as the 1920 presidential campaign got underway. By tapping springs of anti-British sentiment in the U.S., Republicans had managed to discredit Wilsonian foreign policy, and dealt the ailing president the worst political defeat of his life. The only questions which remained were whether the anti-British coalition could be held together and, more importantly, whether it could be used to put a Republican in the White House. It seemed that every group within the coalition had its own choice. The irreconcilables wanted Hiram Johnson, while some midwesterners backed Herbert Hoover, who had gained substantial popularity administering U.S. food relief in postwar Europe. German-Americans became more vocal after the defeat of the Versailles Treaty. The Committee of 96 was formed in early 1920 'to solidify political opinion among Americans of German descent and to create voting units, irrespective of party affiliations in opposition to the Invisible Government'; their choice for Republican candidate was Robert La Follette.[19]

Yet none of these men would receive the G.O.P.'s official nod, mainly because the party's nominating convention remained in the hands of northeastern conservatives who distrusted progressives such as Johnson and La Follette. Their choice went instead to Senator Warren G. Harding of Ohio, who had a reputation for being little more than an average party hack. George Sylvester Viereck, a founding member of the Committee of 96, was particularly unimpressed: upon hearing the news, he wrote, 'The best that can be said for him is that there is little to be said against him.' But what was most important was that he had been an opponent of the League, and when the Democrats nominated a Wilsonian, Governor James Cox (also of Ohio), Viereck and his group officially endorsed Harding.[20]

The support of Johnson and the progressives who had rallied to him was deemed to be vital as well, since most Republicans blamed Wilson's reelection on the California Senator's failure to endorse Charles Evans Hughes in 1916. As a result, Harding based much of his campaign on attacking the League of Nations, but at the same time he had to be careful not to alienate his original northeastern base of support by espousing staunch isolationism. This political highwire-act prompted Sir Arthur Willert, chief Washington correspondent for the London *Times*, to write that Harding 'was not as provincial as might be thought.' Nevertheless, he added, the Ohioan was at heart 'a large and succulent jelly-fish' who was 'susceptible to discipline by the party machine.'[21]

As for Cox, his continuing loyalty to Wilson's League guaranteed that the Democrats would lose the anti-British vote. Irish-Americans, still under the leadership of Daniel Cohalan and his Friends of Irish Freedom, moved *en masse* into the Republican camp, as did progressives, thus (temporarily) healing the split between them and the conservatives that had plagued the G.O.P. since the Taft administration. George Sylvester Viereck, now widely considered the unofficial spokesman of all German-American groups, promised six million of his countrymen's votes for Harding. The liberals, meanwhile, found neither the conservative Harding nor the pro-League Cox acceptable, and they vowed to stay home on Election Day.

Cox decided therefore to try an appeal to the 'pro-American' vote. He accused immigrant groups of putting the interests of foreign countries ahead of those of the United States. His vice presidential candidate, Assistant Navy Secretary Franklin D. Roosevelt, accused Republican leaders of pandering to the 'hyphenated vote,' and seeking the support of 'un-American elements in the electorate.'[22] On the night before the election, Cox stated his position bluntly – 'Every traitor in America will vote tomorrow for Warren G. Harding.' It was an astounding shift in loyalties. The Republicans, the party of immigration restriction and Prohibition, had the backing of most American immigrants, while the Democrats, the party of 'rum, Romanism, and rebellion,' had become the party of Americanism and Anglo-Saxondom. It was a strategy which doomed the Democrats to failure, for outside of the South nearly all the Anglo-Saxons remained staunchly with the G.O.P. Unsurprisingly, Harding won in a landslide.[23]

Thus, by the end of 1920 anglophobia had returned to American political life after its wartime hiatus, and had indeed emerged as a force potent enough both to block Versailles and to put a Republican in the White House. Yet though it proved useful to Republicans, it also proved impossible for them to control. The lack of a natural tie between the anti-British groups and the G.O.P. appeared even during the League fight, when Rhode Island Democrat Peter Gerry introduced a reservation to the Versailles treaty demanding self-determination for Ireland. Though Lodge and most Republican conservatives fought against this – one of their earlier reservations had been designed to keep domestic issues like the Irish question from becoming subjects for League consideration – the reservation passed with the support of northern Democrats and progressive Republicans.[24]

As election day approached, a confident Harding even made some effort to distance himself from the anti-British forces who had rallied to his campaign. On September 18 the Republican candidate asserted that Ireland was a matter for the English to settle, 'not a question for official America.' Furthermore, he criticized 'meddling abroad' on the grounds that it divided Americans into rival groups which are 'led away' by ethnic agitators from 'America first' to 'hyphen first.'[25] The anti-British coalition had proved useful in thwarting Wilson's plans and splitting the Democrats, but it must not be allowed to interfere with foreign policy under a Republican administration. But like the genie released from its bottle, the coalition, once called into existence, would be just as difficult for the G.O.P. to control as it had been for the Democrats to contend with. Anglophobia would remain a potent force in the 1920s, as it would until the early years of the Cold War.

1 'The Most Imperialistic Nation on Earth'

It was not long after the inauguration of Warren G. Harding and the opening of the 67th Congress that the curious ambivalence of the Republican party toward Great Britain became apparent. On the one hand, G.O.P. leaders were faced with the undeniable fact that their victory in 1920 had been due in large part to their success in portraying the Wilson administration as stooges of the British. Yet on the other hand most Republicans, especially those of the Northeast, could not help but feel a certain sense of solidarity with the British. After all, the G.O.P. was still heavily dominated by old-stock Americans of English and Scottish descent, and these familial and cultural ties were not ones that could easily be dismissed. Moreover, Republican politicians from the Northeast represented states that were highly dependent on overseas trade, and there was no getting around the fact that Great Britain was by far America's best international trading partner, especially now that Germany's economy was in shambles.

Nowhere is this ambivalence more apparent than in the attitude of Henry Cabot Lodge, who would remain chairman of the Senate Foreign Relations Committee until his death in 1924. He certainly had a reputation for intense anglophobia; to some extent this was indeed a prerequisite for any seeker of statewide office in Massachusetts, given the size and political strength of the Irish-American community in that state. Yet at the same time it would be doing Lodge an injustice to attribute all of his anglophobia to purely political motives. According to William C. Widenor, his hostility to Great Britain was 'traditional' as well. As an historian, Lodge knew full well that Britain had for years taken advantage of America's vulnerability at sea, and for this reason he advocated the construction of a navy sufficient to defend the nation's trade. Indeed, for Lodge to be able to stand up to Britain was the cornerstone of an effective foreign policy. In

his words, 'Englishmen are prone to mistake civility for ser-
vility, and become offensive, whereas if they are treated with
indifference, rebuke, or even rudeness, they are apt to be re-
spectful and polite.'[1]

But there were substantial differences between the anglophobia of Lodge and that of, say, Hiram Johnson or William
Borah. Lodge never attacked British institutions such as the
monarchy, aristocracy, or the empire, all of which were favorite targets of more visceral anglophobes. He even
described himself as 'in…standards and fashions essentially
English.' He was an ardent admirer of British imperialism
(indeed, he counted among his friends imperialism's arch-
apologist, Rudyard Kipling) and believed that the foundation
of a stable international order was 'a good understanding of
all English-speaking peoples.'[2] In these sentiments Lodge
could very well have spoken for many in the Harding administration.

Certainly, Harding's cabinet choices seemed almost calculated to offend the anti-British sectors of the Republican
coalition of 1920. With the exception of Albert B. Fall, the
president's choice for Secretary of the Interior, there was not
an anglophobe among them. Andrew Mellon, appointed
Secretary of the Treasury, had a reputation as one of the
hated international bankers who had done so much to move
the U.S. so close to Britain during the war, and was moreover widely believed to support the cancellation of Allied war
debts. Charles Evans Hughes, Harding's nominee for
Secretary of State, was also suspect; it was only with a great
deal of prodding that he had been persuaded to drop his
support for U.S. membership in the purportedly British-
dominated League of Nations.[3]

But it was Harding's choice to fill the position of Secretary
of Commerce that aroused the most contempt among
American anglophobes. During his years as a partner in the
English mining firm Bewick, Moreing & Company, Herbert
Hoover had maintained a residence near London from
November 1901 to July 1908. This alone was enough to call
his loyalty into question. Claims soon circulated that he had
at one point begun the process of becoming an English
citizen, and these were bolstered by the appearance of
Hoover's name on a voters' list in Kensington. During the

Senate debates surrounding his confirmation, Tom Watson (D-GA) referred to him derisively as an 'Englishman.' Hiram Johnson (R-CA) went so far as to call him a latter-day 'Benedict Arnold,' a puppet of the House of Morgan and, through them, the British government.[4] Such accusations, however, were soon found to be groundless, and Hoover was quickly confirmed.

Unsurprisingly, Republican foreign policy toward Great Britain reflected the conflict of anglophobia vs. anglophilia which existed within the G.O.P. Problems which might threaten the Anglo-American trading relationship were to be dealt with in good order, but no long-term commitments were to be made. In this curious arrangement, characterized in Michael Hogan's pivotal work as an 'informal entente,' the Departments of the Treasury and Commerce were to play a far more important role than the traditional makers of foreign policy in State.[5] Those engaged in overseas trade and international investment were, after all, not fundamentally hostile toward Great Britain – there might be an occasional squabble over oil rights or foreign markets, but on the whole American merchants sought to emulate the British, not destroy them or even drive them out. If the British were often viewed as rivals, the Anglo-American trade rivalry was for the most part a friendly one in the 1920s; indeed, it was only when His Majesty's Government was viewed as giving unfair advantage to British corporations, as was the case with merchant shipping and the rubber industry, that American businessmen truly cried foul. It was easy for American merchants and bankers to be magnanimous, since, given the trade statistics of the period, they had every reason to believe that time was on their side. Foreign trade, which had amounted to only $4.5 billion in 1913, totalled $10.2 billion by 1929, while America's share of world exports increased from 12.4 percent to 16 percent. Britain's share, meanwhile, slipped from 15.4 percent in 1913 to 11.8 percent in 1929.[6]

In the realm of politics, however, the situation was considerably messier, for the feeling of kinship which international traders and bankers (nearly all of them Republicans and Anglo-Saxons) possessed toward the British was one that was not shared by large sectors of the population. Though publicly Democrats were still denouncing the

German-Americans and Irish 'Sinn Feiners' who had helped
to elevate Harding to the presidency, many privately realized that they had made a grave tactical error in alienating
anti-British forces in 1919–1920. They were eager to reclaim
for their party the standard of anglophobia, and prepared
to seize on any administration approach to the British as evidence of un-American treachery. One early example of this
came in the spring of 1921. On June 7 Admiral William S.
Sims of the U.S. Navy spoke at a luncheon given by the
London chapter of the English-Speaking Union. In his
address he questioned the patriotism of Americans who had
protested British policy in Ireland during the war and its
aftermath:

> There are many in our country who technically are
> Americans, some of them naturalized and born here, but
> none of them Americans at all. They are Americans when
> they want money, but Sinn Feiners when on the platform.
> They are making war on America today. The simple truth
> of it is that they have the blood of English and American
> boys on their hands for the obstructions they placed in the
> way of the most effective operation of the Allied Naval
> forces during the war. They are like zebras, either black
> horses with white stripes or white horses with black stripes.
> But we knew they are not horses – they are asses; but each
> of these asses has a vote and there are lots of them.[7]

For these remarks Sims was immediately taken to task on
the floor of Congress, but by Democrats, not Republicans. In
the House, Rep. Andrew Gallivan (D-MA) introduced legislation to forbid the admiral from returning to the U.S.,
declaring him 'an undesirable alien.' In the Senate, meanwhile, Thomas J. Walsh (D-MT) promised that Sims would
be 'properly trimmed on his return,' and called for an investigation not only of the so-called 'Jackass Speech,' but also
of the English-Speaking Union, which he denounced as 'a
propagandist organization…to undo the work of the
Revolution and restore our country as, or transmute it into,
part of the British Empire.'[8]

Nor was the Republican party united in support of cooperation with Britain. Those of the middle west, who were not
as reliant on overseas markets as their northeastern counter-

parts, were not about to support any close relationship with England. And for western progressives such as Robert La Follette of Wisconsin, William E. Borah of Idaho, and Hiram Johnson of California, Great Britain remained the epitome of all that was corrupt in international politics. Such a combination made any attempt to approach Congress on foreign policy politically risky, to say the least. To the extent that it was feasible, therefore, the Anglo-American relationship, as indeed all foreign relations, had to remain in the hands of the administration and away from the unstable political climate of the House and Senate. Any sort of formal understanding which involved real commitments was thus out of the question, even if the administrations of the 1920s had wanted one.

Yet there were nonetheless several outstanding issues between the U.S. and Great Britain that could not be settled merely by business deals and gentlemen's agreements, and among these the most immediate was the ongoing unrest in Ireland. American concern with the Irish question ran far deeper than simply among the sons and daughters of Erin living in the United States; of course, Irish-Americans could be counted on to denounce 'the savage efforts of England,' but Americans in general were nearly unanimous in support of Irish independence.[9] Midwestern progressives, even those whose districts lay hundreds of miles from any substantial community of Irish-Americans, were quick to cite Ireland as the most egregious example of British imperialism. Even conservatives such as Lodge, who viewed the Empire as a great civilizing force, were unwilling to defend the 'White Man's Burden' in a part of the world whose inhabitants were themselves white. They realized, moreover, that the continued British domination of Ireland provided a ready issue for demagogues and troublemakers to exploit.

Congress began openly supporting efforts toward Irish independence shortly after the end of the war. In March 1919 both the House and Senate passed a resolution extending recognition to Sinn Fein, and by late 1920 eleven senators and thirteen congressmen (as well as five governors, the mayors of fifteen major cities, and a host of Catholic and Protestant clergy) had joined the American Committee for Relief in Ireland. On St. Patrick's Day of 1921, the committee launched a massive fundraising effort aimed at raising $10 million, ostensibly to help rebuild Ireland in the wake of the civil war.[10]

The popularity of the movement placed the Harding administration in a bit of a quandary. On the one hand, the president realized that it was politically unwise to refuse to endorse the committee's goals. At the same time, however, Harding believed Ireland to be a 'purely British internal affair,' and certainly hoped to avoid any kind of international incident. Moreover, the U.S. consul in Dublin continued to claim that the situation in Ireland was not all that bad. Nevertheless, the British ambassador, Auckland Geddes, privately feared that a failure by the State Department to issue some sort of protest to London might lead to a backlash by anti-British forces, and that the reasonably pro-British Hughes might be replaced with an anglophobe such as Interior Secretary Albert B. Fall.[11]

The climax came in June 1921, when Robert La Follette (R-WI), armed with a report by the American Commission on Conditions in Ireland, introduced a joint resolution to recognize an independent Irish state. Comparing Britain's leaders to 'the Tories of 1776,' La Follette charged them with 'barbaric cruelty and oppression which are almost beyond belief.' Nebraska Progressive George Norris joined in the assault, claiming that conditions in Ireland had 'no parallel…in civilization.' Kenneth McKellar (D-TN) suggested stopping all American oil shipments to Great Britain until she agreed to grant independence. The resolution was narrowly defeated, but it did show the strength of anti-British sentiment in Congress as well as the ability of diverse anti-administration elements to use Ireland as a rallying point.[12] Later that year Britain signed an agreement partitioning Ireland, granting most of the island the status of 'Free State,' with only symbolic ties to Britain. The American press enthusiastically endorsed the agreement: the St. Louis *Globe-Democrat* wrote that '"Twisting the lion's tail" will no longer appeal to the Irish vote,' and even predicted that Irish-Americans would suddenly turn pro-English. While this was wishful thinking – Daniel Cohalan of the Friends of Irish Freedom called the deal an attempt to prop up 'the tottering British Empire for the moment by attaching to it an apparently satisfied Ireland' – there is no doubt that for the vast majority of Americans the creation of the Irish Free State eliminated the issue of Ireland as a bone of contention between the U.S. and Great Britain.[13]

Some progressives, realizing that they were losing Ireland as an anti-British issue, attempted to focus attention on India instead. The cause of independence for India had begun to grow in popularity by the end of 1921, evoking concern by Ambassador Geddes that American support might 'make the revolutionary and rebellious elements in India less easy to deal with.' The movement gathered steam in 1922 with the founding of the India Relief Fund, which aimed at raising money to cope with a famine in that country – a famine which the British even denied was taking place.[14]

Yet while Indian independence won support among many American liberals – it was endorsed by Samuel Gompers' American Federation of Labor and a number of church groups – it failed to evoke any real emotion among the American public, and few politicians would pay serious attention to India until the 1940s. India, unlike Ireland, appeared totally foreign to observers from the U.S., and there was virtually no Indian-American community to be won over. Most Americans seemed to second the judgment of the New York *Tribune*, which denounced 'meddling' in relations between Great Britain and India.[15]

If the Irish situation generated high emotions on this side of the Atlantic, the Anglo-Irish agreement for the most part settled the issue. The same cannot be said for the developing naval rivalry between the U.S. and Great Britain, which in the words of one historian promised to 'make the Anglo-German competition of the early 1900s look like a lobster quadrille.'[16] The Republican Congress as well as certain other sectors of anti-British opinion had immediately denounced the Wilson administration's 1919 naval 'truce' with the British, and by 1920 Congress was prepared to toss it aside altogether. Naval authorities in the autumn of that year called for a three-year naval building program of 88 vessels, including three battleships, one battle cruiser, 30 light cruisers, and four aircraft carriers. The navy claimed that the expansion was necessary due to the end of the Anglo-German deadlock, which had presumably been the only consideration which had prevented the full force of the Royal Navy from being set loose against the commerce of the United States. 'Every great commercial rival of the British Empire has eventually found itself at war with Great Britain,' a memorandum circulated by the Navy asserted, 'and has been defeated.' On the floor of the House, congressmen such as H. C. Pell (D-NY) argued that the United States now found itself in 'Germany's position as the chief enemy of England,' and that the time was ripe for America to seize 'the maritime control of the world.' It was an argument that would be repeated many times before the end of the decade.[17]

The Harding administration by and large supported naval expansion, though a number of prominent Republicans (among them Theodore Roosevelt and Henry Cabot Lodge) believed that an essential harmony of interests between the English-speaking powers made it unnecessary for America to have a fleet equal to that of Great Britain. Harding himself announced soon after his inauguration that he favored building the 'most powerful navy in the world.'[18]

Initially, at least, it appeared that Harding would get his wish. When Secretary of the Navy Edwin Denby approached the House for approval of the three-year building plan, he received all that he had hoped for. The announcement in March that Great Britain had begun to work on four 'super-dreadnoughts' (of the *Hood* class) appeared to signal the beginning of a new naval race. Moreover, the continued existence of the Anglo-Japanese Alliance, which tied Great Britain to the one power which Americans most despised, remained a significant irritation. Representative Fred Britten (R-IL) argued persuasively that it was time to break Wilson's naval truce, since to continue it would 'insure to Britain permanent leadership of the seas.' The Naval Appropriation Bill of 1921 passed in April by a vote of 212–15.[19]

However, though it seemed that most Americans supported the idea of having a navy 'second to none,' they were far less interested in actually building the ships necessary to match the Royal Navy. Senator William Borah (R-ID) offered a unique solution to this dilemma – invite the world's leading naval powers to a disarmament conference in which the British might be persuaded to come down to the level of the U.S. Navy. Borah's proposal has been explained in a variety of ways: a reflection of a desire to reduce government expenditures, the hope of finding in disarmament a workable substitute for the League of Nations, his belief that the battleship was obsolete as a weapon of war, or his fear that a large navy would draw the United States into a host of foreign quarrels. There is no doubt some validity to all of these, but the Idaho progressive's personal antipathy toward the British cannot be ignored as a motive. Borah evidently did not believe that the British would ever consent to a disarmament conference, particularly one in which they would be obliged to grant naval parity to the U.S. This would expose the British as hopeless militarists, further proof that membership in the League of Nations would have been a tragic mistake.[20]

No matter what Borah's motives, the idea of a naval disarmament conference quickly caught on among large sections of the American public. The National League of Women Voters, the Federal Council of Churches of Christ, the American Federation of Labor, the National Grange, and a host of other organizations lined up behind the Borah proposal. Even more damaging for the Navy's building plan was the considerable opposition to large military expenditures within the administration itself. Treasury Secretary Mellon claimed that increased arms spending threatened his campaign for greater economy in government. Hoover warned that the building program would drain off capital much needed for postwar development, while Secretary of State Hughes felt that it would serve only to strengthen the hated Anglo-Japanese alliance.[21]

Nonetheless, Harding, buoyed by the passage of the naval bill in the House, announced his opposition to Borah's proposal, arguing that the U.S. should only contemplate a disarmament conference after having built 'the best [fleet] that there is for the advance of our commerce.' Yet by mid-May it was becoming increasingly clear to the President that the Senate would pass the Borah resolution. Progressives embraced the idea enthusiastically, and even many conservative Republicans were being overwhelmed by constituent pressure for disarmament. Democrats, for their part, welcomed it as an opportunity to embarrass the administration. Fearing the end of the naval program and a serious political defeat, Harding struck a deal with Borah – if Borah would endorse the Naval Appropriation Bill, pro-administration Republicans would agree to back the Borah resolution. On May 25 the resolution passed unanimously.[22]

But Borah had badly miscalculated the willingness of both the Harding administration and the British to attend a conference. For Hughes, a conference represented the best opportunity to get Britain to renounce the Anglo-Japanese alliance, and immediately he began to pressure the Foreign Office into doing so. In June he warned Ambassador Geddes that any renewal of the alliance 'could be seized upon by the enemies of Great Britain as indicating an attitude of disregard of…the interests of this country,' and that in particular it might help generate support for recognition of Irish independence, which was before Congress at the time.[23] The British, however, required little convincing, for since the end of the war they had been under intense pressure from the Dominions, especially Australia and Canada, to dump the alliance. In fact, since February the British had even been putting out feelers for some sort of conference. Harding, however, had rebuffed them, fearing that accepting an invitation from the British might inflame anglophobe sentiment in the U.S.[24] To be sure, London had no stomach for an Anglo-American naval race, but saw an even more beneficial outcome for the conference – an arrangement involving not only Japan but the United States to help protect British interests in Asia.

Of the actual conference proceedings, little need concern us here. Both the British and the Americans pledged themselves to destroy a number of capital ships, and the resultant Five Power Pact limited the size of the British, U.S., Japanese, French, and Italian fleets to a tonnage ratio of 5 : 5 : 3 : 1.75 : 1.75 ratio respectively. Far more controversial was the Four Power Pact, a consultative agreement between the U.S., Britain, Japan and France aimed at defending the status quo in Asia.[25] The pact represented the complete opposite of Borah's hopes – instead of his conference proposal being brushed aside by British warmongers, and thus widening the gulf between the U.S. and Britain, it had actually brought the English-speaking powers closer together. As he wrote a friend, he had asked for bread, but had been offered a stone.[26]

As the Washington treaties went before the Senate for ratification, the question of disarmament was pushed aside in favor of a lengthy debate over just how closely the Four Power Pact bound the United States to Great Britain. Opposition came mainly from the old irreconcilables of the fight against the League, but these were also joined by a number of Wilsonian Democrats who felt that the pact was a weak Republican substitute for the League. What seemed to unite both groups was a common willingness to exploit anglophobic sentiment in their rhetoric.

Anti-British arguments against the Four Power Pact generally proceeded in two directions, both of which revealed a great deal about American views not only toward the British, but regarding international affairs in general. They would also remain the standard arguments against cooperation with England until the late 1940s. The first line of attack was to question the morality of aligning with the world's most powerful empire. The Friends of Irish Freedom, for example, passed a resolution denying that any disarmament could take place 'until the system of Imperialism of which England is the great representative shall be destroyed.' In the Senate, Georgia Democrat Tom Watson maintained that ratification would amount to 'consent to the robberies she [Britain] committed during the Great War,' a theme echoed by James E. Reed (D-MO), A. Owsley Stanley (D-KY), and Morris Sheppard (D-TX), as well as progressive Republicans Hiram Johnson and Robert La Follette. Borah, who was now in the ironic position of fighting the fruits of the conference which he in large part had engineered, wrote, 'We are becoming an ally of the most imperialistic nation on earth....'[27] What was strangely absent was any attempt to define American interests abroad or to question why these interests were not served by an Anglo-American partnership. This stood in stark contrast to the foreign policy of most states of the time; for centuries England had been courted as an ally due to her powerful strategic and economic position in the world, but what for most countries appeared attractive was viewed as a liability by American anglophobes. James Reed displayed maps of the world showing the extent of British possessions ('small red pox' which have 'broken out all over the Pacific Ocean'), not for the purpose of showing England's value as an ally, but to attack the notion of any alignment with such a greedy imperialist power.[28]

The other strategy employed by the pact's opponents was directed less toward the British themselves than toward those members of the State Department who negotiated the agreement on the American side. At best, U.S. diplomats were portrayed as naive incompetents, easily tricked by the more experienced and cunning emissaries of England – in James Reed's words, 'somebody put something over on these delegates of ours.' At worst – and this was far more common – American diplomats were accused of being anglophiles, culturally and philosophically disposed toward aligning their country with Great Britain. Some suggested that they had an even more sinister motive, that they were involved in a conspiracy to bring the United States back into the British Empire. John K. Shields (D-TN) fulminated against the Rhodes scholarship program, which he claimed was designed to inculcate promising young Americans with British values, so that they might work toward a union of the English-speaking countries upon their return to America. La Follette and Watson, meanwhile, saw the dark hand of 'the interests,' especially international bankers such as the House of Morgan. La Follette – the great hero of American liberalism – even proposed an investigation of all Englishmen who had been living in the U.S. for more than five years without applying for citizenship, on the theory that they were carrying on subversive activities.[29]

If the cause of the pact's enemies was ultimately doomed, this was not due to any great outpouring of support for Anglo-American partnership. Indeed, conspicuously absent from the speeches of those who supported the pact was any attempt to defend the British Empire or the much-maligned diplomats of the State Department. Lodge, who spearheaded the ratification efforts, spent most of his time on the Senate floor assuring his colleagues that the agreement in no way committed the United States to any particular course of action. This amounted to a tacit endorsement of the opposition's argument that any binding agreement with the British was unacceptable.

But what virtually ensured that the pact would be ratified was Lodge's insistence, which the Senate ultimately found persuasive, that all the treaties concluded at Washington were inseparable. The Senate could therefore not reject the Four Power Pact without also cancelling the Five Power Agreement for Naval Limitation. This most senators, even many with a reputation for anglophobia, were unwilling to do, given the popularity of the disaramament issue. For most Americans, the naval limitation agreement was the only important result of the Washington Conference – the rest was of no particular concern. (The Irish- and German-American communities were notable exceptions to this; Sen. John Williams [D-MS], one of the few genuine anglophiles in the Senate, lamented, 'it is a great pity that Great Britain is a party to it, because if she were not, all the German-American and Irish-American opposition to it would have ceased long ago.'[30]) Groups ranging from the National Milk Producers' Federation to the Parent-Teachers' Association gave their unqualified endorsement. The most important organs of the liberal press – the *Nation* and the *New Republic* – concurred; Bruce Bliven, editor of the latter journal, explained his departure from the anti-British line of 1919 by distinguishing between the immorality of the British Empire and 'the traditional fair-play spirit…of the Englishman.' Faced with such overwhelming popular support, the anti-British coalition of 1919–1920 split. The core of the irreconcilable group – Borah, Johnson, Reed, Watson, et al. – remained true to their anglophobic instincts, as did some senators whose constituencies included many of Irish descent (Peter Gerry [D-RI] and David I. Walsh [D-MA]). Pro-administration Republicans, meanwhile, voted for the treaty, eliciting howls of protest from those who had sided with them against the League. They were joined by most liberals and progressives, who felt that a rapprochement with Britain was an acceptable price to pay for genuine disarmament. On March 25 the Four Power Treaty passed the Senate by a vote of 67 to 27 – the Five Power Pact passed 74 to 1, with only Joseph France (R-MD), an ardent supporter of naval armaments, dissenting.[31] For Hiram Johnson, the vote marked the first step down a treacherous path toward Anglo-American union. Complaining about Ambassador Geddes' open lobbying efforts on behalf of ratification, a disgusted Johnson wrote his son the day after the vote:

How the times have changed! A few years ago, if the British
ambassador had gone about the country making speeches
on a matter pending before the national legislature, there
would have been an outcry that would have resulted forth-
with in the Ambassador's recall.... Today, every public
body does him homage..., creeps and crawls and kisses the
garment of the representative of England.[32]

Another issue which would perennially crop up to poison
Anglo-American relations until the 1940s was that of the
debts stemming from the First World War. While most
European nations owed substantial amounts to the U.S., the
British debt resulted in particular animosity because of its
sheer size. War debts became a campaign issue as early as
1920, when Republicans claimed that their opponents had
lent vast sums with little or no security, and were now unable
even to collect the interest on them. British and French attempts to secure cancellation of the debt merely served to
enhance the image of slick European diplomats 'bambooz-
ling' a naive Wilson. Many Republicans, especially business
leaders, recognized that cancellation of the debt would con-
tribute to the restoration of European purchasing power,
and thus help American exports, but such a stand was politically unfeasible given the high level of taxation. Moreover,
the Allies, especially Great Britain, were believed to have
profited so greatly from the war that repayment should not
have been a problem. There was also the fear in 1921 that if
the British debt were forgiven, the British might spend the
extra money on another naval increase; the *Baltimore Sun*
claimed that it would be foolish indeed 'to turn over
$10,000,000,000 to European governments to be squan-
dered in projects damaging to this country, [and] to the
world in general.'[33]
    After Harding's inauguration, Treasury Secretary Mellon
went before Congress asking for plenary powers to arrange
a war debt settlement, but the legislature was unwilling to
turn the matter over completely to an arm of the executive.
Therefore, on February 9, 1922, Congress passed a bill creating the World War Foreign Debt Commission, made up of
eight members and headed by Mellon. Other members of
the committee were to be appointed by the president and

confirmed by the Senate. The establishing legislation also stipulated that the loans had to be repaid within a twenty-five year period, and that the rate of interest charged was not to be less than 4.25 percent.[34]

The British chose to respond with the so-called Balfour Note, named for former prime minister Arthur Balfour. In the note, Balfour offered to forgive all war debts owed Britain (which were substantial) to the same extent that the United States forgave England's debts. The note was an attempt to link the entire war debt question, placing ultimate responsiblity for its resolution on the U.S. The Balfour Note, coming as it did in the midst of the 1922 election campaign, immediately became a massive political football, with Republicans and Democrats trying to outdo each other in their denunciation of the 'bungling' and 'mischievous' note. Americans widely viewed it as an attempt by the British to escape acknowledgement of their obligations and to make the American government appear as a Shylock. An exasperated Geddes wrote the Foreign Office that the U.S. would continue 'to treat us as a vassal State so long as the debt remains unpaid.'[35]

Despite American rejection of the Balfour Note, the British were still eager to resolve the debt issue as soon as possible in order to restore the City of London's position as the world's banker. As such, the British loan was at the top of the Debt Commission's agenda, but it soon became apparent that no settlement could be reached under the terms mandated by Congress. Negotiations continued, with members of the commission walking a fine line between what the British could pay and what Congress might be willing to accept. When the Americans finally demanded a 3.3 percent interest rate over sixty-two years, the British still complained that it was too high (they had expected that their renunciation of the alliance with Japan would earn them preferential treatment), but were soon convinced that it was the best deal they were likely to get.[36]

There remained, however, a more formidable obstacle to settlement in the form of the United States Senate, which still had to approve the new arrangements. Despite (or perhaps in part because of) a vigorous campaign by prominent bankers and journalists (headed by Thomas W. Lamont of the Morgan bank) to promote a settlement more lenient than that mandated by Congress, the issue was a veritable gift from heaven for more than one Senate demagogue. Hiram Johnson called the entire renegotiation process 'a Hoover-Morgan scheme' to defraud American taxpayers. A number of senators, especially from rural states, were convinced that the British were getting the better end of the deal. Some, like Tennessee Democrat Kenneth McKellar, believed that the members of the debt-funding commission had been completely outmaneuvered by the British; others, such as James Thomas Heflin (D-AL), claimed that the settlement was engineered by 'the bond sharks of Wall Street,' whom the British government would gladly repay once the public debt had been reduced.[37] Stanley Baldwin, British Chancellor of the Exchequer, added fuel to the fire when he attempted to explain the source of Senate opposition to the settlement. Baldwin argued that the problem with the U.S. Senate was that 'the majority of the Members come from agricultural and pastoral communities,' and were thus incapable of understanding the link between the debts and the health of the international economy. 'The people in the West,' he concluded, 'merely sell wheat and hogs and other products and take no further interest in connection with the international debt or international trade.'[38]

Baldwin's ill-timed (even if accurate) statement turned what had originally been an attack on the commission into a full-scale assault on Great Britain and its leaders. McKellar called the chancellor's words 'crude attacks,' an example of the 'sordid parsimony' so characteristic of the British. As for the reference to hogs, it was 'a disgusting attempt at wit and a shining display of ignorance.' This sparked a debate on the Senate floor which the *New York Times* characterized as the 'liveliest two hours which that body has had since the present administration came into power.' As it appeared more and more likely that the settlement would pass, the rhetoric employed by those opposed to it grew more and more vehemently anti-British. La Follette and Reed contended that the agreement would bind the United States more tightly 'to the chariot wheels of British diplomacy,' because as long as the debt went unpaid America would have a vested interest in the survival and success of Britain's 'imperialistic enterprises.' In the meantime, money that should be going into the U.S. Treasury would be used instead to suppress anticolonial movements in India and Egypt.[39] Yet in the end the opposition could muster no more than thirteen votes against the settlement – even Hiram Johnson recognized that it was the best deal that the U.S. could hope for.

Though on some important occasions the Harding administration, as well as the mainstream of the Republican Party, found themselves in support of rapprochement with the British, it was not the case that the administration was unified behind a consistently pro-British policy. When it came to enforcement of Prohibition, for instance, Great Britain and the Republicans could find themselves very much on opposite sides of the fence. Here the problem lay not with German- or Irish-American agitators or liberal critics (who were not about to defend Prohibition), but rather among the very Anglo-Saxons who tended generally to be the most sympathetic to the English. In the process, it led to a serious clash between the needs of domestic law enforcement and the accepted standards of international behavior.

The first signs that the Volstead Act might collide with Anglo-American harmony came in 1921, when arch-prohibitionist and former Secretary of State William Jennings Bryan revealed that a significant amount of liquor smuggled into the U.S. came by way of British territories near the American coast, especially the Bahamas. Senator Thomas Sterling (R-SD) responded by introducing an amendment to the Fordney-McCumber Tariff bill that authorized the Coast Guard to board and search all foreign vessels up to a distance of twelve miles from the coast, and to seize any vessel found to be illegally unloading cargo. The bill passed amended, and the Department of Justice prepared to enforce the new law.[40]

The Sterling amendment, however, flew in the face of one of the standard precepts of international law at the time, which claimed that a nation could only exercise its sovereignty within a limit of three miles from its coast. Any ship further than three miles from shore was considered to be in international waters, and thus not subject to search or seizure. Though in theory the amendment applied to all foreign vessels, the nation quickest to protest was Great Britain, for whom the three-mile limit was a concept vital to its continued control of global sea-lanes. The British, for their part, suspected that the real aim of the amendment was to cripple their overseas trade, or perhaps to generate support for American annexation of the Bahamas. The Foreign Office found it ironic, to say the least, that after more than a century of protesting British search and seizure of American ships on the high seas, the United States now wanted to grant itself the right to do the very same thing.[41]

The stage was thus set, not only for an Anglo-American conflict, but for one within the Harding administration. Secretary of State Hughes, hoping to avoid an international incident, tried to block enforcement of the new twelve-mile rule. Against him stood Assistant Attorney General Mabel Walker Willebrandt, a former California prosecutor, an ardent dry, and the first woman ever to hold a subcabinet position. Willebrandt attacked the State Department's obstructionism as an attempt 'to give "aid and comfort" to the British Embassy,' and argued that 'the time is right to thrash it out' with the British.[42]

Actually, the British proved more willing to negotiate on the issue than either Hughes or Willebrandt expected. After issuing a number of diplomatic protests arising from the seizure of British vessels, Whitehall began dropping hints via the American charge that some sort of deal might be reached. Despite its attachment to the three-mile limit, and in spite of the importance of the liquor trade to the British economy, the Foreign Office was never comfortable defending liquor smugglers. Moreover, there was an important privilege that the British hoped to gain from any bargain regarding prohibition enforcement – the right of British passenger liners carrying liquor to call at American ports, provided the liquor was sealed and stored (so as not to be brought ashore). Since American passenger liners were prohibited from serving liquor, even in international waters, such an arrangement would give the British a powerful advantage in the competition for the overseas tourist trade. On January 23, 1924, a treaty was signed in Washington giving both sides essentially what they wanted. In the Senate, there was some opposition from representatives of maritime states, but when the Anti-Saloon League endorsed the treaty it passed easily, by a vote of 61 to 7.[43]

The administration also proved willing to use anti-British rhetoric in Congress in order to pursue its own domestic agenda. A case in point involved Harding's attempt in 1923 to privatize a large part of the American merchant marine. During the war, the U.S. had constructed thousands of vessels in order to supply Allied forces in Europe, with the result that after the armistice the government found itself in possession of a huge merchant marine. However, the ready availability of vessels on all sides made competition in shipping quite intense, and Great Britain quickly regained its dominance in overseas trade while American ships rusted in port. In the summer of 1921 Senators Robert La Follette and William S. Kenyon (R-IA) charged that the United States Shipping Board (USSB) had fallen under British influence, and that American financiers were conspiring with English shipowners to perpetuate British dominance of the high seas. Nothing officially came of these charges, but they did help plant in the public mind the idea that it was only through treachery that the British were able to defeat the U.S. in the competition for shipping.[44] It was thus hardly surprising that the administration would use a similar tactic when proposing its own solution.

Harding, who during the campaign had promised to make the United States 'the leading maritime nation of the world,' appointed Albert Lasker as chairman of the USSB. Lasker had no previous experience in shipping, but was adept in the growing field of advertising. As a former campaign adviser to Harding, he had a particular knack for using patriotic themes in defense of his arguments. Lasker proposed the establishment of a fund to subsidize private purchase of USSB vessels and Harding, seeing an opportunity to strengthen the merchant marine while at the same time reducing government expenditures, quickly endorsed the plan. The ship subsidy went before Congress in March 1922, portrayed as America's only hope against the British shipping menace. Sen. Wesley L. Jones (R-WA), who sponsored the legislation, claimed that Great Britain had been subsidizing its own private shipping firms for years; now it was time for the United States to retaliate in kind. Joseph

Frelinghuysen (R-NJ) concurred, and then reminded his
colleagues that 'our English cousins...hardly waited for the
formalities of the peace before they turned to...regaining
her maritime supremacy.'[45]

Yet while this appeal to anglophobia found willing ears
among representatives of coastal states, it ultimately persuaded neither populist Democrats nor progressive Republicans,
who saw in the ship subsidy a massive giveaway to wealthy
shipowners. George Norris of Nebraska, certainly no friend
of the British Empire, claimed that he preferred to keep the
ships under government control, even if they could only be
operated at a loss, than to see them in private hands. La
Follette also opposed the subsidy, and moreover denied that
it would solve what for him was the basic problem – namely,
British influence over the Shipping Board. According to the
Wisconsin progressive, American shipowners often had close
ties to their English counterparts. Opponents of the subsidy
launched a successful filibuster, and the proposal was with-
drawn on February 28.[46]

By the end of 1923 it seemed that practically every point of
contention between Great Britain and the United States had
been settled. Ireland had been granted its independence,
and important agreements had been reached on the issues of
naval armament, war debts, and enforcement of prohibition
laws. Nor did the death of Harding and the succession of
Calvin Coolidge to the presidency in that year threaten to
change matters. Though 'Silent Cal' seemed thoroughly un-
interested in foreign affairs (it is a telling fact that he never
even broached the subject in his autobiography), Harding's
foreign policy establishment remained intact; moreover,
Coolidge himself, when he did deign to address foreign
affairs, spoke often of the need to maintain a strong Anglo-
American relationship, and the new British ambassador, Sir
Esme Howard, always believed him to be pro-British in his
sympathies.[47] In November 1923 David Lloyd George
became the first British former prime minister to travel to the
United States, and so successful was his visit that it prompted
renewed discussion on the merits of closer Anglo-American
partnership. 'Since the end of the war Great Britain has consented to one costly sacrifice after another in the hope of
removing obstacles to a better understanding with the

United States,' the *New Republic* wrote in the wake of Lloyd George's speaking tour. 'When [the British]...propose co-operation between the two countries, they are entitled to a friendly and attentive hearing from the American government and people.' In the summer of 1924 an article in the popular periodical *Harper's* entitled 'England and America: Their Misunderstandings and Their Opportunity' urged Americans to ignore their 'historic prejudices, ancient grudges and misunderstandings,' since there were no 'concrete grounds of antagonism' between the two countries.[48]

But those predicting a new era of harmony between the two English-speaking great powers were engaged in a bit of wishful thinking, for most of the presumed sacrifices made on the part of the British were, upon closer inspection, nothing of the sort. The Washington Treaties, for example, gave the Foreign Office what it believed to be a meaningful substitute for the Anglo-Japanese alliance, which according to many in the British government had outlived its usefulness in any case, while naval limitation extended only to capital ships, which most of the British Admiralty believed were obsolete anyway. The war debt settlement produced a great deal of grumbling in England about 'Uncle Shylock,' and would last fewer than ten years. In the liquor treaty Britain did concede the three-mile limit, but only partially, and in return received a far more valuable concession in the right to carry liquor on passenger liners calling at U.S. ports. Finally, while the granting of independence to Ireland was done in part to assuage American sensibilities, it is hard to argue that Britain's unloading of one of its least profitable territories, and historically its most troublesome one, amounted to any great sacrifice to secure good relations with America.

Yet even if the difficulties that might have generated actual crises in Anglo-American relations had been resolved, 'historic prejudices, ancient grudges and misunderstandings' died hard in any event. If the atmosphere in Washington, D.C. in 1923–1924 lacked much of the open anglophobia that had reigned since 1919, there were a number of trends elsewhere in the country that militated against any close relationship between the two nations. One was the growing movement to accentuate the distinction between the language used by Americans and the English of the British Isles, an assertion of what might be called 'linguistic nationalism.' In 1923 the Illinois legislature passed a resolution stating:

> Whereas, since the creation of the American Republic there have been certain Tory elements in our country who have never become reconciled to our Republican institutions and have ever clung to the tradition of King and Empire...the...official language of the State of Illinois shall be known hereafter as the 'American' language, and not as the 'English' language.[49]

Similar pieces of legislation passed in Texas, Ohio, and Wisconsin. Even certain intellectuals could become jingoistic when it came to their native tongue. H. L. Mencken fought tirelessly against American use of English linguistic habits; for the irascible Mencken, English pronunciation had 'a mauve, Episcopalian, and ephebian ring.' A correspondent for the *New York World* boasted in the spring of 1923, 'Was it Washington Irving who said that the best English is spoken here? I myself would say that the best English is written here.' *Collier's* sounded the tocsin even more loudly: 'Under American treatment English has become the richest of all languages, whereas under purely British control it ran about fourth.'[50]

Perhaps unsurprisingly, this movement eventually found expression on Capitol Hill when Rep. Washington McCormick (R-MT) spoke out on the House floor in favor of America's 'literary independence.' 'It was only when Cooper, Irving, Mark Twain, Whitman, and O. Henry dropped the Order of the Garter and began to write American that their wings of immortality sprouted,' McCormick proclaimed. He furthermore exhorted 'our writers' to 'drop their top-coats, spats, and swagger-sticks, and assume occasionally their buckskin, moccasins, and tomahawks.'[51]

Somewhat more troubling for Anglo-American relations was the development of historical revisionism regarding the origins of the World War. A number of historians such as Sidney Fay, Harry Elmer Barnes, and Charles A. Beard had as early as 1919 begun to challenge the accepted thesis on the origins of the war, namely, that Germany provoked it in pursuit of European hegemony and world empire.

Revisionist historians examined the documents of all of the major powers involved, and, while they often differed on exactly who was to blame, all generally agreed that Germany did not deserve to shoulder the entire burden of guilt.[52]

Revisionism initially had no significant political impact; when Rep. M. Alfred Michaelson (R-IL) introduced a resolution in 1921 calling for an investigation of 'why the Yanks came in 1917,' his words were damned as 'scandalous' and 'treasonable.' Yet by the end of 1923 the time was ripe for a more dispassionate assessment. Sen. Robert Latham Owen (D-OK), a Virginia-born liberal who had voted for U.S. entry in 1917, traveled to Europe in the summer of 1923, and during his trip he read a number of revisionist works by French, German, and British authors. He returned to the United States convinced that the Allies 'had greatly deceived the people of the United States' by telling them that the war was being fought 'in defense of American ideals.' On December 18 Owen took the Senate floor; in a speech which filled over forty pages of the *Congressional Record*, Owen accused Russia and France of starting the war. He later proposed the establishment of a committee of historians to investigate the issue further.[53]

In its early stages, it should be noted, historical revisionism was not particularly anti-British, as it remained exclusively focused on the origins of the war, and none of the revisionists tried to argue that Great Britain was responsible for provoking it. Nor did Owen have a reputation for anglophobia. Nevertheless, it was undeniable that British speakers, authors, and diplomats in the United States from 1914 to 1917 expended a great deal of money and effort to convince Americans that the war was Germany's fault, and that it was being fought to make the world 'safe for democracy.' Thus originated the theory, later taken up as a topic of study in its own right by later revisionists, that 'British propaganda' had lured the U.S. into a war in which it had no vital interest. Nor, according to this account, had the propaganda mills stopped with the end of the war – in April of 1922 Hiram Johnson wrote to his son about the 'fixed policy of Great Britain to conquer the public opinion of the United States and make it subservient to British interests....Great Britain...[is] striving to do insidiously and by propaganda that which she had failed to accomplish in two wars with the United States.'[54]

The most common manifestation of the fear of British propaganda during these years was the concern over school textbooks, which had been a very prominent feature of the campaign to 'rehabilitate' Great Britain during the war. The outcry began with a series of articles in the Hearst newspapers in 1921 by Charles Grant Miller, former editor-in-chief of the *Cleveland Plain Dealer* and the *Christian Herald*, who charged that American children were being exposed to falsifications of history composed by men of what he called 'the British mind' – not necessarily Englishmen, but authors who were 'more British than American.' The Knights of Columbus took up this line with a vengeance; at its 1921 convention in San Francisco a 'Historical Commission' was set up under the chairmanship of Edward F. McSweeney. McSweeney's committee, which included several prominent journalists and politicians but no historians, produced a collection of anti-British essays entitled *Studies in History*, which explained how through propaganda in textbooks, children were being 'weaned away from national patriotism by the internationally minded.' In the words of the Reverend P. J. Cormican of Fordham University, this was part of 'a systematic effort to "de-Americanize" America and ultimately to bring it back within the British Empire.'[55]

The effort to root out British propaganda in textbooks soon spread beyond the Knights of Columbus, whose (largely Irish) anglophobia was to be expected. By the end of 1921 the American Legion was denouncing authors who, 'in their efforts to "be fair" to a foreign nation...[had] fallen over backward and...untruthfully condemned the position of their own country.' The American Legion, after all, could hardly allow themselves to have their patriotism challenged by a band of 'hyphenated Americans'! Over the next two years they were joined by a chorus of groups made up almost exclusively of Anglo-Saxons; in 1923 the Daughters of the American Revolution, the Veterans of Foreign Wars, the Grand Army of the Republic, the Descendants of the Signers of the Declaration of Independence, and the United Spanish War Veterans all called for the suppression of 'un-American and unpatriotic' history texts. By 1928 pressures for revision had led to the passage of new laws in Wisconsin and Oregon, and to investigations, and in some cases actual removal, of books from libraries in California, Kentucky, Tennessee, Idaho, Alabama, Iowa, Illinois, New York, New Jersey, Massachusetts, Minnesota, Michigan, and Washington, D.C.[56]

Therefore, while on the surface Anglo-American relations appeared smoother than ever, there were strong hints of the stormy period to come. Despite the willingness of American businessmen and diplomats to reach understandings with Great Britain, most Americans in and out of Congress were not prepared to move their country closer to what was still perceived as 'perfidious Albion.' The anti-British coalition was indeed unsteady, as shown by the ratification of the Washington Treaties in spite of the Four Power Pact, but was capable of regrouping if the need presented itself. Moreover, as the decade wore on and a genuine naval race developed between the two powers, the coalition would attract new members, growing both in size and in political clout. The anglophobia of the late 1920s would, indeed, make that of the early part of the decade appear mild.

2 'The English Navy has Gone Mad'

A perceptive observer in the final months of 1924 might have noticed dark clouds on the horizon of Anglo-American relations, most of which stemmed from the presidential campaign of that year. James W. Davis was unquestionably the most conservative Democratic presidential candidate of the twentieth century. There was, therefore, practically no difference between Davis and Coolidge on most issues of domestic policy; the challenge for the Democrats was to accentuate the differences that did exist between the two – namely Prohibition and, especially, foreign policy.

The key to this strategy was to attack the Washington Treaties of 1922. In addition to undermining what was undoubtedly the most important foreign policy initiative of the Harding Administration, this had the added benefit of perhaps winning back some of the anti-British hyphenate groups which had defected from the Democratic party in 1920.

The only problem was which treaty to criticize. Unfortunately for the Democrats, the only truly controversial agreement – and, indeed, the only one to generate any opposition among Congressional Democrats – was the Four Power Pact. Since they could hardly hope to win popular support for an attack on a treaty whose provisions had never been invoked, they instead chose to focus their assault on the Five Power Naval Agreement, which they argued was a classic example of cunning British diplomats outsmarting their naive American counterparts. Rumors abounded to the effect that, despite the promise of naval parity which the Washington Conference had seemed to offer, the Royal Navy remained far superior to that of the United States in almost every category – its guns were larger, and elevated so as to give them increased range; it had not lived up to its promise to scrap certain capital ships; it was frantically building smaller ships, not covered under the Five Power

Agreement; it was making plans for the immediate armament of merchant vessels in time of war. Most of these
charges were soon proven false, but taken together they
helped create the lingering suspicion that the British
Government could not be trusted to live up to its solemn
promises.[1]

This is not to suggest, however, that Davis himself was any
sort of anglophobe. Indeed, since he was unwilling to part
with Wilsonian orthodoxy and renounce the League of
Nations, the Democratic candidate for president never made
any serious inroads among anti-British ethnic groups, and
thus ensured that Coolidge would be elected by wide
margins. German-Americans rallied instead to the independent Progressive candidacy of inveterate anglophobe
Robert La Follette, who not only promised to keep America
out of the League, but demanded the immediate revision of
Versailles in Germany's favor. La Follette, however, remained on the political fringe, and his death soon after
Election Day removed this irritant to Anglo-American relations.[2]

Even more disturbing in the long run than the accusations
of the Democrats and La Follette was the death of Henry
Cabot Lodge on November 9, and the succession of William
Borah as the new chairman of the Senate Foreign Relations
Committee. As discussed in the last chapter, though no
anglophile, Lodge had consistently worked to keep anti-
British sentiment under control in the upper house. Indeed,
the Massachusetts Republican deserves much of the credit
for the ratification of the Washington treaties. Borah, by contrast, was both an irreconcilable and a thoroughgoing
anglophobe. His new position – gained, according to a dis-
approving Coolidge, 'by accident of seniority' – made it all
the more important that the administration keep foreign
affairs as far from the congressional docket as possible.
Unlike the reliable Lodge, Borah was likely to cause a great
deal of trouble.[3]

Just how much trouble the Idaho progressive could generate soon became obvious on March 15, 1926, when he
introduced a resolution demanding that the Secretary of
State (now Frank Kellogg, who replaced Hughes when the
latter was appointed to the Supreme Court), report to the

Senate on the progress of the negotiations for settlement of claims arising from the World War. Most of these claims were from shipowners whose cargoes had been seized by the British Navy in its blockade of Germany before the U.S. had entered the war. Several major newspapers denounced this move, accusing Borah of 'twisting the lion's tail.' The *Chicago Tribune*, not generally known for excessive kindness to the British Empire, warned that it would lead to 'a flood of claims against the United States by other neutrals who suffered from the blockade after we joined forces with Britain and France.' Nevertheless, the resolution was politically popular, reflecting the fact that the issue of freedom of the seas had never been resolved. Not only was Borah's resolution reported out of the Foreign Relations Committee unamended on June 15, but it was immediately approved by the Senate without debate or division.[4]

Borah's resolution frightened both Kellogg and the British, who had been for some time negotiating what was already a complicated and difficult issue. Pressure from Congress could only make things worse. The American ambassador to Britain warned Kellogg that if London were forced to pay the claims the result would be 'a wave of bitterness and anger against us whose duration and effect will be difficult to measure.' Ambassador Howard, for his part, called the pressing of the claims 'unprecedented,' given that after the U.S. entered the war Americans actually benefited from the blockade. Nevertheless, both sides were anxious to come to some sort of agreement, and this was finally announced in November. A list of fifteen jointly drafted conditions was applied to each individual claim, reducing the total valid number of claims to 157 out of the 2658 which had originally been made. Furthermore, only eleven of these were deemed by the State Department to have 'conspicuous merit,' and the other 146 were thrown out. The response by the anti-British forces was predictable – a clear example of a 'sell-out' of American interests to Britain. The *Nation* called this 'surrender...a fitting climax to the arbitrariness of 1917.'[5]

Yet such criticisms came from predictable sources – progressives friendly to Borah, the jingoistic press, as exemplified by the Hearst papers, and of course Irish- and

German-Americans. Most Americans found it difficult to get terribly excited about the claims of a few shipowners from a decade ago. Nevertheless public resentment toward Great Britain increased dramatically between 1924 and 1928. There were two main reasons for this – the controversy over rubber created by the British Stevenson Plan, and a renewed Anglo-American naval race.

The rubber problem had its origins in a postwar glut which had caused prices for crude rubber to plummet from a prewar high of three dollars a pound to fifteen cents per pound in 1922. With British planters in Ceylon and Malaya facing bankruptcy, a committee was appointed by the Colonial Office to investigate the problem. This committee, led by Sir James Stevenson, recommended in that year a series of government regulations to restrict rubber exports to a maximum of sixty percent of standard production in 1920. Not only would this stabilize the price of rubber, but, in the words of Colonial Secretary Winston Churchill, 'making the Americans pay' more for rubber would 'contribute materially to stabilizing the dollar exchange.'[6]

As expected, the country most affected by the Stevenson Plan was the United States, since Americans were at the time consuming more than seventy percent of the world's rubber output. Since the most important use of rubber by far was in automobile tires, it came as no surprise when Harvey S. Firestone, America's leading tiremaker, became the latest convert to the anti-British line. Even before the end of 1922, Firestone was predicting that, thanks to the artificial shortage created by the Stevenson Act, by 1929 world demand for rubber would outstrip supply by 25 000 tons. He soon found ample support for his position from certain members of the House and Senate. Sen. Joseph Ransdell of Louisiana called the Stevenson Plan 'an example of British discrimination that reaches even into the American farm.' In February 1923 the House appropriated half a million dollars to investigate the possibility of growing crude rubber in the Philippines or Latin America in order 'to free [Americans] from the shackles of British monopoly.'[7]

Yet while such efforts did begin to bear some fruit – the Amazon basin was deemed to be a promising area for the production of crude rubber – the British appeared to have no intention of easing the restrictions under the plan. The price of rubber soon began to soar – to 36 cents per pound at the beginning of 1925, 77.3 cents per pound by June, and up to $1.09 at the beginning of November. Many in Congress began to demand that the Coolidge administration do something; in late December 1925 John Q. Tilson (R-CT) proposed a resolution 'to investigate…the means and methods of the control of production and exportation of crude rubber, and its effects upon the commerce of the United States.' Rep. Cordell Hull (D-TN), complaining of the 'excessive and extortionate prices' being paid to the British, claimed that 'all of Europe is laughing in her sleeve at the manner in which we are being held up by this unholy combination.' What Hull, and, indeed, most Democrats wanted was a reduction in the tariff. They believed that the British were using high prices for rubber as a means of re-taliating against what one southerner called 'the nonsensical, outrageous, damnable rates in the Fordney-McCumber tariff law.'[8]

But the administration's plan had nothing at all to do with tariff reduction; instead the job fell to Commerce Secretary Herbert Hoover to organize an American pressure campaign against the Stevenson Plan. The assignment corresponded well with Hoover's own attitudes toward the relationship between government and business; the idea of government-backed monopolies was an affront to his ideas of 'rugged individualism,' especially when such monopolies threatened the growth of the American economy. It also afforded him the opportunity to take a strong public stand against the British government, and thus perhaps dispel the persistent rumors that Hoover was excessively pro-English.

Hoover's assault began with an open letter to longtime pol-itical ally Senator Arthur Capper (R-KS), in which he declared that the rubber situation required immediate atten-tion. He proposed a nationwide campaign to combat the restrictions by reducing consumption, eliminating waste, de-veloping new sources for crude rubber, and, most controversially, allowing American manufacturers to form syndicates in order to pool purchases, and thus to negotiate a better price. The following week Capper introduced an amendment to the Webb-Pomerene Act of 1918, which would allow the 'cooperative buying of raw materials controlled by foreign monopolies.' Though progressives predicted a return to the giant trusts of the 1890s, the measure quickly passed.[9]

More important in the long run, however, was Hoover's publicity campaign to encourage Americans to use less rubber, which one observer called 'perhaps the most effective propaganda campaign against a foreign nation ever undertaken by a Washington Government in peace time.' Bus signs in cities across the country carried messages such as 'Economize on Rubber,' 'Help Hoover Against English Rubber Trust,' and '1776–1925.' For the secretary, there was far more than the rubber issue at stake – he repeatedly contrasted the virtues of America's free enterprise system, in which business prospered without government interference, with the British system of state-subsidized monopoly. And clearly it was having some effect – in February 1926 the British government, while refusing to abandon the principle of restriction, increased production quotas temporarily for the first half of the year; by March the price of crude rubber had dropped to 60 cents per pound, but Hoover pledged to continue his campaign until all restrictions on rubber were lifted.[10]

Not all Americans supported Hoover in his fight against the Stevenson Plan. Congressional liberals and progressives, seldom inclined to leap to the defense of Great Britain, nonetheless professed themselves amused to see the Secretary of Commerce, a man with ties to American big business, denouncing foreign monopolies. The Democratic delegate from Alaska, Dan A. Sutherland, sneered that '[t]he high priest of American monopoly twisting the India-rubber tail of the British lion is really a spectacle for people to behold.' Representative James A. Frear (R-WI) called the British scheme 'primitive and guileless' compared to 'such shining examples of unregulated international monopoly…as the Aluminum Company of America.' He was joined by Loring Black (D-NY), who claimed that tire manufacturers were only using the Stevenson Plan as 'an alibi to gouge the public' through increased prices. 'Why try to legislate for Great Britain,' he concluded, 'when we can not legislate for ourselves?'[11]

The British finally abandoned the Stevenson Plan in 1928, but this decision can only be attributed in part to Hoover's efforts. Certainly, there was some decline in American rubber consumption as a result of efforts toward conservation, but more important was the fact that the Dutch refused to go along with the British restrictions. From 1922 to 1928 the Dutch increased their output by 150 percent, and Great Britain's share of the world rubber market fell from 72 to 53 percent during the same period. Nevertheless, few Americans mourned the lifting of the restrictions. The *Saturday Evening Post* hailed it as the defeat of a British plan to control the world rubber market, while *Literary Digest* noted the general sense of relief among the American press – the Stevenson Plan, they believed, had 'constituted the most serious bone of contention that Great Britain and the United States have experienced since the war.'[12]

Yet even by the time these words were written, a new bone of contention had arisen, which by the end of 1928 would loom even more serious than the rubber controversy, and would have politicians and diplomats on both sides of the Atlantic suggesting what had seemed unthinkable since the late nineteenth century – an Anglo-American war.

The first stirrings of a renewed naval race could be heard in 1924. In response to a new building program by Japan, the British government in that year began construction on five 10 000-ton cruisers carrying 8-inch guns. The United States soon followed suit; in May the Navy Department presented a budget to Congress that would modernize the six oldest battleships in the fleet, build eight 10 000-ton cruisers and six gunboats. It passed the Naval Affairs Committee almost unanimously, though an amendment was inserted to suspend the program should a new arms conference be called. The measure then narrowly passed the House, 168–138, but sailed through the Senate without debate or division. Though actual construction on the new vessels would not begin until late October of 1926, the passage of the authorization clearly showed the extent to which congressional opinion was shifting on the subject of naval armament.[13]

The main cause of this change of heart was the continuing barrage launched against the Washington Conference, an assault which grew in intensity after the 1924 elections. Sen. Kenneth McKellar (D-TN) asserted that England had received the better end of the deal; the British, he contended, recognized that they could not compete against the U.S. in naval construction, and so designed an agreement which would guarantee continued supremacy on the seas. The promise of parity was completely bogus – the British were to maintain 22 battleships, most of which had been built within the past ten years, while the United States kept only 18, many of which were obsolescent. Sen. William H. King (D-UT), who had been one of the leading advocates of disarmament in 1921, seemed to have completely changed his mind three years later; in signing the naval limitation pact, he claimed, 'we relinquished...the field in which we were superior [i.e., battleships] and left the other nations predominant in other fields of naval craft.' Humorist Will Rogers quipped that Charles Evans Hughes had told the British at Washington, 'For every battleship you fellows build America will sink one.'[14]

This placed Republicans in a dilemma, for they had been the chief supporters of naval construction in 1921. The Washington Conference had promised parity between the British and American navies, but obviously the Royal Navy remained much larger than the American. At the same time, however, the G.O.P. could not attack the Five Power Agreement given that it was the product of a Republican administration. They thus responded that the fault lay not with the treaty, which was of course intended to grant parity – it lay rather with the British, who by their continued naval construction were violating the spirit if not the letter of the agreement. Rep. Fred Britten (R-IL), who was soon to become chairman of the House Naval Affairs Committee, claimed that 'Japan and England, just about as soon as the ink on the Washington Treaty was dry, started to do what Europeans and Old World diplomats always do – to evade the thing they have just agreed to.' The only alternative was to build more and more cruisers. Hiram Johnson agreed: 'While America scrapped warships,' he wrote disgustedly, 'Britain scrapped blueprints.'[15]

This new enthusiasm for naval construction was both applauded and aided by a coalition of naval officers, publicists, journalists, and industrialists which came to be known as the 'Big Navy' party. Mostly Republican and anti-British, the Big-Navyites coalesced into an effective pressure group for greater expenditure on naval construction, and against any new arms limitation agreement with the British. At the core of the movement was a large part of the U.S. Navy itself – 'older naval officers mainly retired' and 'younger officers of strong racial and religious prejudices' according to the magazine *Scientific American* – as well as the Navy's powerful civilian lobbying organization, the Navy League of the United States. Both had been among the first opponents of the Washington Conference; for many naval officers, the conference was the greatest British victory since Trafalgar. The United States, they charged, gave up the chance to become the world's greatest naval power without securing any guarantees regarding neutral rights. In a future war, they believed, the Royal Navy was free to harass American shipping as it had in the World War. The Navy League, for its part, claimed to support arms limitation in principle, but accused American delegates at Washington of laying the foundation for a U.S. Navy based not on the needs of the country but on the financial situation of Great Britain.[16]

The British building program of 1924, along with Democratic attacks on the Washington Treaties, were god-sends for the Navy League, which soon attracted the support of a number of prominent journalists (chief among them Frank Simonds, prolific author and editor of the influential journal *Review of Reviews*),[17] newspapers (such as the *Chicago Tribune*, the *New York Herald Tribune*, the *Baltimore Sun*, and, of course, the Hearst chain), and politicians. Moreover, the League's new anti-British assault quickly won over the loyalties of German- and Irish-Americans. George Sylvester Viereck, writing in the popular magazine *American Monthly*, claimed that the Five Power Agreement was an element in the State Department's strategy to reduce the navy so as 'to weaken America to such an extent that we can never question the right of John Bull to bulldoze us on the seas.' The ultimate goal, he charged, was to reduce the United States 'to the status of a colony of Great Britain.' Under the leadership of the Big Navy party, then, the anti-British coalition found new strength.[18]

By the end of 1926 the navalists were ready to make their move. On December 18 Thomas S. Butler (R-PA), chairman of the House Naval Affairs Committee, introduced a bill authorizing the construction of ten new cruisers. Ambassador Howard reported that naval expansion had widespread support across the country; even some peace groups supported it as a means of coercing Britain into attending another disarmament conference.[19]

But the call for increased naval spending ran into powerful opposition in the form of President Coolidge, who in February 1927 proposed calling a conference which might extend the Washington ratios to cruisers and auxiliary vessels. Though personally no less committed to naval parity than his predecessor, Coolidge balked at the size of the government expenditure which would be required to build up to England's level, and thus hoped instead to limit the size of the Royal Navy through international agreement.[20]

Yet while many peace organizations favored a conference, Coolidge's proposal met with a less than enthusiastic response among many sectors of American opinion. The Navy, for one, was no longer willing to accept mere parity. In the words of Rear Admiral Phelps, parity with the Royal Navy would still mean that 'Great Britain, by reason of overwhelming superiority in merchant marine and bases, would completely dominate the seas.' The popular magazine *Liberty*, published by the anti-British and pro-Navy editor of the *Chicago Tribune*, Colonel Robert McCormick, printed an article entitled 'The Coming Naval Disarmament Conference, and What We Won't Get Out of It.' The article prominently featured a map of the Western Hemisphere which showed the vulnerability of the Panama Canal, and, indeed, the American East Coast, to an attack from British Bermuda or Jamaica. Its author, Hugh Fullerton, morosely concluded that '[w]e probably are in for a diplomatic trimming so that the administration may make a pacific gesture to please the church people in the next Presidential campaign.'[21]

Navalists in the House and Senate were equally hostile to the idea. Sen. Frederick Hale (R-ME) claimed that, unlike in 1921, when the U.S. possessed 'a great preponderance of capital-ship strength,' the navy in 1927 was far weaker than that of Great Britain. 'We must, therefore, approach the question of a new conference on limitation of armaments not as a great country willing to make a great sacrifice in the interests of world limitation of armament but as a country asking others to make the sacrifice.' A conference now, in Hale's opinion, would 'be worse than useless.' Hiram Johnson, scornful of the very idea – 'What an age of bunk this is!' he wrote to his son – claimed that it was 'simply ridiculous to imagine' that the British would scrap cruisers which they had actually built. Kenneth McKellar, meanwhile, reminded his colleagues that the Washington conference dealt 'one of the greatest blows that was ever struck to the American Navy.'[22]

Nevertheless Coolidge had determined on another conference that might prevent a full-scale armaments race, and three days of intense negotiation between the president and pro-Navy Republicans ensued. The result was a compromise similar to that reached between Harding and Borah in 1921 – Coolidge promised to withdraw his opposition to Butler's cruiser program, provided that the congressional navalists dropped their hostility to a conference, and delayed the actual appropriation of funds for the construction of new vessels until after the conference had been held. Unlike the agreement which paved the way for the Washington Conference, however, this compromise heavily favored the Big Navyites; as Ambassador Howard pointed out, they had nothing to lose from a conference. At worst, the battleship ratios set at Washington would be extended to cruisers and other auxiliary craft, allowing for a massive buildup in everything but capital ships. At best (and, in the minds of most navalists, the most likely outcome), the British would hold out against the extension of ratios and the conference would collapse. The pro-Navy forces could then continue to exploit anti-British themes in order to marshal public opinion in support of a much larger building program. Either way, the navalists would gain equality with Britain.[23]

The Geneva Disarmament Conference got underway in July 1927, and, as the pro-Navy forces hoped, the American and British delegations were unable to come to any agreement. The main sticking point was the definition of what actually constituted a 'cruiser.' The true strength of the

British Navy lay in its large numbers of small, fast cruisers, armed with 6-inch guns. The U.S. Navy, by contrast, favored large cruisers with 8-inch guns, sometimes called 'treaty cruisers,' since they weighed in at just under the tonnage that would classify them as battleships. (They would later come to be known as 'heavy cruisers.') The British feared that if the Americans were allowed to build enough of these larger vessels to match the Royal Navy's tonnage in light cruisers, the U.S. Navy would actually gain supremacy, not parity, on the high seas. Their definition of 'parity,' therefore, meant that both sides could have roughly equal tonnage, but only in light cruisers.

This offer, however, was wholly unacceptable to the General Board of the U.S. Navy. Light cruisers, the admirals argued, were quite valuable for the British, who after all had naval bases all over the world. For the United States, however, they would prove useless. Without an extensive network of bases beyond the American coastline, the U.S. Navy had to rely on bigger ships which could carry enough fuel to allow them to operate at longer range. Moreover, the General Board feared that light cruisers would be insufficient to take on large numbers of armed merchantmen, a pressing concern given Britain's preponderance in merchant vessels. It soon became obvious that no agreement would be reached. By July 19 Secretary Kellogg had reached the conclusion that the British were no longer negotiating in earnest; as he wired Hugh Gibson, chairman of the American delegation, '[w]e do not believe that the British actually intend to limit tonnage of cruisers to extent which will be satisfactory, but have in mind to break up Conference on matter of size of guns and cruisers.' Three days later he wrote Coolidge that 'much to the surprise of everybody [sic], Great Britain's demands as to the tonnage of cruisers were exorbitant.'[24]

Why did the Geneva Conference fail? One common explanation has been that the General Board of the Navy was allowed to decide what America's position would be, and that the civilian negotiators were overruled at every turn.[25] This is no doubt true, but it does not tell the full story, for there were pressures on the negotiators from sources aside from the navy. Public opinion, as already mentioned, was not unanimous in favor of a conference in the first place, and many Americans were insistent that the U.S. get a better deal in 1927 than it had received in 1922. The British, hoping for a renewal of the pro-disarmament sentiment which had accompanied the proceedings at Washington, made an appeal to the American public. This time, as David Carlton has pointed out, the appeal failed, since most Americans suspected that the British were merely trying to perpetuate their superiority over the U.S. in cruisers. In any case the English side was drowned out by a chorus of pro-Navy agitation in the press, not only from the traditional sources but even from formerly reliable pro-British papers such as the *New York Times*.[26] Lord Bridgeman, head of the British delegation, complained that 'every little incident has been used to make mischief.' Soon afterward he wrote to King George V that it was 'evident that no agreement which did not humiliate the British Empire was likely to find acceptance' on the American side.[27]

The delegates also had to worry about the Senate, which of course had to ratify any treaty which the conference produced. The strength of the Democrats in both houses of Congress had greatly improved since 1922, and they could be expected to paint any agreement launched by a Republican administration as a sell-out to British interests. Nor were the navalists among the Republicans to be trusted, since (as discussed earlier) they had only consented to a conference on the assumption that it would fail. Therefore when Kellogg informed Coolidge of the impending failure of the conference, he claimed that the reason for this was that Great Britain refused 'to make any agreement which our Navy officials would be willing to make and which we could get ratified by the Senate.' A few weeks later he wrote his *post mortem* on the affair: 'Either the British Navy has gone mad or Great Britain has felt compelled to continue ship building to furnish employment.'[28]

Whatever the cause, Americans were nearly unanimous in proclaiming the British guilty of wrecking the conference, and the American press soon unleashed a barrage of anti-British rhetoric. Typical was the response of the Chicago *Daily News*, which wrote that 'responsibility for the most deplorable outcome rests primarily with the British experts and their reactionary supporters in the Baldwin Cabinet.' The *New York Herald Tribune* reminded its readers that Britain 'gains relatively with every reduction in the size of fighting units' while the *Philadelphia Inquirer* accused the British of exploiting well-meaning but misguided pro-disarmament sentiment in the U.S. One editor remarked that Britain was experiencing 'the worst press in America since the Venezuela dispute' of the early 1890s.[29]

Not surprisingly, such sentiments were echoed in Congress. Sen. Thomas J. Walsh (D-MT) called Geneva 'a grievous disappointment.' Though he had hoped that it would not be necessary to spend 'hundreds of millions to attain parity with Great Britain,' he now claimed to believe that this was the only alternative to 'remaining inferior to her in naval strength.' Even some liberals and pacifists pointed the finger of blame toward London; Sen. Frederick H. Gillett (R-MA), who had voted against the Butler bill of 1926, now called for a larger navy. Apparently, he announced, England's 'traditional impulse that Britannia shall rule the waves was stronger than her economic necessities, and she preferred to excite our rivalry rather than our cooperation.'[30]

This, of course, was welcome news for Big Navy advocates, and the House Naval Affairs Committee immediately set about writing a naval authorization bill that would make the Butler bill of 1926 look like small potatoes, indeed. Even Coolidge appeared to be on board; in his annual message to Congress on December 6, he wrote: 'While the results of the Conference were of considerable value, they were mostly of a negative character. We know now that no agreement can be reached which will be inconsistent with a considerable building program on our part.' The original bill provided for everything that the General Board wanted – 25 new heavy cruisers, five aircraft carriers, nine destroyer leaders, and 32 submarines – to be built over a nine-year period at an estimated cost of $740 000 000. After consultations with the White House, however, the bill was watered down significantly; in the wake of Geneva Coolidge was prepared to support increased naval expenditures, but he was not prepared to bankrupt the country in the process. Therefore the Naval Affairs Committee introduced a new bill on February

28, 1928, authorizing the construction of 15 cruisers and one aircraft carrier. The Cruiser Bill, as it soon came to be called, attracted widespread support in the press and among both parties in the House, and it passed by a wide margin on March 17.[31]

But the Cruiser Bill ran into a snag when it it reached the Senate, as opposition from church groups and peace societies began to mount. The new naval program, they argued, would trigger similar construction by other countries. Moreover, it would fly in the face of the Kellogg-Briand Pact for the Outlawry of War, which was being negotiated at the same time. Hiram Johnson scornfully dismissed critics of naval armament as a collection of 'pacifist ladies' associations, Friday morning clubs, Tuesday noon clubs, Wednesday 9 o'clock clubs, and Thursday 6 o'clock in the evening clubs.' Most senators, however, continued to take the peace groups seriously. Fearful of a backlash at the polls, the Senate decided to delay action on the bill until after the 1928 elections.[32]

In the meantime, however, events were transpiring abroad which would give the Cruiser Bill added support. If Americans were disappointed by the apparent unwillingness of the British to grant parity at Geneva, they were outraged when it was revealed that Great Britain and France had reached a 'compromise' regarding arms limitation. The agreement was an attempt to link the cruiser issue to the larger question of European disarmament. Talks had stalled due to Germany's insistence that France reduce the size of its army, which the French steadfastly refused to do. According to the Anglo-French agreement, Britain would support France's position on land armaments, and the French would back the British in their dispute over cruisers with the United States.

Though the terms of the compromise were telegraphed to Rome, Tokyo, and Washington on July 30, the world found out about it by accident, before the transmissions had been received. In a particularly heated session of the House of Commons, Foreign Secretary Austen Chamberlain found himself under heavy fire regarding the recent failure of arms-limitation discussions. In an attempt to defend himself, and, indeed, fighting a bout of pneumonia which would soon force him into more than three months' convalescence, Chamberlain mentioned the compromise. Immediately the American press went on the attack, led by the redoubtable William Randolph Hearst, who printed a leaked copy of the compromise in his *New York American* on September 21. Big Navy advocates, of course, had a field day – the British, it appeared, were trying to build a diplomatic coalition aimed at limiting large cruisers (which the U.S. Navy favored) while leaving untouched England's huge numbers of smaller vessels. Fred Britten took to the floor of Congress to insist that the agreement represented a British attempt to 'retain domination of the high seas by subversive diplomacy.' Their position was helped enormously by the publication of an article by an Englishman, J. M. Kenworthy, which claimed that the Anglo-French compromise was just another example of Britain seeking allies against any nation that threatened her maritime supremacy. The Navy League had more than 3500 copies of the article distributed to influential people throughout the country.[33]

Nor were navalists the only Americans upset over the compromise. Although the State Department made no official protest – claiming by mid-September to 'see a molehill where we formerly saw a mountain' – the accord seemed to convert President Coolidge to the Big Navy cause. He ordered Kellogg to cancel a scheduled visit to London, substituting a trip to Dublin instead – a calculated insult to the British Tories, many of whom still smarted over Irish independence. He further vented his frustration in an Armistice Day speech before the American Legion. After pointing out how America had saved Europe from 'starvation and ruin' in the aftermath of the World War, he explained that the country's long coastlines, extended trade routes, and large population required the use of heavy cruisers: 'Having few fueling stations, we require ships of large tonnage, and having scarcely any merchant vessels capable of mounting five or six-inch guns, it is obvious that, based on needs, we are entitled to a larger number of warships than a nation having these advantages.'[34] Meanwhile those who normally fought against any increase in the navy – liberals – felt betrayed by the British. Not only did they view the agreement as an attempt to manipulate pro-disarmament sentiment in

America, but they also saw it as a throwback to the days of the 'secret diplomacy' so despised by Woodrow Wilson.[35]

The most important effect of the Anglo-French compromise, however, was the added impetus which it gave to the Cruiser Bill, which was stalled in the Senate at the time. Public outrage over British diplomacy swept nearly all opposition to it aside. The Navy League assured its friends in Congress that the American press was nearly eight to one in favor of the bill, and President-elect Herbert Hoover publicly endorsed it. Sen. Claude Swanson (D-VA), claiming that the Anglo-French agreement only underlined 'the unfairness of...[Britain's] proposals at Geneva,' led southern Democrats in their unanimous support, adding their strength to pro-Navy Republicans. The result, recorded on February 13, 1929, was a landslide victory for the navalists, with a vote of 68 to 12. Only the progressives of the upper midwest refused to back the new construction.[36]

The passage of the Cruiser Bill, however, represented more than simply an interest in the navy, for in late 1928 and early 1929 the prospect of war between the United States and Great Britain, dismissed in the early 1920s as 'unthinkable,' was now beginning to appear a distinct possibility. The *New York World* asserted that war was, indeed, 'thinkable,' while the *Washington News* wrote that 'the specter of war hovers black and ugly in the background' of Anglo-American relations. Meanwhile the War Plans Division of the Navy Department, in its annual 'Estimate of the Situation' for 1928, recommended the 'development and refinement' of Plans Red and Red-Orange, which envisioned a war against either Britain alone or against a revived Anglo-Japanese alliance. Talk of war could be heard even in the Senate. Simeon Fess (R-OH), claimed that 'we are not wholly exempt from any danger of war' with Britain. James Reed (D-MO) went further, warning that '[f]rom the island of Jamaica in five and one-half hours' time...[Britain] can destroy with her airplanes the Panama Canal.'[37]

War may have been 'thinkable,' but how likely was it? There were some, indeed, who believed it was inevitable. Certain members of the Navy's General Board and the Irish-American community had been claiming since the early part of the decade that the question of naval supremacy could only be settled by war between the English-speaking powers. Rear Admiral Charles P. Plunkett, commandant of the Brooklyn Navy Yard, announced at a Republican club luncheon in early 1928 that 'we are nearer war to-day than ever before,' and that such a war was 'absolutely inevitable.' By early 1929 he was joined in this assessment by some prominent figures on the Left. Wisconsin Representative Victor Berger, the Socialist Party's only congressman, claimed that '[w]hat is taking place between Great Britain and America is almost exactly what took place between Britain and Germany in the decade that preceded the war.' America's quest for naval equality and access to world markets, he predicted, would lead to armed conflict. Ludwell Denny, in his 1930 book *America Conquers Britain*, asserted that 'economic war' had been taking place between the two countries ever since the end of the World War. He pointed to the results of the 1920 census, which showed that barely one-third of all Americans were of British stock, as an ominous sign of things to come. American capitalists, he predicted, would manipulate the growing non-British population – already by nature anti-British – into fighting a war for profits. He pointed specifically to the rubber controversy and to Big Navy agitation as two examples of business and industry playing to traditional anglophobia in pursuit of their interests. 'We were Britain's colony once,' Denny concluded. 'She will be our colony before she is done; not in name, but in fact.... If Britain is foolish enough to fight us, she will go down more quickly, that is all.'[38]

Others felt that war might come about as a result of continuing Anglo-American differences over neutral rights during wartime. Indeed, supporters of increased naval construction repeatedly reminded Americans of how during the last war Great Britain had claimed the right of search and seizure of neutral vessels on the high seas. The British had been able to get away with this outrage, they argued, because the U.S. Navy had been too small to prevent it. In 1928 Frank Simonds warned that if the navy were not enlarged significantly, 'Great Britain will continue to exercise the power to impose her will upon us and upon all other neutrals in case of war.' This argument ultimately proved persuasive in the Senate: Great Britain, said Thomas J.

Walsh (D-MT), was 'ruthless in the restrictions she imposes and entirely regardless of the principles of international law generally recognized.' This concern was believed to be so pressing that it was even written into the Cruiser Bill, in an amendment drafted by William Borah. The Idaho progressive, heavily influenced by the writings of Yale law professor Edwin M. Borchard, claimed that unless the powers were able to meet and codify international law regarding the rights of belligerents versus the rights of neutrals, 'we must not only build against England, but we must build against any combination at sea that England can make.' His amendment, therefore, called for 'a treaty, or treaties, with all the principal maritime nations regulating the conduct of belligerents and neutrals in war at sea, including the inviolability of private property thereon.' It passed, with only one dissenting vote.[39]

Those predicting war between Great Britain and the United States, however, overlooked a number of factors. The first was the essential opposition to war felt by the vast majority of the American people, even among those of non-British origin. It is significant that at almost precisely the same time when the Cruiser Bill was being debated, the Kellogg-Briand Pact for the Outlawry of War reached the Senate for ratification. There was no question that the bill would be passed; many Americans believed it was a means of guaranteeing peace without any particular commitment on the part of the U.S. There was one sticking point, however, concerning a reservation which the British Foreign Office had made before agreeing to the treaty, which justified war for self-defense only. Foreign Secretary Chamberlain added an interpretation of 'self-defense' which included 'certain regions of the world the welfare and integrity of which constitute a special and vital interest for our peace and safety.' In effect, Chamberlain had reserved the right of Great Britain to intervene in any part of the world where British dominion was challenged. The U.S. ambassador to England complained that this 'British Monroe Doctrine' opened 'a veritable Pandora's box of difficulties.' In the Senate, a long procession of statesmen protested that the treaty granted special rights to the British; William Cabell Bruce (D-MD) insisted that 'Great Britain has not become a party to the pact

at all.' Even Borah, the pact's main supporter, claimed that
with such a reservation 'the treaty would not be worth a
damn.' Hiram Johnson, meanwhile, dismissed the entire
agreement as 'just a great big piece of American bunk.'[40]
Yet despite their personal feelings toward the pact, the
senators of the 70th Congress had to take into account the
overwhelming support it had from the American public –
polls showed that some 95 percent supported its ratification.
The senators, therefore, found reason to cast their reluctant
votes in favor of the treaty. Bruce, despite his denunciation
of the British 'Monroe Doctrine,' justified his vote as a step
toward membership in the League of Nations. David I.
Walsh (D-MA), certainly no friend of the British Empire,
claimed that the failure of the Senate to ratify Kellogg-
Briand would be misunderstood by the world, and 'place the
United States...in the position of an obstructionist.' In the
end there was only one vote against ratification, that of
Wisconsin Progressive John J. Blaine, who called the treaty
'a one-sided declaration of British policy.' American support
for the pact, he claimed, would help to prop up 'a power that
is not only a menace to the peace of the world, but, as well, a
menace to civilization itself.' Most Americans, however, were
unwilling to rise to this height of anglophobia, even during
this period of Anglo-American tension. One newspaper, in
fact, called Blaine the spokesman for the 'lost cause of un-
compromising parochialism.'[41]
Nor were American businessmen eager to go to war. As
mentioned in the previous chapter, the vast majority believed that foreign markets and raw materials would
eventually come under American control without the need
for armed conflict. In fact, as Michael Hogan points out,
there was continued collaboration between British and
American businessmen throughout the period, including a
cooperative effort to protect the pound in 1927.[42]
Finally, although the Big Navy party quickly found itself at
the head of a revitalized anti-British coalition, its own anglophobia was never particularly sentimental or deep. As
historian Gerald Wheeler has argued, most naval officers
and members of the Navy League saw Japan, not Great
Britain, as the real enemy; however, since the Japanese fleet
remained considerably smaller than that of the U.S. in 1925,

it would be difficult to convince the American public –
despite the considerable anti-Japanese sentiment which
existed – that Japan was any sort of a threat to the United
States. Appealing to the old 'freedom of the seas' issue, in
addition to winning over the traditional anti-British forces,
would have a greater effect on the public at large. As Wilson's
old confidant, Colonel House, explained to Ambassador
Howard in late 1924, 'the American public was not really interested in armaments,' but that

> [T]he best way to interest them and make them willing to
> spend money on armaments…[is] for a foreign govern-
> ment to oppose such armaments, and so give some colour
> to the accusations in the Hearst and other papers that the
> United States government are bowing to the will of a
> foreign Power in not acceding to the demands of the Big
> Navy School.

House went on to predict that if Britain protested American
naval construction, 'a spirit of national antagonism would at
once be aroused which would carry Congress off its feet.'[43]

Moreover, in their writings many of the most ardent navalists seemed more like frustrated anglo*philes* than twisters of
the lion's tail. Despite his talk of the threat of the Royal Navy
to American shipping, Frank Simonds proposed canceling
the entire British war debt in one of his books. William
Howard Gardiner, Chairman of the Navy League, assured
the readers of *Harper's* that current difficulties with Britain
reflected nothing more than the ongoing 'rivalries that continue among the powers'; he only wished that 'the English in
general, and their Tories in particular,' would wake up to
the fact that 'America has overseas interests and outlooks
many of which are very similar to those of England.' Among
those in the Senate, Virginia Democrat Claude Swanson
agreed wholeheartedly, arguing that naval parity served 'the
best interests of the United States *and* Great Britain.' For
these men the most dangerous consequence of an Anglo-
American naval race was that the British Navy's stubborn
refusal to concede real parity to the American fleet might
stand in the way of future cooperation between the two
English-speaking powers.[44]

Yet though predictions of an Anglo-American war may

have been exaggerated, there is no denying that anglophobia was a widespread phenomenon in the political life of the late 1920s. One politician who liked the way the winds were blowing was William Hale Thompson, better known to his friends and cronies as 'Big Bill.' Thompson had served as mayor of Chicago from 1915 to 1923, remaining in power largely due to the appeal of his anti-British and anti-League of Nations rhetoric among Chicago's considerable population of German- and Irish-Americans. In 1923, however, even his ethnic support could not save him from evidence of widespread corruption within his administration, and he was unceremoniously turned out of office. Now, four years later, 'Big Bill' was ready to make a political comeback, and announced a new run for mayor. This time, however, he had an explosive issue that linked the anglophobe sentiments of the ethnic community with more local concerns, for the furor over allegedly pro-British school textbooks was in full swing. In New York City that same year hearings were held to determine whether materials being used in public schools were 'unpatriotic'; among those who testified was Edward F. McSweeney of the Knights of Columbus. The controversy made its way into the American press with the publication of an article by Judge Frederick Bausman entitled 'Under Which Flag?' which claimed that the British were using 'our literary class' as well as 'our own bejeweled class' to circulate propaganda in textbooks.[45]

The controversy finally reached Chicago with the formation of a 'Citizen's Committee on School Histories,' made up largely of citizens of German and Irish descent. The group drafted a petition calling upon Superintendent of Schools William McAndrew to remove from the curriculum a list of books defined as 'pro-British'; when McAndrew (an appointee of the incumbent Democratic mayor) failed to take any action, Thompson was handed a ready-made campaign issue. Largely ignoring his opponent, 'Big Bill' concentrated his fire on King George V, whom he warned to 'keep his snoot out of America,' as well as his 'stool pigeon,' McAndrew, whom he promised to 'fire…back to Wall Street.' It is eloquent testimony to the extent of American anglophobia that a mayoral candidate in the nation's second-largest city could use this issue as the basis for a campaign; that he won (albeit with considerable help from his ally, Al Capone) says a great deal about the appeal of anti-British rhetoric at the time.[46]

After a brief speaking tour in the wake of the election, Thompson returned home to begin civil service proceedings against McAndrew. First he suspended the superintendent on charges of insubordination, then he forced the resignation of several school board members so that he could pack the board with his own appointees. The formal accusations were numerous: that McAndrew had recommended certain textbooks that contained pro-British propaganda, 'all for the purpose of promoting propaganda for the English-Speaking Union'; that he had removed from school walls the famous picture 'The Spirit of '76' in order to carry out 'his purpose of perverting and distorting the ideals and patriotic instincts of our schoolchildren'; that he refused to allow children in the public schools to make contributions for the preservation of 'Old Ironsides,' the U.S.S. *Constitution*; and finally, that he had entered a conspiracy with Charles Judd, professor of history at the University of Chicago, to 'destroy the love of America in the hearts of children by encouraging teachers to attend special classes at Chicago University at which a textbook was used which pictured George Washington as a rebel and a great disloyalist.' The board voted six to five in favor of dismissing McAndrew, pending a formal trial.[47]

The trial itself was largely a procession of 'expert witnesses,' such as Frederick Bausman and anti-British former congressman John J. Gorman (R-IL), all of whom spent far more time attacking the American historical profession than anything McAndrew may have done. One witness, Chicago history teacher Rosalie Didier, claimed that historian Arthur M. Schlesinger should be imprisoned for calling Washington a rebel; another, Charles Grant Miller, head of the Patriotic League for the Preservation of American History, denounced Columbia University as a 'font of treasonous history.' Finally, in March 1928 the board voted eight to two to dismiss McAndrew, but the following year the ruling was overturned in the local courts.[48]

Thompson next turned against the Chicago Public Library, which he claimed was infested with British propaganda. 'I will not rest,' he announced, 'until I have purged this entire city of the poison that's being injected into the heart of American youth to eulogize England at the expense of their own country.' He assigned the investigation to his friend Urbine J. 'Sport' Herrmann, who informed the public of his intention to burn every pro-British work in the library. The project came to an ignominious halt, however, when it was discovered that, in the wake of the disastrous fire of 1871, approximately 12 000 volumes had been contributed to the Chicago library by English benefactors, including Gladstone, Disraeli, and even Queen Victoria herself.[49]

The press was almost uniformly critical of Thompson's actions. *Collier's*, for example, called him a 'flag-flapper,' while the editors of the Detroit *News* sarcastically asked, 'What British propagandist was it who disguised himself as Mrs. O'Leary's cow and started the Chicago fire?' Even the usually anti-British *Chicago Tribune* called the mayor 'a buffoon in a tommyrot factory.' Many suspected that the whole campaign might be a publicity stunt designed to put him in the running for the Republican presidential nomination in 1928. Only the Hearst papers defended him, claiming that his 'effort to keep the detractors out of American schools is a noble effort...worthy of emulation in other cities and other states.'[50]

But even though most of the national press ridiculed Thompson's antics, his essential point – that British propaganda was alive and well in American society – was taken quite seriously. In January 1927 Garet Garrett, an editor for both the *New York Times* and the *New York Herald Tribune*, compared the wartime propaganda efforts of Germany and Britain, concluding that the English were propagandists 'who do it intuitively with a kind of genius.' And even 'Big Bill's' accusations were regarded seriously enough to be entered into the *Congressional Record* by Sen. James E. Watson (R-IN).[51]

It was therefore in an atmosphere of intense anglophobia that the presidential elections of 1928 were held. The campaign pitted the popular former governor of New York, Al Smith, against Secretary of Commerce Herbert Hoover. Unsurprisingly, the question of Hoover's citizenship and his presumed pro-British orientation became an issue once more. A number of Republicans, claiming to place 'country before party,' opposed his candidacy, among them 'Big Bill'

Thompson. Progressive Republican John J. Blaine publicly endorsed Smith, calling Hoover's campaign 'the first step to make the so-called "American cousins" internationally a fact, and bind America to the imperialism of the British Empire.' At the same time, the fact that Smith was not particularly anti-British did not prevent the Democrats from twisting the lion's tail, especially in the cities. The National Democratic Club issued a series of pamphlets calling Hoover 'Lord Balfour's candidate; Sir Austen Chamberlain's candidate; King George's candidate.' One of Smith's campaign ditties, sung to the tune of 'Yankee Doodle,' used a similar appeal:

> We'll elect our own Al. Smith,
> We'll crown him, boys, with glory
> And Hoover he may go to ——
> We'll have no English Tory.[52]

Yet the force of anglophobia alone was insufficient to defeat Hoover, for Smith lacked appeal outside the largest cities; he was a Catholic, for one, and he spoke with a New York Irish brogue which, in an age of radio, worked against him in the Midwest and South. Though he did succeed in re-capturing the ethnic vote for the Democratic Party, this gain was offset by victories by Hoover in the formerly 'solid South.' Hoover was elected, and for the first time since Wilson a man with a reputation for being an anglophile went to the White House. Most of the important groups within the anti-British coalition had opposed him: the ethnic communi-ty had returned to the Democrats, while the progressives identified him (from his days as Secretary of Commerce) with big business. Jingoistic nationalists such as William Randolph Hearst continued to refer to him as 'a loyal and law-respect-ing subject of His Majesty, King George V,' while Colonel Robert McCormick, the conservative editor of the *Chicago Tribune*, announced at his inauguration, 'This man won't do.'[53] Pro-Navy forces were equally apprehensive; although Hoover had spoken in favor of the Cruiser Bill during the campaign, he had been an opponent of naval expenditures throughout the decade, and he made no secret of his desire to resume disarmament talks with the British. The anglo-phobes had indeed been dealt a severe defeat in the election of Hoover, and their influence would continue to wane during the first half of his presidency. Hostility to Britain, however, did not disappear, and would soon make a dramatic comeback with the help of the Great Depression.

3 'An Alien Administration'

One student of Herbert Hoover's foreign policy has characterized Hoover's attitude toward the British as 'colored by a
feeling of kinship but...not overly enthusiastic.' Though he
was no admirer of England's class-based social structure or of
the Empire, he trusted the British and regarded them personally as friends. Certainly he preferred the English to
other foreigners; he once claimed that he 'would rather have
an Englishman's mere confirmation letter of a verbal agreement than the most elaborate contract with any European
national.' Hoover had lived a good portion of his adult life
abroad, including a stint in England, and thus brought to the
White House a level of cosmopolitanism that stood in
marked contrast to his two predecessors. He listed among
British virtues '[i]ntimate professional associations, loyal
friendships, generous hospitality, constant glimpses of moral
sturdiness, great courage, a high sense of sportsmanship,
and cultivated minds.' Hoover's campaign against British
rubber restrictions during his tenure as Secretary of
Commerce was no evidence of any real anglophobia on his
part, but rather of his disdain for government involvement
in the 'bickerings and higgling of the market.'[1]

Indeed, the British themselves welcomed Hoover's election, and were doubly encouraged when in a conversation
with Ambassador Esme Howard the new president spoke ur-
gently of the need to improve relations between the
English-speaking powers. Hoover appointed financier
Charles Dawes, a man of known pro-British sympathies, as
ambassador to the Court of St. James, and immediately
began calling for a new international naval disarmament
conference. This time, he promised, the so-called 'naval
experts' would only be brought in on technical matters; they
would have no real say in the formulation of the American
position. Moreover, he spoke of the need to resolve the
cruiser issue through the use of a 'naval yardstick' by which
comparisons could be made between American heavy cruisers and smaller British vessels. The British, for their part,

were more than prepared to reopen talks. The new Labour Prime Minister, Ramsay MacDonald, was just as eager as Hoover to bring an end to the burgeoning naval competition, though Stanley Baldwin's Conservative Cabinet had reached the same conclusion several months before being voted out of office.[2]

But before any new negotiations could be conducted, Hoover felt it necessary to discredit the Big Navy party, whom he held responsible for the heady atmosphere of jingoism which reigned in early 1929. The president believed – as did the British – that the navalists were being funded by shipbuilding and steel concerns eagerly seeking lucrative government contracts, but solid evidence of this connection was not forthcoming until August of that year. It was in that month that William B. Shearer brought civil suit against the Bethlehem Shipbuilding Corporation, the Newport News Shipbuilding and Drydock Company, and the American Brown Boveri Electric Corporation on the grounds that they owed him over $250 000 for 'professional services' rendered by him during the years 1926 to 1929. During these years Shearer had been a prominent lobbyist for the Big Navy cause, and had played an important role in formulating the intransigent American position at the Geneva Conference.[3]

Hoover saw his opportunity, and instructed his Secretary of State, Henry Stimson, to launch an investigation of Shearer's activities. 'It may be a useful public example,' the president added, 'and one that we will need before we are finished.' He then called upon the companies named in the suit to answer the charge, and when they denied Shearer's claims he ordered a full investigation by the Justice Department. Hoover was reported as saying that he wished Great Britain could find a Shearer as well. Soon the Senate joined the fray, and Borah demanded further investigation by a subcommittee of the Naval Affairs Committee. Senate hearings opened on September 20 and continued intermittently until mid-January 1930. During these hearings, which featured testimony by directors of most major American shipbuilding concerns, it was established that Shearer had indeed been paid as a lobbyist in Washington and as an 'observer' at Geneva. Furthermore he was found to have connections with the Navy Department – he was reported to have been engaged in frequent conversations with at least four U.S. naval experts in Geneva.[4]

When Shearer himself appeared before the subcommittee he succeeded only in making the navalist cause look ridiculous. When asked to state his name, he responded, 'William Benton Shearer, American, Christian, Protestant, Nationalist.' He produced what he called an 'amazing secret document,' which contained a vicious British attack on the United States, but which actually turned out to be written by an Irish-American propagandist. He proudly claimed authorship of a host of anti-British pamphlets with titles such as *The Cloak of Benedict Arnold*. And the funds for his activities, it was revealed, came not only from the shipbuilding industry but from William Randolph Hearst, who paid him $2000 per month to agitate against the League of Nations and for increased naval expenditures.[5]

Now that the Big Navyites were somewhat discredited in the public mind, the next step toward ending the arms race was a visit to the United States by Prime Minister MacDonald in preparation for a new naval conference. Some in the administration felt that such a visit, which would be the first by a sitting prime minister, might backfire given the current anti-British mood. Ambassador Dawes, for instance, felt that it should be postponed until the cruiser issue was settled; he feared that it might create the impression that the differences between the two countries were greater than they actually were. The Senate, he claimed, was particularly susceptible to such an impression, being a 'breeding ground of imaginative and ingenious deviltry of the rarest order.' Hoover agreed to some extent, expressing the concern that 'our whole great program might in public mind degenerate into a huckster's quibble,' but feared the British reaction should the press find out that MacDonald had been told not to come.[6]

Dawes' and Hoover's concerns proved groundless, however. In a letter to Dawes written just days before his departure, MacDonald appeared to give in entirely to the American position on cruisers. 'This parity business is of Satan himself,' he wrote, further calling it 'an attempt to clothe unreality in the garb of mathematical reality.' While he refused to maintain anything less than a navy capable of defending the empire, he admitted that he was not really concerned with the size of the U.S. Navy – it was the rest of the world that he was worried about. On the American side, the *New Republic* saw the upcoming visit 'as an indication of the friendly intentions and peaceful attitude of the Labor Government of Great Britain.'[7]

The visit itself was a complete success, though more as an act of public relations than a feat of diplomacy. The talks themselves, conducted between Hoover and MacDonald at the presidential retreat at Rapidan, were largely inconsequential. Indeed, Sir Robert Vansittart, Undersecretary for Foreign Affairs, described them as horribly dull. The two leaders signed a joint declaration of faith in the Kellogg Pact and affirmed that war was no longer possible between their two countries. A formal conference was scheduled for London in the following year, to which all the important naval powers would be invited. The most important outcome of the visit, however, was its effect on American public opinion. MacDonald was treated to a ticker-tape parade through the streets of New York, and spoke before the Senate in Washington. A Scottish socialist who had opposed the war in 1914, he did not fit the American stereotype of the British politician – aristocratic, polished, and cunning – and he managed to convince Americans that his desire to end the arms race was indeed sincere. The *New York Times* called the visit 'an overpowering success.' An overjoyed Stimson, meanwhile, claimed that 'even the most blatant jingoes and British haters were temporarily in the great wave of good feeling which swept over the country.'[8]

Thanks largely to MacDonald's visit, the British had accumulated a substantial stock of goodwill among Americans by the time the London Naval Conference convened in January 1930. Negotiators on the U.S. side would therefore feel few of the pressures to 'get tough with John Bull' that their counterparts at Geneva had endured in 1926. Moreover, since the naval establishments of both countries were kept at arm's length, it was far easier for civilian delegates to reach some sort of accord. Most important of all, however, was the fact that the British were now openly and publicly offering naval parity in all classes of vessels; as MacDonald himself announced during his visit, 'What is all this bother about parity? Parity? Take it without reserve, heaped up and flowing over.'⁹

Such sentiments notwithstanding, however, the means of determining parity between Great Britain's preferred light cruisers and the heavier ones favored by the U.S. Navy remained unclear. For all Hoover's determination to find a 'yardstick' by which the two could be compared, the idea was far simpler in principle than in actual execution. Indeed, even before the conference began Stimson and MacDonald 'had come to the conclusion that it was impossible to find a scientific yardstick which could be agreed upon by the Admiralties of both sides.' But though the idea of the yardstick was rejected as a technical device, it still remained a powerful tool for winning over the American public. As Hugh Gibson, head of the American delegation, explained, 'The first thing is to find out how little the British can get along with, and how much we are obliged to build in order to attain a reasonable parity that will satisfy the Senate and the man-in-the-street; then all we have to do is to make a yardstick to fit that situation.'¹⁰

Reaching an agreement, therefore, was relatively simple. The British steadfastly refused to scrap any of their vessels, but promised to limit their total cruiser tonnage to 339 000. The U.S., meanwhile, would be permitted to build its heavier cruisers up to a total tonnage of 327 000; however, American negotiators promised to delay completion of their cruiser program until after 1936, when the question would be reopened at another conference. The cruiser issue finally seemed to be resolved: as Stimson wrote on February 23, the treaty had 'clearly accomplished one of our chief purposes, that of healing the serious friction which had arisen between America and Britain over cruisers.'¹¹

But could the American public, and the Senate in particular, be convinced that the British offer of parity was genuine? Long before the treaty had been signed attacks on its provisions could be heard in Congress and in the press. Arthur Sears Henning, correspondent for the *Chicago Tribune*, wired home accounts of the conference's proceedings that were markedly anti-British in tone; at home they were capped with such suggestive headlines as 'BRITISH FIGURES BARE DRIVE TO "SINK" U.S. NAVY' and 'BRITISH

GIGGLE AS UNCLE SAM GIVES UP SHIRT.' Stimson himself wrote to Ambassador Dawes in May warning of a concerted effort in some sectors of public opinion 'to confuse and discredit the treaty.' In the Senate, meanwhile, several of the Big Navyites registered their opposition, insisting that, far from guaranteeing parity, the treaty actually institution-alized American inferiority at sea. Hiram Johnson wrote that 'there never was such an outrage attempted to be put over on the American people since the League of Nations.' Tennessee Democrat Kenneth McKellar furthermore an-nounced that he would not vote to ratify any naval treaty which ignored the issue of neutral rights. 'It can not make for peace,' he claimed, 'to leave Great Britain in command of the seas in times of war.' Traditional enemies of England, such as the Irish-American community, leapt into the fray as well. The American Association for the Recognition of the Irish Republic adopted a special resolution denouncing the treaty, charging that 'the British Empire seeks to gain by flat-tery and chicanery what it cannot provide out of its own resources.'[12]

A special session of the Senate was called in July to delib-erate the London treaty, and there was some fear among certain British observers (Ambassador Howard chief among them) that the anglophobes in the upper house might close ranks and block ratification. Of special concern was Borah, who as chairman of the Foreign Relations Committee had a great deal of say over whether the treaty would pass. Borah, like McKellar, had objected to the failure of the conference to address the 'freedom of the seas' issue, and therefore, 'is quite capable of joining forces with the Big Navyites in order to smash up the whole agreement in the Senate.' MacDonald, in fact, took it upon himself to write to Borah personally, asking him not to oppose the settlement. There was, moreover, the chance that Democrats might use the op-portunity to scuttle what was, after all, an initiative from a Republican president. Yet it soon became apparent that no such troubles would arise. Democrats for the most part lined up behind their minority leader, Joseph D. Robinson of Arkansas, in support of the agreement; even many of the more moderate navalists (Claude Swanson of Virginia, for example) did not object to the pact, since it would take over a billion dollars in new construction just to reach the levels mandated under the treaty. Nor would Borah pose an obstacle – 'I have been unable to see any real merit to the Naval Treaty,' he wrote on May 19, 'I have no enthusiasm for it and yet I doubt if it would be helpful to defeat it.' As McKellar morosely concluded by mid-July, '[w]e have got a hopeless fight as I think British propaganda has brought out enough votes to ratify the treaty.'[13]

This left only the most ardent among the Big Navy party, as well as the most virulent anglophobes, in opposition to the London treaty. American negotiators, they claimed, had been 'outsmarted' or 'euchred' in the British capital; George Higgins Moses (R-NH) accused them of having 'announced in advance that they would accept whatever our British cousins chose to hand out to us.' Arthur Robinson (R-IN) agreed, calling the treaty a British 'ultimatum...given to the world.' Hiram Johnson aired his suspicions that American negotiators had spent too much time in England, associating with Englishmen and aping British ways. '[S]ometimes I think,' he said on the Senate floor, 'that the greatest foe of the American Navy is the English napkin.' Frederick Hale (R-ME), chairman of the Senate Naval Affairs Committee, warned that the treaty would bring upon the United States 'the contempt that a supine nation invariably gets and deserves to get.'[14]

Nor were the negotiators the only ones singled out for criticism; the British themselves came in for their share as well. Henrik Shipstead (R-MN) claimed that they were 'conspiring to control the governments of the world...in the name of peace.' McKellar warned that '[t]he ambition of Great Britain is to take the lands of other nations wherever she can take them,' while Nevada Democrat Key Pittman argued that the treaty would leave to Britain control of 'everything, from the vicinity of its coast clear around to Singapore, the Mediterranean, the Indian Ocean.' Finally John J. Blaine (R-WI), though inclined to support naval limitations, used the occasion to lambast the British for their behavior in India – 'the most atrocious conduct known to history on the part of a nation' – and introduced an amendment to the treaty demanding Indian self-rule.[15]

Yet in the end the treaty passed by a lopsided vote of 58 to

9. 'There never was any question of the outcome,' Johnson wrote to his sons, 'but I never have felt more proud of a contest in which I engaged.' McKellar wrote a friend that he was becoming disillusioned about internationalism, adding that '[o]ne or two more such treaties and America will have no Navy worthy of the name.'[16]

Thus in just over one year did the nation move from a storm of anti-British indignation to a new agreement with Great Britain. The Big Navy party, such an impressive movement in 1928 and 1929, and a rallying point for anglophobes across the country, was now in disarray. The nation had grown tired of the cruiser issue and other naval questions; when a new naval authorization bill came up in 1932, aimed at building the navy up to treaty levels, it failed in the House of Representatives. What had caused this shift of opinion? Part of the answer, to be sure, is that Hoover and MacDonald were both passionately committed to arms limitation, but this does not tell the complete story. The real key to the decline of navalism was the state of the world economy, which was then in the early throes of the Great Depression. The need to reduce government expenditure on armaments was one issue on which many Democrats and Republicans alike were willing to agree. George Norris (R-NE) put it simply: 'I would rather feed people than build battleships.' And though Big Navy advocates such as Frederick Hale complained that the navy was being allowed 'to go absolutely on the rocks,' Americans were feeling less and less sympathetic to their cause.[17]

In the short run, of course, these changing attitudes gave a boost to Anglo-American relations. For the first time since the end of World War I, senators could be heard speaking of the 'invisible ties' that connected the English-speaking powers. Prime Minister MacDonald even referred to Anglo-American cooperation as 'one of the few bright spots in this gloomy world.'[18]

But anglophobia was far from dead; it would emerge as an even more potent force by the mid-1930s. It is, however, accurate to say that anglophobia was changing. Led as it had been by the Big Navy party in the 1920s, the anti-British coalition was marked by a spirit of militant nationalism which saw the navy as the outward sign of America's status as a world power. By the early 1930s, however, attitudes had changed. No longer was the United States viewed as the next Germany, rising up to challenge John Bull. Now, in a period of world economic depression, Americans no longer feared the British as a potential enemy, but as a potential ally. Old issues like parity and freedom of the seas were declining in importance; what was crucial now was that England not be allowed to lure the United States into a war to protect the interests of the British Empire.

This sentiment was not exactly new; it had, in fact, begun to gain strength in the mid-1920s. World War revisionism as early as 1926 was beginning to take a more overtly anti-British course as it turned its attention away from the origins of the war itself and toward the motives behind U.S. intervention. Actually, the revisionists were far from united. Some, such as Charles A. Beard and Harry Elmer Barnes, blamed American banks, which wanted U.S. involvement to protect their investments in Britain and France. Others, primarily Judge Frederick Bausman and C. Hartley Grattan, charged that the British themselves tricked Americans into believing that the war was a struggle for democratic ideals. 'The British propagandists,' Grattan wrote in his 1929 *Why We Fought*, 'counted heavily on the naivete of the...American public.' Both Grattan and Bausman believed in a conspiracy between British agents and the pro-British American State Department to bring America into a war to defend the British Empire. Some observers professed to see the same thing happening in the late 1920s. In a rare moment of agreement, both H. L. Mencken and the editors of the *Nation* claimed that the Empire was falling apart, that England's leaders were 'pathetically fourth-rate.' The only logical course for them to follow, then, was to appeal to 'the great young empire of the Western Hemisphere, rich America, the new marvel, the traditional friend of democracy and of oppressed peoples' to help them restore their former imperial glory.[19]

The Depression served only to strengthen such convictions, as the public often blamed the troubled times on England's failure to manage the world economy effectively. As D. C. Watt has written, 'American opinion had concluded that Britain as a partner in American purposes was unreliable, immoral, corrupt and invariably ended with the lion's share (in both the proverbial and the symbolic sense).' By the early 1930s, moreover, suspicions of British intentions had merged with popular resentment toward big business, and banks in particular – America's pro-British business and banking community was operating hand-in-glove with the State Department, the Hoover administration, and the British government to design a foreign policy which favored British over American interests.[20]

Nor was it only the mass of the American public that had become increasingly distrustful of Great Britain by 1932. Elites, especially within the foreign policy establishment, were becoming disillusioned as well, thanks in large part to the so-called Stimson Note of January 7, 1932. During the previous September the Japanese army had occupied Manchuria and set up a puppet regime there. Secretary of State Stimson's response was an announcement that the United States would not recognize the Japanese conquest, or the legality of the puppet state of Manchukuo. Furthermore he called upon the British government to make a similar declaration. He was to be sorely disappointed by the response of the Foreign Office, and the result was a sticking point in Anglo-American relations which would remain until the Second World War. Foreign Secretary Sir John Simon claimed that this was an issue for the League of Nations, or that at the very least the other signatories to the Nine Power Pact of 1922 had to be brought into any discussion of a response to the Japanese occupation.[21]

For Stimson this response amounted to a complete rebuff. He followed up his nonrecognition note with a public letter to Borah on February 24, in which he invited other nations to join the U.S. in denouncing the Japanese violation of the Washington Treaties. He claimed that he had made an honest attempt at Anglo-American cooperation to confront the Far Eastern crisis, but that the British 'preferred to take refuge in the inconspicuousness of League action among the flock of European nations.' He furthermore accused the Foreign Office of siding with Japan on the issue, complaining of 'a strong tendency on the part of one group in Britain [the Tories] to defend Japan's actions.'[22]

This interpretation, however, was not entirely accurate. As

Robert Ferrell has pointed out, the Foreign Office had never intended its response to the Stimson Note as a rebuff. The note had been hurriedly read, and a response hastily written and cabled, on a Saturday afternoon , as most of the staff of the office's Far Eastern Section were about to leave for the rest of the weekend. 'They did not realize until the following Monday,' Ferrell writes, 'that it read like a rebuff to America.' Nor was Stimson acting under anything but his own authority; it is far from likely that he would have had any support among the administration, let alone from the Congress, for a joint Anglo-American policy toward the Far East.[23]

Nevertheless most Americans believed in Stimson's interpretation of the affair – that the note had been an offer of good faith thrown back in his face by a pro-Japanese British Empire. Even those who, like Hiram Johnson, denounced Stimson as a hated internationalist, but were in any case inclined to believe the worst about the British, accepted the Secretary of State's version of the story. Indeed, the legend would grow throughout the decade, and by 1940 the British ambassador, Lord Lothian, complained of 'the universal conviction in America that Manchuria would have been saved if it had not been for Simon's opposition.'[24]

This renewed sense of distrust of things British helped to hamstring Hoover's attempts to deal with the war debt situation in the last two years of his presidency. Much of this involved partisan politics as well, since the 1930 congressional elections had left him facing a Democratic House and a Senate in which the Republican majority was so slim that Progressive Republicans could conspire with Democrats to torpedo almost any presidential initiative. Hoover nonetheless believed that some revision of the debt settlement was necessary in order to revive the world economy. This reflected his belief that the causes of the Depression were largely foreign, and could be alleviated by some compromise on war debts and reparations. In late spring of 1931 the British government decided to force his hand. When Germany went into default on its reparations to Britain and France, the Chancellor of the Exchequer announced that England would withdraw all of its funds from the German Reichsbank if the United States did not agree to a temporary suspension of war

debts. Ray Atherton, the American chargé in London, suggested an effort 'toward a postponement of payments,' and
wrote Stimson that such a proposal 'should...contemplate at
least two years.'[25]

Hoover realized that in its current mood the Senate (which
still claimed the final word over war debt policy) would be unlikely to support any suspension of payments that might still
be in effect during the 1932 elections. However, as Stimson
reported to MacDonald, the president enjoyed 'gratifying
success' in garnering the support of the Senate's leadership
for a one-year moratorium. Even such anglophobes as Borah,
George Higgins Moses, David I. Walsh, and James E. Watson
of Indiana recognized that failure to take action would
further damage the international economy. As it turned out,
the moratorium did not come up for approval on the Senate
floor until mid-December, six months after it had gone into
effect, and was thus unlikely to be overturned in any event.
Most senators agreed with Majority Leader Walter E. Edge
(R-NJ) when he argued that, 'failure to ratify would entail the
loss of the political authority of the United States in world
affairs.'[26]

Though ratification of the moratorium was practically
assured, the temptation to criticize Great Britain and France
proved too strong for some to resist. The *Chicago Tribune* ap-
provingly reported how Hiram Johnson 'ripped to pieces'
the idea on the Senate floor. Nebraska's George Norris proposed an amendment that would make the moratorium
apply only to those nations which agreed to the revision of
the Treaty of Versailles, including, he added, 'the return to
the German Government of its former but now mandated
colonies.' John Blaine was quick to agree, contending that,
aided by that treaty, the British were 'restricting and circum-
scribing, step by step, America's future wealth and
prosperity' by expanding their empire and raising tariffs.
The amendment failed, and the moratorium passed by a vote
of 69 to 12 on December 23. In order that their intentions
might not be misunderstood, however, the House and Senate
approved a joint resolution on the same day, expressly for-
bidding any cancellation or reduction of the debts. Thus the
moratorium represented at best a delay of the inevitable, far
less than the British had hoped. Stimson tried to explain to

the new British ambassador, Sir John Lindsay, that the news was good – that 'we think we got along as well as we could possibly expect.' The joint resolution, he claimed, 'simply indicates the difficulties which any American President faces when he goes into foreign affairs.'[27] Lindsay, however, remained pessimistic on the subject of war debt revision. As he wrote back to the Foreign Office,

> The average congressman will return to Washington next month, his ears ringing with cries of distress, his pockets stuffed with repudiated bonds. His views are usually superficial, and he is surprisingly ignorant of extra-American affairs. He may be expected to approach his legislative task in a mood distinctly anti-administration and anti-foreign, indisposed to ask 'how can we help the world?' but arguing that for the current year America has remitted everything she can remit with confusion worse confounded as the result.[28]

Still, Congress and the public constantly suspected that the administration would try to cancel the debts. A visit by Stimson to MacDonald's home in Scotland in August 1931 led to a barrage of rumors, as did the appointment of Andrew Mellon, former Secretary of the Treasury and outspoken advocate of cancellation, as ambassador to the Court of St. James in early 1932. These suspicions were heightened further with the publication in April of the British budget for the following year, which included no provision for the payment of the debt. Hoover's proposal to reestablish the old World War Debt Financing Committee led Senate Minority Leader Joseph T. Robinson to ask, 'Is the interest of the British taxpayer the primary concern of the administration in this distressing period?' Hoover quickly withdrew the plan, advising Britain and France to disarm. If they did, he offered, Congress might change its mind; if not, he warned, 'Heaven help the British and French when they come to America about their debts next December.'[29]

Hoover was not the only one recommending disarmament in 1932. A common theme in the debate over war debts in the Senate was that the British government could hardly plead poverty when it was spending upwards of half a billion dollars each year on military expenditures. England, Borah claimed, was more heavily armed than 'at any time except in the midst of the great World War.' An editorial cartoon in the *Chicago Tribune* showed two unemployed men talking about the situation, worrying over 'Poor England with scarcely money enough to maintain the largest navy in the world....An' us rolling in the lap of luxury with scarcely 10 million idle.' In a letter to Lindsay, Stimson admitted that renegotiation of the debt would contribute to economic recovery, but reminded the ambassador that 'in the American mind' it was impossible to separate the issues of debt and disarmament. To Lindsay, however, this amounted to 'Open your mouth and shut your eyes and see what I will give you.'[30]

Of course, all of this was going on against the backdrop of the 1932 presidential election campaign, which pitted a thoroughly unpopular Hoover against Franklin Delano Roosevelt, a man whose foreign policy views were somewhat unclear. He had been a diligent supporter of Wilson's League of Nations in 1919, leading some of his opponents to label him an internationalist. He was defended against this charge by Senators Clarence Dill (D-WA) and Burton K. Wheeler (D-MT), who predicted that Roosevelt would come out against the League, which he did in February 1932.[31] It soon became clear that it was Hoover, not Roosevelt, who would have to defend himself against charges of internationalism and anglophilia. Not surprisingly, the old stories of his supposed attempts to gain British citizenship popped up once again, this time aided by the publication of a screed entitled *The Strange Career of Mr. Hoover Under Two Flags.* Raymond Moley, Roosevelt's chief economic adviser, claimed that the president had promised cancellation of England's war debts if reelected. After all, a plank had been inserted in the Democratic party platform opposing cancellation, while the Republican platform included no such pledge.[32]

Despite all this, and despite the high esteem in which the British government held Hoover, the Foreign Office pinned its hopes on Roosevelt. For one thing, Hoover seemed doomed to defeat anyway, and Roosevelt seemed to be the least objectionable of the Democrats; he was certainly preferable to vice presidential candidate John Nance Garner, whom Lindsay described as 'a man after Mr. Hearst's heart, with a closed mind and the xenophobia of a Boxer.' Moreover, the British found the current situation – with Hoover facing a hostile Congress – intolerable. Since any effort made by Hoover toward greater Anglo-American co-operation was likely to be used as an opportunity for demagoguery anyway, Roosevelt was unlikely to do any worse. Still, in Lindsay's opinion, not much was to be expected from him, as he was 'hardly a great enough man' to 'guide policy on national rather than local lines.'[33]

Of course, it would be misleading to imply that foreign affairs *per se* had any real effect on the outcome of the election of 1932, which not only sent Roosevelt to the White House but also gave the Democrats control of both houses of Congress. The state of the American economy, and Hoover's failure to bring about any sort of recovery, was more than enough to guarantee his defeat. It is also true, however, that Hoover's known fondness for things British helped con-tribute to the negative image which many Americans had of him by 1932. After all, at a time when he consistently held out against large-scale relief for unemployed Americans, he appeared to be moving heaven and earth to forgive England's war debts.

Moreover, the charge of 'anglophilia' had come full circle by the early 1930s – for the first time since the war it was being associated in the popular mind with the Republican Party rather than with the Democrats. This was especially dis-turbing to conservatives such as Colonel Robert McCormick of the *Chicago Tribune*, who actually endorsed Roosevelt and would continue to blame Hoover's pro-British policies for the Republican rout of 1932. This theme was taken up in Congress by Representative George Holden Tinkham (R-MA), who in February 1933 attacked 'those who would denationalize the United States.' He proceeded to name 'dis-loyal and seditious organizations' such as the Carnegie Endowment for International Peace and the Rockefeller Foundation' as promoters of a 'subversive, disloyal, and sedi-tious movement against American independence....' He concluded by attributing Hoover's defeat in large part to 'the opinion of the American people that this administration had been an alien adminstration, devoted to the interest of Europe and not to the interest of America,' and called upon the Republican Party to 'purge itself' of the influence of anglophiles such as Hoover. Neither party, it seemed, was likely to be overly friendly toward Great Britain in the years to come.[34]

4 'Tail to the British Kite'

In an address before the Women's National Republican Club in New York on January 21, 1933, outgoing Assistant Secretary of State William R. Castle argued that '[i]n general, the Democratic Party has been more parochial than the Republican, more in favor of a policy of isolation.' Furthermore, he contended, 'Senator Reed of Missouri was really more representative of Party feeling than was President Wilson....' While he may have been overestimating the internationalism of Republicans outside the Hoover administration, his characterization of the Democrats was nonetheless accurate. The elections of 1930, 1932 and 1934 had so reduced the power of the Republican party in Congress that mainstream Republicans would have no significant influence over foreign affairs until 1939. The Roosevelt administration and Congress, dominated thoroughly by Democrats and progressive Republicans, would set the agenda on foreign policy for most of the 1930s, putting a stamp on it that was both anti-interventionist in general and anti-British in particular.[1]

As for Franklin Roosevelt himself, there has been a strong tendency in the popular mind to portray him as a strident anglophile, based mainly on his close working relationship with Winston Churchill. Yet though the president had a definite fondness for British culture, and indeed had traveled widely and had made many acquaintances in Great Britain before taking office, he did hold many views toward the mother country that might be defined as traditionally American. He had long been a critic of the British Empire, even heading a movement for Boer relief in his days at Harvard. Later in his presidency, the British Embassy would routinely warn English visitors to the White House that Roosevelt was likely to make some snide comment about the empire in any meeting. He also distrusted the upper classes, whom both he and his wife Eleanor characterized as arrogant and selfish, and he was always prepared to ascribe British setbacks to 'too much Eton and Oxford.' He felt the

84

same way toward the tactics of Foreign Office diplomacy, observing in 1936 that 'when you sit around a table with a Britisher he usually gets 80% out of the deal and you get what is left.' In his dealings with English diplomats he was, in the words of J. M. Blum, 'always afraid of losing a round in negotiation to London, always conscious that British and American interests were not identical.' Nor would this attitude change, even when the United States and Great Britain were clearly growing closer in the late 1930s. He was always concerned that the U.S. maintain the upper hand in any Anglo-American partnership, that any cooperation would be on his terms; above all, that the U.S. be prevented from becoming 'a tail to the British kite.'[2]

The British themselves had strong reservations regarding Roosevelt's closest advisers. The British ambassador, Sir John Lindsay, warned his superiors at Whitehall that Rexford G. Tugwell possessed 'a distinct anti-British bias,' while Raymond Moley was a man of 'definitely second-rate ability.' Both men were economic nationalists, suspicious of what they saw as an alliance of Wall Street and the City of London which they blamed for many of America's problems. The president's cabinet choices also reflected a certain disregard of British sensitivities. His appointee for Secretary of the Navy was longtime Big Navyite Senator Claude Swanson of Virginia; for Attorney General Thomas J. Walsh of Montana, who had been one of the most outspoken champions of the movement for Irish independence (Walsh would, however, be killed in a train wreck on his way back to Washington to accept the nomination). Roosevelt's choice for Interior Secretary was none other than arch-anglophobe Hiram Johnson, who nevertheless turned down the appointment on the grounds that it would limit his cherished political independence. Even Tennessee Senator Cordell Hull, a longtime internationalist and the nominee for Secretary of State, was less than satisfactory in Lindsay's eyes; though he was a man of 'utmost integrity, dignity and charm' who would speak at length to diplomatic visitors, 'when they return to their houses they usually have difficulty in remembering anything he has said which deserves to be reported.'[3]

One of the first issues of foreign policy which Roosevelt had to face was the lingering debt situation. In December

1932 the British had made a payment of 95 million dollars in gold, but made it clear that this was 'not to be regarded as a resumption of the annual payments,' since in the eyes of the British government the repayment schedule established in 1923 'cannot be revived without disaster.' Hoover had invited the president-elect to the White House in November in an attempt to establish some sort of continuity on debt policy, but the meeting failed completely when Roosevelt, quite understandably, refused to make any commitment which might associate himself with the outgoing administration. Hoover dejectedly concluded that the president-elect 'did not get it at all,' while Lindsay remarked that 'in these complex economic matters' Roosevelt was 'an almost complete amateur and an opportunist.'[4]

Nevertheless, Roosevelt promised to send a delegation when the British announced a World Economic Conference in London scheduled for the summer. Some senators, especially Illinois Democrat J.Hamilton Lewis, opposed even this, calling such a conference 'outrageous' and 'rarely paralleled in the relations of a debtor to his creditor.' Even those who did not protest American participation were careful to warn the president that the renegotiation of the debt was the prerogative of Congress. Sen. Arthur Robinson (R-IN) claimed that there was 'nothing to discuss' when it came to the debts, and Patrick McCarran (D-NV) warned against a revival of 'the propaganda that prevailed in this country and was broadcast here under British dominance and under British money before the war was declared.' These men had little to fear from the president, however; not only was he determined not to allow international economic concerns (i.e., war debts, reparations, and monetary stabilization) to hinder his program for domestic national recovery, but he even recommended Hiram Johnson as a member of the American delegation to London. Unsurprisingly, the conference was a failure, in large part due to intransigence on the part of the United States.[5]

Thus the United States and Great Britain remained at an impasse on the debt issue, with the Roosevelt administration and Congress refusing to discuss renegotiation and the British government insisting that it could not pay. In June the British announced that they would make a 'token payment' of ten million dollars, what Lindsay called 'an acknowledgement of the debt pending a final settlement.' When Roosevelt accepted this he was met with a storm of protest from members of Congress who insisted that the 'token payment' amounted to a default. Sen. David Reed (R-PA) called it 'a contemptuous gesture,' while Hiram Johnson referred to it as 'a fraud, a farce, and a delusion.' By accepting it, they insisted, the administration had unilaterally canceled some 90 percent of the war debt, at a time when Great Britain was running a budget surplus.[6]

It was in response to the failure of the London Economic Conference and the announcement of the 'token payment' that Johnson revived an old piece of legislation which he had sponsored in February of 1932. Originally aimed at protecting private American investors from the sale of unstable Latin American bonds, the bill would ban all loans to countries which had defaulted on previous debts. In early 1932 it had no relevance to the European situation, as no country had yet defaulted on its war debts, but in mid-1934 it could serve as an effective bludgeon against America's former allies. It immediately ran into opposition from the Departments of State and Treasury, both of which hoped to use debt remission as a lever to win a more favorable trade agreement from the British. The British themselves viewed the proposed ban as a decidedly unfriendly gesture. The Johnson Act, as it had come to be known, made no distinction between those who were in complete default, such as France, and those who, like Britain, were making token payments on the debt. Lindsay warned Secretary of State Hull that such an act would be 'bitterly resented' in London. Roosevelt had some initial reservations, but promised full support as long as the bill would only apply to private loans, and would continue to allow the government to float loans to nations in default; indeed, even Hull offered no objection to the Johnson Act in this form. As for Congress, there was almost no opposition, and the bill passed by a voice vote. And despite Lindsay's warnings of 'repercussions,' Roosevelt signed the bill on April 13.[7]

Since the Johnson Act banned loans both to those in complete default and those making token payments, it came as no surprise that Great Britain stopped making even the token payments. Hull even suggested that the British might be able to avoid default through 'special payments in the form of...certain strategic raw materials' such as tin and nickel – a suggestion which the Foreign Office indignantly refused to countenance. Johnson would be widely criticized for having introduced a bill which cut off even the small flow of repayments which still existed in 1934; many claimed that he had effectively forgiven the war debts, something which he had constantly accused his opponents of attempting. Indeed, Lindsay would derisively refer to him thereafter as the 'Iron Canceller.' However, these critics missed the essential point. By 1934 Johnson was convinced that America's debtors would never repay the loans from the Great War; the Johnson Act had nothing to do with forcing them to resume payments. His motives were rather to prevent the extension of further loans to the former allies, and thus to avoid an economic incentive for entering any future European conflict, and to prevent the British from getting away with making only token payments. The Johnson Act succeeded on both counts.[8]

Another of Roosevelt's concerns during his first term was the expansion of the navy. The president had long been a 'Big Navy' enthusiast, but the Depression gave naval construction a new urgency as a public works program which even many conservatives could favor. The moratorium on new capital ships, a key part of the London Naval Treaty of 1930, was due to expire at the end of 1936, and the administration envisioned a massive building program aimed at bringing the U.S. Navy up to the strength allowed under the treaty. In January 1934 the Vinson-Trammell Bill was introduced into Congress, authorizing construction of (but not allocating funds for) 102 new ships and 1184 naval aircraft over a seven-year period. Though the new construction was aimed primarily at Japan, the British government protested that it might trigger a new Anglo-American naval race. Of special concern were American plans to construct four 10 000-ton cruisers carrying six-inch guns. British Foreign Minister Sir John Simon argued that this amounted to 'creating a new type' of vessel, one not covered under the London treaty and thus in violation of the spirit, if not the letter of the agreement. The State Department replied tersely that the U.S. had no intention of altering the construction program, since, as veteran negotiator Norman Davis pointed out, 'we had gotten so much below the treaty limit there could be no question raised by anyone regarding our taking steps to bring up our strength....'[9]

In Congress the Vinson-Trammell Bill had the enthusiastic support of most Democrats and what remained of the Big Navy Republicans, while progressives of both parties mounted a spirited opposition. Most interesting about the debate, however, was that both sides attempted to play the anti-British card. Supporters of Vinson-Trammell used Simon's protest over the new type of cruiser as the bill's biggest selling point, and pro-navy congressmen such as Louis T. McFadden (R-PA) and Fred Britten (R-IL) denounced pacifistic organizations opposed to the naval buildup (for instance, the Federal Council of Churches of Christ of America, the American Civil Liberties Union, the Socialist Party and the League of Women Voters) as 'more British than American.' At the same time, progressives such as Wisconsin's James A. Frear accused the navalists of wanting a large navy in order to help Britain in its next war. And in 1936, when it came time to allocate the actual funds for the program, Senators Gerald Prentiss Nye (R-ND), Homer T. Bone (D-WA), Robert M. La Follette, Jr. (R-WI) and Bennett Champ Clark (D-MO) accused the administration of dragging the U.S. 'into a secret alliance with England,' claiming that the new vessels would be used 'to pull British irons out of the fire in the Far East.' There was no stopping the impetus for naval construction, however, and both Vinson-Trammell and the allocation bill passed by wide margins.[10]

But though the new naval program was a setback for the pacifist movement, it was not a serious one, for the peace movement remained strong. In 1933, for example, 15 000 students from 65 colleges around the country signed a pledge not to fight unless the United States were actually invaded. In 1934 their cause was helped immeasurably by the publication of *Merchants of Death* by H. C. Engelbrecht and F. C. Hanighen. A Book-of-the-Month Club selection and an almost immediate bestseller, *Merchants of Death* showed the role of munitions-makers and arms dealers in starting and prolonging wars. The attack on arms merchants, coming at a time when the popularity of businessmen was already low, gained wide appeal, and corporations such as DuPont soon found themselves depicted alongside British propagandists and international bankers as part of a mammoth conspiracy to lure the United States into war.[11]

The formation and hearings of the Nye Committee came about in part as a result of the emotions aroused by *Merchants of Death*. This Senate committee, headed by progressive Republican Gerald Nye of North Dakota conducted an ongoing investigation from September 1934 to February 1936 into the role played by arms makers, as well as by international bankers and financiers, in the entry of the U.S. into the World War. The committee met with the blessings of Roosevelt, who claimed to have 'come around entirely to the ideas of Mr. [William Jennings] Bryan' on the issue. Indeed, inasmuch as the targets of the investigation were wealthy businessmen – the same group that Roosevelt was attempting to use as scapegoats for the Depression – they could serve the president's purposes well. The president therefore approved a generous budget for the Nye Committee, and allowed them access to numerous presidential files which were otherwise confidential.[12]

The early proceedings were largely exercises in the anti-business rhetoric that characterized so much of the political culture of the period. The committee's focus soon shifted, however, to the connections of certain American concerns with the British government. Part of this stemmed from Nye's own hostility toward Great Britain, which he associated with eastern financial and industrial interests such as J. P. Morgan and Company. When in March 1935 the committee subpoenaed the files of the Guaranty Trust Company relating to loans made to Great Britain, the Foreign Office protested loudly. Lindsay complained that the committee was treating his government 'as a circus animal which would be made to perform tricks for the spectators.' Hull and Roosevelt met again with the committee, asking that this part of the investigation be dropped, but received nothing but assurances that the contents of the files in question would not be made public.[13]

The Nye Committee, however, soon met with an ignominious end. On January 15, 1936, Nye accused the late

President Wilson of having lied to the American people regarding his knowledge of the existence and terms of secret treaties among the Allies during the World War. Even Hiram Johnson, certainly no great defender of Wilson, called the charge 'unnecessary and unrestrained' and suggested that he was 'exploiting his position' on the committee. The Democrats, as might be expected, were even harsher in their characterizations of Nye. Senators Tom Connally (D-TX) and Carter Glass (D-VA) led much of the Senate leadership in attacking the North Dakota progressive and the committee, and the hearings soon collapsed amidst partisan bickering. Yet the final report of the committee included a veritable laundry list of British sins during the war, mentioning not only English violations of neutral rights, but also the charging of rental fees to American soldiers for use of British trenches ('We fought their war and had to pay for the privilege of giving us a battle ground.') and the diversion to the British Isles of military supplies earmarked for American forces in France.[14]

Although the proceedings of the Nye Committee came to a halt amidst a storm of recrimination, its findings led to the introduction and passage of the Neutrality Acts of 1935 and 1936. Taken together, these two pieces of legislation sought to keep the United States out of future wars by avoiding the circumstances which most Americans believed had led to American involvement in the last war. Sponsored by Nye and Bennett Champ Clark (D-MO), the 1935 bill prohibited all arms shipments to belligerents, and permitted American citizens to travel on belligerent ships only on the condition that they did so at their own risk. The act of 1936 compounded this by adding a prohibition of loans to nations at war.

As had been the case with the Nye Committee proceedings, Roosevelt had little quarrel with the spirit and intent of the Neutrality Laws. However, the administration differed with the Nye-Clark version of the legislation on the subject of the arms embargo. The president feared that a blanket embargo on all belligerents would needlessly hamstring the executive, and thus proposed – by way of Key Pittman (D-NV), chairman of the Senate Foreign Relations Committee – a discretionary embargo which could be placed on either or both combatants. Congress, however, was not about to stand for this, and Roosevelt was attacked for wanting to take sides in future conflicts.[15]

Yet even though the Pittman resolution never found its way out of the Senate Foreign Relations Committee, Roosevelt dutifully signed both Neutrality Acts. Part of the reason for this was that a veto would almost certainly have been overturned, and that he was unwilling to risk defeat over an issue which, after all, remained for him a fairly low priority. It is also important to remember that the purpose of the bill – to keep America out of any foreign war – was one that Roosevelt supported no less than Nye or Clark.[16]

The battle over neutrality legislation, then, was thus not particularly important as a contest between Congress and the administration; that Roosevelt would prefer a discretionary embargo to one that was mandatory and impartial merely reflected his natural inclination to defend the prerogatives of his office. Far more revealing was the clash between two competing notions of neutrality that emerged during the Senate debate over the 1936 act. Recalling that sinkings of American merchant vessels by German submarines had been one of the prime causes of U.S. entry into the Great War, Nye and Clark hoped to include in their revised neutrality legislation the provision that those engaged in trade with belligerents must do so at their own risk. This was anathema to those who, like Borah and Johnson, had championed the cause of freedom of the seas in the 1920s. Johnson called the idea 'illogical and harmful,' the work of the 'pacifist societies' in collusion with pro-British internationalist organizations such as the Carnegie Endowment for Peace. For his part Borah refused to believe 'that neutrality is synonymous with cowardice.' '[I]f we provide by law what shall be legitimate,' he wrote in January, 'then we are duty bound to protect our citizens in carrying on that trade.' They were joined in their fight by international lawyers such as Edwin Borchard and John Bassett Moore, who testified before the Senate Foreign Relations Committee that it was 'inconceivable' that the United States consider abandoning its historic position as defender of the freedom of the seas in favor of 'a gopher-like policy of seclusion.' Borchard, who in the following year would publish his *magnum opus*, *Neutrality for the United States*, argued that it was not America's enforcement of neutral rights that brought the U.S. into war, but rather the unwillingness of American diplomats to stand up to the British in defense of those rights.[17]

Though Nye's 'trade-at-your-own-risk' proposal was voted down, the issue remained far from settled in late 1936. Nye, ever the moral crusader, continued to deny that 'private American citizens in pursuit of fat profits had a right to involve us in war,' and to regard the concept of freedom of the seas as illusory. Johnson, who regarded Nye as 'a well-meaning boy, without any great capacity,' warned that the battle had merely been postponed, and not won. Pacifist groups, he warned, were forming 'a militant, aggressive army' with the active support of the internationalists. Johnson would soon be proven correct, and the debate resumed the following year over the 'cash-and-carry' provisions of the 1937 Neutrality Act.[18]

The whole incident illustrates a central fact about American thinking on foreign policy in the mid-1930s. Most Americans believed that U.S. involvement in the World War had been a profound mistake, and one which must not be repeated. Beyond this, though, there was a great deal of disagreement over why the United States had been dragged into war, and how such a thing might be prevented from happening again. The debate, in short, was not over whether or not the U.S. should take a more active role in world affairs – the fabled duel of 'isolationist vs. internationalist' – but over the best way in which to remain disengaged.

In such an environment anglophobia was bound to thrive. To be sure, there was little American goodwill toward any foreign country at the time, and to this extent historian Manfred Jonas's definition of isolationism as 'studied indifference' to the rest of the world is accurate. However, Great Britain occupied a special place in the American view of the world in the 1930s. Many nations owed war debts, for example, but the British debt was the largest by far. Many nations felt threatened by the rise of militant nationalist powers such as Germany, Italy, and Japan, but only the British were at the same time engaged in the suppression of nationalist movements in Egypt and India. And, most importantly, though it seemed a distinct possibility that another war might break out in Europe, Great Britain was the only nation likely to try to involve the United States. Thus by 1935 anti-British sectors of public opinion were once again clearly in the ascendant.

At the heart of this new coalition, of course, remained the ethnic anglophobes. The immigrant population, it should be remembered, amounted to a considerable force in itself; as late as 1940, for example, it was estimated that nearly half the adult population of Chicago did not usually speak English in their homes. Many Irish-Americans had retained their traditional animosity toward Great Britain despite the settlement of 1923. By 1935 they had made quite a few friends among the Italian-American community as well. Members of this group, many of whom were sympathetic to the regime of Benito Mussolini in their mother country, were outraged by British opposition to Italy's invasion of Ethiopia. Given Britain's history of colonial exploitation in Africa, the apparent unwillingness of the Foreign Office to allow Rome its share of the pie seemed an act of sheer hypocrisy. Moreover, Americans of Irish and Italian descent had gained a new level of political significance through connections at the local level with the Roosevelt administration. On the radio, meanwhile, the militant Irish Catholic priest Charles Coughlin sounded the alarm against British imperialism. He blamed American involvement in the World War on 'a barrage of lying British propaganda,' and denounced the League of Nations as the 'catspaw of the international bankers of the British Empire.' In Congress Representative Martin L. Sweeney (D-OH) eagerly embraced the standard of ethnic anglophobia. Calling himself 'Father Coughlin's man in Congress,' Sweeney distinguished himself in January 1936 as the only member of Congress to oppose a House resolution offering condolences on the death of King George V. The king, he argued, was a 'symbol of imperialism' who had sent the black and tans to Ireland.[19]

Sentiment among Americans of German ancestry remained equally hostile toward Britain, even though by the end of 1934 most had become disenchanted with Adolf Hitler's new regime in Berlin. By the mid-1930s more than 75 percent of the German-American population was born in the United States; of the 1.6 billion German immigrants in the country, two thirds had arrived prior to the Great War, and thus their connections with the mother country had begun to weaken considerably. This did not, however, imply a more generous attitude toward London, nor toward America's Anglo-Saxon elites, and organizations such as the Steuben Society professed their continuing vigilance against British propaganda.[20]

But as in the 1920s, ethnic animosities were not the only manifestations of anglophobia in mid-1930s America. There had emerged by this time a profound rift in liberal opinion on issues of U.S. foreign policy. Most supported a position of strict neutrality as put forward in publications like the *New Republic*, which dismissed any notion of a joint enterprise between the U.S. and Britain as 'a bandits' partnership' to defend colonial swag. When a British diplomat visited the U.S. in 1935 and suggested cooperation in the Far East, veteran *TNR* writer Oswald Garrison Villard rejected the idea as 'preposterous.' After all, he asked his readers, 'who could possibly think that any American would be willing to see our government make the cause of...the exploiters of China its own?' At the same time, some liberals had begun to echo the call of the Soviet Union for a 'popular front' against fascism. This brand of opinion found its most respectable outlet in the *Nation*, which began to call for increased American participation in an anti-German coalition. Yet despite this critical difference in editorial policy, the attitude of both journals regarding Great Britain remained essentially the same. Both, for example, maintained a deep hostility toward British imperialism, easily devoting as much ink and space to denouncing colonial exploitation in Egypt and India as they did to attacking the Italian invasion of Ethiopia. Moreover, liberals of all stripes grew even more suspicious when the coalition government of Ramsey MacDonald gave way to a new Tory cabinet under Stanley Baldwin in June 1935. Both the *New Republic* and the *Nation* feared that the political shift indicated an entente between England and Nazi Germany, fears which would grow stronger as the Foreign Office began to move toward a policy of appeasement. Incredibly, the *Nation* coupled its denunciation of Baldwin's unwillingness to join a popular front against Hitler with an attack on the Conservatives' programs for increased military expenditures, thereby simultaneously demanding

stronger action against Germany while vitiating the only
policy which might make any such action possible.[21]

The third partner in the new anti-British coalition were
progressives from the Middle and Far West. Progressives
had, of course, played a pivotal role in the derailing of the
Versailles Treaty in the Senate, and had formed the core of
the opposition to the Five Power Treaty in 1922. However,
their hostility to large military expenditures made them the
chief opponents of the Big Navy party, and thus some were
actually accused of being pro-British. By the early 1930s,
however, they had returned to the vanguard of anglophobia,
denouncing all efforts to reduce war debts or otherwise aid
Great Britain. Their shift out of, and then back into the anti-
British camp can be explained in part by the return of the
Conservatives to power in London, but more importantly by
the fact that the progressives viewed American financial and
industrial interests as their chief enemies. Men such as Gerald
Nye of North Dakota and Burton Wheeler of Montana believed that these interests were natural allies of the British.
When East Coast shipbuilding concerns and steel magnates
preached the gospel of naval rivalry with Britain, the progressives saw only a cynical ploy to promote their narrow
self-interest, not any genuine feeling of hostility toward the
British Empire. When, during the Hoover administration,
Wall Street bankers renewed their calls for war debt cancellation, they saw their suspicions confirmed.[22]

It bears noting that the anglophobia of the 1930s was a far
cry from that of the late 1920s. The rallying cries of the anti-
British forces in 1927 – naval parity, access to overseas
markets, freedom of the seas – had lost much of their old
appeal. In the Senate, their leadership was passing from the
Big Navyites to progressives such as Nye and Wheeler. If Big
Navy anglophobia was revealed in the writings of Frank
Simonds and William Benton Shearer, the 1930s variety
found its most cogent expression in Quincy Howe's *England
Expects Every American to Do His Duty* (1937). Whereas the
navalist writings had warned Americans about British
strength, it was England's weakness that concerned Howe.
The British Empire, he claimed, 'needs the aid of the United
States to maintain its rule over one-quarter of the earth's
surface.' The U.S. gained nothing from an Anglo-American

partnership, yet Howe identified a 'British network,' made up of groups such as the English-Speaking Union, the Foreign Policy Association, the Council on Foreign Relations, and the Carnegie Endowment for International Peace, dedicated to subordinating American interests 'to the needs and desires of the British Foreign Office.'[23]

For at least the first two years of the Roosevelt administration, liberal and progressive anglophobes had good reason to believe that the president was on their side. FDR's torpedoing of the London Economic Conference and his apparent support for both the Johnson Act and the activities of the Nye Committee indicated a complete break with the supposed pro-British policies of the Hoover administration. In early 1935, however, the president annoyed his anti-British and isolationist supporters by proposing U.S. membership on the World Court at the Hague. The idea was nothing new – public sentiment had strongly supported participation since 1923, and indeed it was endorsed in the political platforms of both parties in 1932. Roosevelt initially avoided committing himself; indeed, soon after his inauguration he assured Hiram Johnson that he had no personal interest in the matter. Yet when a poll taken at the start of 1935 showed sixty-five senators in favor of U.S. participation, and only sixteen on record as opposed, the president decided that it was time to act. Johnson was livid at what he felt to be a personal betrayal by the president, and attacked the court as an 'infernal foreign contraption.' But, he concluded, the legislation providing for U.S. membership was sure to pass, since most of the Democrats had 'neither the knowledge of the subject, nor sufficient mentality, to do otherwise than they are told.'[24]

But what neither Roosevelt nor Johnson had counted upon was the tremendous groundswell of anti-World Court public opinion which ensued. The Hearst papers printed editorial after editorial denouncing the court as a tool of the British Foreign Office. In the Senate Johnson was joined by Borah, Henrik Shipstead of Minnesota, and Huey Long, the colorful and popular former governor of Louisiana. But what really turned the tide against the court were the efforts of Father Coughlin, who charged that the 'British-run' court represented 'an internationalism which is a greater menace to our prosperity than the type advocated by the Soviet Third International.' In response to his radio program, approximately 200 000 telegrams flowed into the Senate office buildings, demanding that the U.S. stay out. While a majority in the Senate continued to support membership, the final vote amounted to only 52 in favor – seven votes short of the required two-thirds. Johnson was predictably elated; as he wrote to his son two days after the vote, 'I won the toughest and the biggest and most far-reaching contest legislatively in which ever I have been engaged.'[25]

Even more controversial than Roosevelt's support for the World Court was his response to the Italian invasion of Ethiopia. The invasion was the first test of the 1935 Neutrality Act, which the president promptly called into effect. However, FDR sought to go further in punishing Italy. As an aggressor, his reasoning went, Italy would not particularly suffer from an American arms embargo, since presumably Mussolini would have stockpiled a sufficient number of weapons to carry on his campaign without imports from the United States. Roosevelt therefore decided to follow the lead of the League of Nations in declaring a trade quota on certain goods deemed important to the Italian war effort. The sanctions were not legally binding – that would have required an act of Congress, which the president realized was unlikely – but amounted to, in his terms, a 'moral embargo.'

The embargo unleashed an immediate storm of controversy. Some of the opposition, to be sure, came from those sympathetic to Mussolini – Father Coughlin, for example, charged that Ethiopia was merely a 'camouflaging marauder,' a puppet state of Great Britain. Many Italian-Americans, as previously mentioned, were of similar mind, blaming Roosevelt's pro-Ethiopian policy on 'the trickery, the deception and designs of…British diplomats.' The trade quota, they maintained, was not an act of neutrality but rather 'an insurance policy for the British Empire.' Most of those who challenged the embargo, however, did so out of concern that it was placed at the behest of the British Foreign Office. 'Sanctions if universally applied would go a long way toward bringing the so-called civilized nations back to their senses,' admitted Congressman Martin Sweeney of

Ohio, 'but sanctions that are the brain children of Great Britain...is [*sic*] a move that every American must look upon with suspicion.' Liberals in particular were convinced that British denunciations of the invasion were less a reflection of their concern for world peace than of their fears about an Italian threat to the empire. The League sanctions, which Roosevelt had heartily seconded by means of the embargo, were merely another example of British diplomacy using the League of Nations to advance its own ends. The *New Republic* compared Italian conduct in Ethiopia to British repression in Arabia and India, while Oswald Garrison Villard made light of the whole affair. '[I]f there had been wealth in Ethiopia,' he wrote, 'England would have stolen it years ago....' Even the *Nation*, which supported the embargo, continued publishing its series of articles attacking British rule in India.[26]

Nor was this sort of thinking limited to the liberal journals. One British observer reported that the 'belief that England cared less for the integrity of Ethiopia than for the preservation...of the All-Red Route to India' was shared by nearly all Americans. Edwin Borchard wrote to Borah that the 'moral embargo' was the product of 'gentlemen [who]...always want to do what Great Britain wants done.' Even some in the State Department – the ambassador to Rome, for example – believed that the British were out to start a war in defense of their empire.[27]

As it turned out, the embargo had no measurable impact on the Italian war effort, especially since it lacked any legal means of enforcing compliance, and by the summer of 1936 Ethiopia had succumbed to Mussolini's armed forces. Faced with this inescapable fact, Roosevelt terminated the embargo, though he refused to recognize the conquest. The moral embargo, in the end, served no purpose except to open the administration up to charges that American foreign policy was being made in London. Edwin Borchard warned that the U.S. was 'in danger of becoming a puppet nation, with the strings in European hands.' Rep. George Holden Tinkham (R-MA) went further, declaring in 1935 that 'The President of the United States and the Department of State, his agent, are under the domination and control of the British Foreign Office.'[28]

One other event served to heighten American hostility toward Britain in 1936. King Edward VII announced his intention of marrying Wallis Simpson, an American divorcee. When he refused to be swayed from this position by, among others, Prime Minister Baldwin and the Archbishop of Canterbury, Edward was forced to abdicate in favor of his younger brother, who assumed the throne as George VI. The concern among Britons was that a king ought not marry a divorced woman. Americans, however, interpreted the affair in a different manner, believing that the English upper class objected to having an American as their queen. The *Chicago Tribune* used the story to attack the Baldwin government, claiming that the abdication was an attempt to keep a popular, reform-minded monarch out of Buckingham Palace. For liberals such as Quincy Howe, meanwhile, the crisis 'made it quite plain that the same British aristocrats who had shouted themselves hoarse' to bring the U.S. into the Great War 'actually in their heart of hearts despised the United States as the "alien" source of Edward's corruption.'[29]

It was just as the abdication crisis was getting underway that Roosevelt faced his first attempt at reelection. Edwin Borchard suggested that the president might be vulnerable on foreign policy, and urged Republicans to make it the centerpiece of their campaign. The leaders of the G.O.P. rejected this advice, believing that it was still the national economy which remained uppermost in the minds of the voters. Their nominee was thus Alfred Landon, governor of Kansas, a man with no experience in foreign policy, and, apparently, no strong opinions on the subject. The challenge to Roosevelt's conduct of foreign affairs, if there was to be one, would come instead from a third party. The Union Party was formed by an alliance between the supporters of the president's two most influential and popular critics – Senator Huey Long and Father Charles Coughlin. Both were staunch anglophobes, enemies of what they called, in the true spirit of progressivism, the 'Wall Street-Downing Street Axis.' By 1935 Long himself was leaning toward a run for the presidency, but his hopes were cut short by an assassin's bullet that same year.[30] The chosen standard-bearer of the Union Party was instead William Lemke, an obscure congressman from North Dakota. Lemke was every bit as anti-British as Coughlin and

Long, a function both of his progressive mentality and his German-American heritage, yet foreign policy did not play a significant role in his quest for the presidency. The Union Party, however, attracted a number of political adventurers and opportunists to its ranks, among them William Hale Thompson. Claiming to have broken with the Republican party over Hoover's pro-British sympathies, Big Bill ran for the governorship of Illinois. However, his promises 'to find out whether this country is a tail to England's kite' failed to call sufficient attention away from the corruption and scandal which had been such prominent features of his two terms as mayor of Chicago. By late summer Thompson was so desperate for a base of support that he attended the annual picnic of the Chicago Nazi Clubs, where he won the acclaim of the crowd by denouncing not only the British but Jewish bankers as well.[31]

In the end, neither Landon nor Lemke posed any particular challenge to the president's prospects for reelection, though this was not so much an indication of support for his foreign policy as it was an affirmation of how low a priority international affairs remained for president and public alike. Roosevelt's support for the World Court and the moral embargo on Italy cost him the votes of some progressive Republicans (who preferred the mildly progressive Landon), and it certainly hurt his standing among anti-British ethnic groups (who tended to favor the more anglophobic Union Party), but the election of 1936 nevertheless strengthened the Roosevelt coalition's hold over national politics. Yet at the same time it was dangerous to assume – as the president apparently did – that the outcome represented a mandate for bold new initiatives in foreign affairs, or especially for a closer relationship with Great Britain and the League of Nations. Though 1936 had brought him a smashing victory, a showdown between Roosevelt and the anglophobes was soon to follow.[32]

5 'Whom He Loveth He Chastiseth'

In May 1937, when Neville Chamberlain became Prime Minister, Great Britain was confronted by an international environment which was far from friendly. The British Empire faced three potential threats simultaneously – from Germany in Europe, Italy in the Mediterranean and Africa, and Japan in the Far East. The Foreign Office, meanwhile, could not bring itself to trust either France or the Soviet Union, the only two European Powers who might have an interest in restraining the aggressors. This left only the United States as a possible ally, and thus the British Government hatched a strategy in that year to win over Americans to the cause of joint cooperation. The Foreign Office had already concluded that there was no chance of luring the U.S. into European affairs, but hoped that the Americans could be persuaded to help defend the status quo in Asia and the Pacific, leaving Britain free to deal with the situation closer to home. Ambassador Lindsay believed that this might be possible, but only if Britain managed to stand out from the rest of Europe in the popular mind. Americans, he contended, regarded the European countries as 'so many cats in the bag'; British policy, he believed, must be calculated 'to appear as a force seeking to preserve peace rather than as one yielding to jealousy or selfishness or mere panic.'[1]

There was at least some ground for optimism on this score; British observers of United States had been cheered by a Gallup poll taken in April, which asked American voters which 'European country' they 'liked best.' Fifty-five percent answered, 'Great Britain,' while France came in a very distant second, with 11 percent. But this was no guarantee of U.S. aid in case of war, as the British ambassador was fond of pointing out, American impressions of Great Britain were formed almost entirely from Hollywood movies, and the reality would always prove a disappointment. The typical American, he warned, 'expects much of England, almost superhuman wisdom; and when something goes wrong, even though it be something which does not affect American interests, he is loud in his condemnation, for "Whom he loveth he chastiseth."'[2]

Another problem for Chamberlain's government was the Prime Minister himself, who had developed a reputation across the Atlantic as the archetypal 'anti-American Englishman' during his tenure as Chancellor of the Exchequer. Moreover, the abdication crisis was still fresh in many American minds. Indeed, in September, an editorial in the *Nation* reported the existence of 'a suspicion of British foreign policy which is almost hysterical in intensity.' 'There is a widespread feeling,' it went on to argue, 'that the present British government may ultimately be on the side of Hitler.'[3]

At the same time, the increasingly threatening state of world affairs was convincing most Americans that what was needed was stronger neutrality legislation, not new commitments abroad. The administration's response to this demand was the Neutrality Act of 1937, which reaffirmed the terms of the 1935 and 1936 acts, as well as stipulating that they would apply to the Spanish Civil War, which had broken out the previous year. The most important part of the 1937 act, however, was a bit of political legerdemain known commonly as 'cash-and-carry.' Formulated by Wall Street banker and Roosevelt supporter Bernard Baruch, 'cash-and-carry' stipulated that goods could only be exported to belligerent nations if payment were made in hard currency, and that such goods could only be carried on the ships of that same nation. For most anti-interventionists, this was a means of avoiding the sort of incident that brought the United States into the World War – a goal similar to that pursued by Nye and Clark in 1936. 'Cash-and-carry' at the same time appealed to advocates of collective security, since if war broke out in Europe only Britain and France would have sufficient command of the sea lanes to take advantage of American exports. It was precisely this fact which caused Borah and Johnson to oppose the bill. Joined once again by international lawyers Edwin Borchard and John Bassett Moore in defense of traditional neutral rights, the two former irreconcilables called it a 'British measure,' designed not to protect American neutrality but to defend the British Empire. Even worse, in their eyes, was the fact that 'cash-and-carry' invalidated any notions of freedom of the seas. 'What sort of government is this and what sort of men are we,' Johnson demanded to know, 'to accept a formula which will enable us to sell goods and then hide?'[4]

But though the appeal to neutral rights had still been effective in 1936, the Senate of 1937 would not be swayed by such arguments. Hitler's remilitarization of the Rhineland and the outbreak of the Spanish Civil War made a European war appear to be a far more realistic possibility than it had seemed only the year before. It also did not help the cause of the advocates of traditional neutrality that Johnson had only recently suffered a stroke, which significantly reduced his oratorical abilities. In the end only four senators, all from the New England states, joined Johnson and Borah in voting against cash-and-carry: Henry Cabot Lodge, Jr. (R-MA), Warren Austin (R-VT), Peter Gerry (D-RI), and Styles Bridges (R-NH). The Neutrality Act itself passed by a vote of 41 to 15, but most of those voting against it did so not out of devotion to the rights of neutrals in time of war, but because they believed the bill did not go far enough. It had become clear to all, particularly the British, that Borah and Johnson, since 1919 the pillars of the American anti-interventionist movement, had lost control of it.[5]

The Neutrality Act of 1937 aimed at preventing U.S. involvement in a European war, but it was in Asia that the next international crisis erupted. In July the Japanese reopened hostilities against China, launching a campaign which quickly captured most of that country's coastal cities. American opinion had long been more sympathetic toward China than it had toward Britain or France – China was, after all, viewed as a victim of European imperialism. Moreover, the sack of Nanking, in which as many as 100 000 Chinese soldiers and civilians were murdered by Japanese troops, aroused American passions in a way that the invasion of Ethiopia and the occupation of the Rhineland had not. Roosevelt at first followed a dual policy. He refused to invoke the neutrality laws, realizing that cash-and-carry would in this case only help Japan, but at the same time rejected British calls for joint mediation of the conflict.

But then the president grew bolder. Believing that public

opinion was ready to support a more vigorous foreign policy, Roosevelt on October 5 gave a speech in Chicago in which he denounced 'the present reign of terror and international lawlessness,' and called for an international 'quarantine' of aggressors. The speech was on the whole warmly received, mainly because it offered no concrete plan. British Foreign Minister Sir Anthony Eden eagerly seized on the speech, and asked whether the United States might participate in an international boycott of Japan, but was quickly rebuffed. '"[S]anctions" is a terrible word to use,' he responded when asked to clarify his position. 'They are out of the window.' Ultimately the only step Roosevelt was willing to take was to second the League of Nations denunciation of Japanese actions. All that the quarantine speech amounted to, then, was, in the words of one correspondent, 'an attitude without a program.'[6]

Yet for some in Congress even the attitude went too far. Rep. Hamilton Fish (R-NY) called the speech 'sheer hysteria,' and accused Roosevelt of trying to involve the United States in an Asian war 'to pull British chestnuts from the fire.' William B. Barry (D-NY) seconded this, asking his colleagues, '[I]s not Japan merely doing today what Great Britain…[has] done in the past…[in] building up its empire…?' When American naval vessels called at Singapore a few months later, the *Chicago Tribune* asked, 'Is the United States in a secret alliance with Great Britain?' Many liberals also objected to the increasingly anti-Japanese tone emanating from the White House. 'Could England and America fight Japan with clean hands?' Bruce Bliven wrote in the pages of the *New Republic*. 'What Japan is doing is merely to continue on a larger scale and with more brutal candor what the Great Powers did in China for a hundred years. The British are not so far from the Amritsar massacre that they can afford very much righteous wrath about the bombing of Shanghai.'[7]

Nor did the situation change substantially when Japanese planes sank the U.S. gunboat *Panay* on December 12. In London there were high hopes that American opinion might become outraged over the attack and take a harder stance against Tokyo, and indeed a sizeable body of opinion in the navy wanted to, in the words of Admiral Leahy, 'get the fleet ready for sea,…make an agreement with the British Navy for joint action and...inform the Japanese that we expect to protect our nationals.' But in Congress the sinking of the *Panay* had precisely the opposite effect, since it began to be rumored that U.S. armed forces were in China for the sole purpose of defending British interests there. Fears that America was on the verge of being drawn into a war in Asia gave new impetus to the Ludlow Resolution, a proposed amendment to the Constitution which would require a national referendum in order to go to war. The *Panay* incident rapidly pushed the resolution out of committee onto the floor of the House, and it was debated immediately after Christmas recess. Though it failed to gain the necessary two-thirds vote required to send it on to the states, the vote of 209–188 showed just how strong anti-interventionist sentiment remained in the House of Representatives.[8]

Thus already by the end of 1937 Britain's strategy to increase American involvement in Asia had failed. A large part of this stemmed from the simple fact that the vast majority of the American people were afraid of getting into a war, especially a war in which nothing more than 'British chestnuts' seemed to be at stake. There was widespread agreement with the conclusions of A. Whitney Griswold, professor of international relations in Yale, who in his 1938 book *Far Eastern Policy of the United States* maintained that there was no community of interests between the U.S. and Great Britain in Asia. Similar objections to a joint Anglo-American policy in the Pacific were to be found among the policymakers of the State Department as well. There were, first of all, continuing suspicions that Great Britain and Japan might reach some sort of *rapprochement* independently of the U.S.; fears that the two powers were about to divide China into spheres of influence were especially strong in 1937. And secondly, even if the British did not mend fences with Tokyo, diplomats such as Norman Davis feared that it would be the United States, and not Great Britain, which would be forced to bear the brunt of any Japanese retaliation. It should be noted finally that even those pressing for a more vigorous Asian policy were seldom doing so out of love for the British. Nelson Trusler Johnson, ambassador to China, for example, wrote to the president in 1939 that the end of the British Empire in Asia was imminent, which meant that '[t]he frontiers of the

United States are the world.' While no fan of the British – he rejoiced that 'the day of colonial empires is past' – he saw it as the duty of the United States to aid China against Japan. 'It is not a question of saving British chestnuts,' he concluded, 'our own chestnuts are involved.'[9]

The reopening of the war in Asia and the *Panay* incident did, however, have one consequence which could be considered positive from the British point of view – it awakened a majority in Congress to the need for a larger navy. This was a welcome sign for the Foreign Office, which hoped it might serve as a signal to aggressors that the United States had not abandoned all interest in the outside world. In early 1938 a new naval expansion bill came before the House and Senate providing for two billion dollars in new construction and an increase in tonnage by 20 percent. The bill effectively divided critics of Roosevelt's foreign policy, since many had also been longtime supporters of the navy, and thus there was little doubt about its ability to pass. What is interesting about the debate on the bill are the tactics which its opponents chose to adopt. Whereas in earlier congressional battles over naval authorizations and appropriations the opposition concentrated its assault on the familiar demons of liberalism and progressivism – the Navy League, the 'steel trust', the shipping magnates, etc. – in 1938 they seemed more concerned about the uses to which an expanded navy might be put. 'These battleships are not for national defense, but for international meddling,' claimed William Lemke, now back in Congress. 'They are for assault upon other Nations, not in our own waters, but in foreign waters.' Senators Burton Wheeler (D-MT), Bennett Champ Clark (D-MO), Rush Dew Holt (D-WV) and many others argued that the enlarged fleet was the first step toward an alliance with Great Britain. 'The whole naval policy of the United States today is built on the theory of being an auxiliary of the British Navy,' Clark contended, while Holt once again raised fears 'that the foreign policy of America is not made in the State Department but is made in Downing Street.' A number of conservative Republicans, whose animus toward Roosevelt had by this time grown far stronger than any commitment they had to the navy, joined in the chorus, creating a strange political alliance of the far left and the far right against the center. The *New Republic*, for instance, found itself lavishing praise on the arch-conservative Representative Hamilton Fish (R-NY) for opposing the bill, while denouncing its sponsor, Carl Vinson (D-GA) as 'a Roosevelt idolator.'[10]

The debate over the naval program of 1938 was thus a complete reversal of similar legislative battles from the late 1920s. Ten years earlier, it had been the navalists who were conjuring the specter of Britain menacing the East Coast and cutting off American trade with the rest of the world. This time it was the progressives and liberals who were warning of a British threat, not to trade but to the independence of U.S. foreign policy. Indeed, fears that the navy might be used as an instrument for 'pulling British chestnuts from the fire' were not uncommon even among those in favor of the proposed construction. Senator David I. Walsh (D-MA) reminded his colleagues that though 'there is need of an expanded naval defense program,' it should be 'an American program...independent of the actions of any other nation.' In a letter to his son Hiram Johnson summarized the feelings of all those who remained pro-navy yet anti-British: 'We may need it to whip the Japs,' the acerbic Californian wrote of the proposed fleet, 'but we don't need it as an auxiliary of Great Britain.' Despite these lingering fears, the bill passed the House on March 21 by a margin of 294 votes to 100, and the Senate on May 3 by a vote of 56 to 22.[11]

Yet though the British welcomed the new naval program, there was no getting around the fact that Britain's popularity was in steady decline in 1937 and 1938, thanks in large part to the Foreign Office's policy of appeasement of Germany and Italy. As early as the spring of 1936, after England's acquiescence to Hitler's remilitarization of the Rhineland, Ambassador Bingham wrote from London that the Tory government was 'so lacking in strong and courageous leadership' that Germany would be tempted toward greater acts of aggression. A visit by Lord Halifax to Berlin in November 1937 convinced William C. Bullitt, ambassador to the Soviet Union, that Chamberlain would 'finally, deviously, by silences and tacit approvals,' allow Hitler to take Austria and the Sudeten region of Czechoslovakia. The *New Republic's* Bruce Bliven, meanwhile, asserted that 'left to themselves the English under their present government would, I think, join the Fascist bloc.'[12]

American opinion grew increasingly unfriendly in the spring of 1938. In March the first part of Bullitt's prediction came true as the German army marched into Vienna; when the Chamberlain cabinet joined the French in doing nothing, the British Embassy was deluged with letters from private American citizens accusing London of 'bolstering up the European dictatorships.' Nor was the situation helped when in the following month the prime minister announced British recognition of Italy's conquest of Ethiopia, despite Roosevelt's warnings of a 'serious effect upon public opinion.' Congressional anglophobes had a field day. British willingness to deal with the dictators, Hiram Johnson claimed, laid bare 'the realistic policy of Britain in all its nakedness.' Borah agreed, asserting in late April that 'Great Britain has swung back to the old 'balance of power' idea.... Neither treaties nor the rights of small nations,...nor the calls of justice and humanity stand in the way of power politics.' Criticizing those who clung to the idea of collective security, Oswald Garrison Villard blamed Great Britain – 'a great empire ruled at present by cold-blooded reactionary imperialists' – for creating an international environment in which Hitler and Mussolini were able to thrive. How can we save Europe, Villard asked, when Europe is unwilling to save itself?[13]

Roosevelt's attitude toward appeasement was far more ambivalent. On the one hand, he often seemed eager to criticize what he called the 'national selfishness' which underlay British policy. He even suggested to Treasury Secretary Henry Morgenthau that England and Germany had reached an agreement for joint domination of Europe. Furthermore, in March 1938, in response to the annexation of Austria, he wrote:

> If a Chief of Police makes a deal with the leading gangsters and the deal results in no more hold-ups, that Chief of Police will be called a great man, but if the gangsters do not live up to their word, the Chief of Police will go to jail. Some people are, I think, taking very long chances.[14]

Yet on the other hand, even as he continued to fault the British for not standing up to Hitler, he refused to take any concrete action which might have encouraged them to do so.

In 1936 the president failed even to lodge a protest over Germany's reoccupation of the Rhineland; indeed, his wife, Eleanor, wrote an article defending the move. He steadfastly refused to suggest any modification of the neutrality laws in 1938, nor would he consider renegotiation of the war debts. And not only did he resist public demands for an accelerated rearmament program (one poll taken in January 1938 showed 69 percent in favor of a larger army, 74 percent supporting an increased navy, and a whopping 80 percent favoring an expanded air force), but he went so far as to advocate a new round of arms control agreements.[15]

Compared to quite a few others, however, Roosevelt's anti-British stance in 1938 was mild indeed. For some, in fact, Britain's inclination to appease Hitler and Mussolini was a sign that the Chamberlain government was actually sympathetic to fascism. At best this would manifest itself in an alliance with the dictators; at worst it meant that Britain was on the verge of becoming a fascist power, if it was not one already. This line of argument was especially popular among writers of the far left, socialists such as Norman Thomas and the Englishman Robert Briffault. Briffault particularly, in his 1938 book *The Decline and Fall of the British Empire* (described in the *Nation* as 'the most hostile and pitiless book on England and the English that has been written for many years') wrote that 'England, if not a Fascist country, is a Fascist power. . . . He who hates the scourge of Fascist infamy must logically regard England with hundredfold horror. But for England there would be no Fascism.' He went on to call Great Britain 'the archetype of crooked and callous duplicity, nameless self-sufficiency, and fulsome hypocrisy.' It should be mentioned here, however, that American Communists avoided this argument in the months prior to the conclusion of the Nazi-Soviet Pact in August 1939. The Soviet Union, after all, was still pursuing the tactics of the popular front, which would presumably include Great Britain, and Stalin's American supporters were not ones to deviate from the party line.[16]

The legend of a fascist-dominated Britain was not limited to left-wing sources: the conservative *Chicago Tribune*, for example, used it quite frequently in the late 1930s. In the summer of 1937 Colonel Robert McCormick, the *Tribune*'s flamboyant publisher, returned from a trip to England (he himself had attended Eton) with a new interpretation of the abdication crisis of the previous year. 'WHY DID EDWARD FALL?' a *Tribune* headline asked on August 22, answering, 'FASCISTS DEPOSED HIM: A PICTURE OF BRITAIN UNDER NAZI YOKE.' British appeasement of Hitler and Mussolini, of course, only strengthened McCormick's belief that England's leaders 'would rather deal with a reasonable Fascist government than with an unpredictable democracy.' Indeed, by late 1938 disparaging headlines about 'Nazi England' had become commonplace in the pages of the *Tribune*.[17]

Even many who were not willing to go so far as to claim England had gone fascist were prepared to make some unflattering comparisons between Great Britain on the one hand and Germany and Italy on the other. Congressman Herbert S. Bigelow (D-OH) argued that the only difference between British and Italian imperialism was that 'Italy is less hypocritical. Italy makes no professions of democracy, while England boasts of liberties for herself which she denies to others.' Liberal author Randolph Leigh, in his 1938 book *Conscript Europe*, pointed out that only one Briton in 1013 attended college, while one in 878 Germans and one in 808 Italians did so. '[W]hile England still makes education a class privilege,' he admiringly concluded, 'Germany has shut out incompetent rich boys from the universities and is making a strenuous effort to see that a limited number of the most talented in all groups, rich or poor, receive an education.' Jerome Frank, a former New Deal lawyer, topped them all: at one point in his *Save America First: How to Make our Democracy Work*, he wrote that Britain's 'treatment of the Irish, *for at least a hundred years,*... was only slightly (if at all) better than Germany's treatment of the Jews *for the last five years* [author's italics].'[18]

In Congress this sentiment translated into an even more marked resistance to the idea of cooperation with Britain. There was, for instance, a growing desire among some legislators to lift the arms embargo on Spain. Part of this may be explained by a genuine sympathy among many liberals and progressives for the plight of loyalist Spain, threatened as it was by the prospect of a proto-fascist dictatorship. But

animus toward British policy cannot be ignored as a significant factor, since Britain was at the time calling for
international nonintervention in the civil war. Gerald Nye
now emerged as the leading advocate of lifting the embargo,
denouncing what he called 'the practice of following
...British ideas and wishes as a faithful dog follows its
master.' He found a ready ally in Borah, who announced that
he was 'no more desirous of cooperating with Great Britain
than I am with Italy.'[19]

But it was in the wake of the Czech crisis of 1938, which cul-
minated in the Munich Agreement of September 29, that
American regard for Great Britain fell to its lowest point of
the entire interwar period. The crisis began in May, when
Hitler, ostensibly attempting to unite all of Central Europe's
Germans within his Third Reich, began making demands for
control of the Sudeten region of Czechoslovakia. Ambassador
Lindsay had warned the Foreign Office in the midst of the
crisis that any new capitulation to Hitler would result in 'a
certain letdown of American friendliness,' and this certainly
seemed to be the case with Roosevelt. While negotiations
took place at Hitler's retreat at Berchtesgaden, the president
took the opportunity to call Chamberlain 'slippery,' and to
accuse him of 'playing the usual game of the British, peace at
any price.' If negotiations failed, he predicted, the prime
minister would find some way of blaming the Americans. By
mid-September he despaired that Hitler would simply take
whatever he wanted from Czechoslovakia, while Britain and
France 'washed the blood from their Judas Iscariot hands.'
Yet when, at the end of the month, it looked as though the
crisis might erupt in war, Roosevelt was quick to counsel a
peaceful settlement. He sent each of the participants a letter
urging them to keep negotiating, lest 'reason is banished and
force asserts itself,' and even made a personal appeal to
Hitler, suggesting a conference be held at some neutral loca-
tion. Privately, he told Lindsay that he would be 'the first to
cheer' if Czechoslovakia could be persuaded to give up the
Sudetenland.[20]

But when the terms of the Munich Agreement, which appeared to give Hitler all that he had demanded, reached the
American public, Roosevelt was hardly the only one cheer-
ing. A poll taken in early October showed that 59 percent of

those surveyed believed that Britain and France had done 'the best thing in giving in to Germany instead of going to war.' The administration, for its part, sounded positively enthusiastic about the sacrifice of Czechoslovakia. Under Secretary of State Sumner Welles, for example, announced that the world now had an opportunity to establish 'a new world order based upon justice and upon law.' The president, meanwhile, confided to Ambassador William Phillips that 'I am not a bit upset over the final result.' In a letter to Canadian Prime Minister Mackenzie King several days later, Roosevelt announced, 'I can assure you that we in the United States rejoice with you, and the world at large, that the outbreak of war was averted.' Even some notorious anglophobes found some nice things to say about Neville Chamberlain. The *Chicago Tribune*, for example, rejoiced that all cause for war in western Europe was removed, allowing Hitler to focus exclusively on the East. A war between Hitler and Stalin, Colonel McCormick reasoned, might destroy both regimes while the United States remained completely aloof. Representative Hamilton Fish also praised the Munich agreement. At a German Day rally in Madison Square Garden, Fish, speaking from a podium decorated with Nazi flags, called Chamberlain 'a great statesman.'[21]

American support for the agreement, however, was short-lived. Some, indeed, recognized from the start that Hitler would not be satisfied merely with the Sudetenland, and that any chance for collective security had been destroyed at Munich. Assistant Secretary of State George Messersmith called the agreement 'a cynical sellout of principle,' asking rhetorically if there were any moral distinction between one who takes something that does not belong to him and one who gives away something which is not his. Claude Bowers, ambassador to Spain, called it 'the most shameless thing that has happened since the partition of Poland.' In the weeks that followed more and more were won over to this argument. Assistant Secretary of State Adolf A. Berle now maintained that the United States had no choice but to 'go it alone,' since the British government obviously could not be trusted. The widespread sense of betrayal arising from Munich is perhaps best summed up in a poem which made the rounds in the offices of the State Department at the end of 1938:

Meine Herren and Signori,
Clients of the British Tory,
Kindly note that No. 10
Requests your patronage again.
Opening as from today,
As Chamberlain et Daladier,
Messrs. Hoare, Laval, successors,
For doing business with aggressors.

Frontiers promptly liquidated;
Coups d'etats consolidated;
Pledges taken and exchanged;
Acquisitions re-arranged;
Loans on Fascist risks advanced;
Nazi enterprise financed.
European intervention
Given personal attention.
Have you problems with partition?
Let us send a British Mission.

Breaking with Geneva's firms
We offer Nazis favored terms.
Let us lend, to back your name,
England's honorable fame.
For dirty deals both great and small
Our representatives will call.
Orders carried out with speed,
Satisfaction guaranteed.
We obsequiously remain,
Daladier and Chamberlain.[22]

But the real turning point for American opinion came five weeks after Munich, when the Nazi government staged a massive pogrom against the Jews. Americans were outraged, but they directed much of their anger toward Great Britain. Almost overnight they came to view the Munich agreement as a prime example of European perfidy, with British and French diplomats (though the British always figured more prominently in American accounts) sacrificing a small nation in order to protect their empires. One public opinion poll showed that 60 percent of respondents believed that the agreement actually made war more, and not less, likely. Borah, in a letter to Walter Lippmann, accused the British and French of plotting with Germany to destroy the only true democracy in Europe. He then went on to predict that Britain would encourage Hitler to expand further in central and eastern Europe, using Germany as a bulwark against the Soviet Union. Vice President Henry Wallace wrote that he 'would not be at all surprised if she [Britain] would suggest at the most appropriate moment giving Germany a foothold in such a spot as to most embarrass us.' For Robert Briffault the events at Munich finally dispersed '[t]he decent, but inconvenient, fiction of antagonism between pretended "democracies" and Fascist barbarism.' The result, he concluded, was 'the coalition of international Fascism and Fascistic "democracies".'[23]

President Roosevelt, meanwhile, promptly backed away from his former support of the agreement. Now instead of congratulating Chamberlain, Roosevelt accused him and other British leaders of having an inordinate fear of communism which kept them from appreciating the extent of the German threat, the result, he believed, of 'too much Eton and Oxford.' As he wrote to Herbert C. Pell in November, 'Our British friends must begin to fish or cut bait. The dictator threat from Europe is a good deal closer to the United States and the American Continent than it was before.' He nevertheless rejected the idea that the U.S. should take over Britain's international role, arguing that the current precarious situation stemmed from a lack of nerve, not a lack of power. 'What the British need today,' he wrote in February 1939, 'is a good stiff grog, inducing not only the desire to save civilization but the continued belief that they can do it.' He repeated these arguments in an interview with the Marquis of Lothian, the former viceroy of India who would succeed Sir John Lindsay as ambassador to the U.S. in the summer of 1939. Roosevelt told Lothian that while he was willing to help the British in a war against Germany, he would not take any action if Great Britain 'cringed like a coward.' What was required was a policy of 'robust self-help,' since anything else would only strengthen the hand of those fighting against Anglo-American cooperation.[24]

This tactic – using public suspicion of Great Britain as a

club with which to bludgeon London into doing what he wanted – had become a favorite of Roosevelt's by late 1938. For example, after four years of trying to craft an Anglo-American trade agreement in the teeth of Britain's policy of 'imperial preference,' some well-placed warnings that failure to compromise might move Americans 'toward political and economic isolation' quickly led the British to a less intransigent position in the wake of Munich.[25]

However, the dispute between the administration and the Foreign Office that received the most attention in 1937–8 involved the Canton and Enderbury Islands in the Pacific. These islands were mere specks in the ocean; bereft of natural resources, they had been ignored in the colonial grabs of the 19th century. But by the late 1930s American and British policymakers had begun to see a use for them as vital refueling stations for military and commercial flights across the Pacific. The dispute began in the summer of 1937, when a U.S. minesweeper visited Canton Island and raised the flag there, despite the fact that Britain had claimed the islet in March. When the Foreign Office protested, Roosevelt dismissed British claims as 'a sheer case of bluff.' It was not sufficient, he wrote to Hull, to advance a claim on the basis of discovery alone, unless the discovery is 'followed within a reasonable period of time by permanent occupation.' Thus ensued a race to land settlers on Canton and Enderbury, though the Foreign Office continued to insist that both islands were 'definitely British territory.' Roosevelt complained that the British had 'an attitude of grabbing everything in sight'; Great Britain always tried to take 90 percent of everything, but this time it was not even willing to offer the United States 10 percent. Unless the British agreed to negotiate for joint control of the islands, the president threatened to sign an Executive Order placing all the currently unoccupied islands between Samoa and Hawaii under the jurisdiction of the U.S. Department of the Interior. Furthermore, he outraged the Foreign Office by issuing a license to Pan-American Airways allowing that company the use of Canton Island as a base.[26]

Finally the British had little choice but to back down, unable to afford a serious diplomatic rift with the United States at such a dangerous time. In Lindsay's words, it was important to keep 'a mere pimple from developing into a boil.' The Foreign Office agreed to joint control of the islands as a token of goodwill, but warned that such tactics as employed by the United States during the dispute would not be looked upon as favorably in the future. The result was thus a complete American victory; when British demands for landing rights in Hawaii were rebuffed, Lindsay claimed that the prevailing opinion in London was that 'Great Britain had come out on the short end of the stick.'[27]

But foreign affairs clearly took a back seat to Roosevelt's domestic problems in 1937 and 1938. His relationship with progressive Republicans, already weakened by his rather timid bows in the direction of collective security, collapsed altogether over his ill-fated plan to expand the Supreme Court. A sharp economic downturn in 1937 caused a significant drop in the president's public approval ratings, and his ability to maintain party discipline was faltering in the face of growing opposition to the New Deal by southern Democrats. His attempt during the 1938 primaries to 'purge' members of his own party whom he regarded as disloyal backfired, making the administration's position vis-à-vis Congress all the more tenuous. All of these setbacks contributed to a debacle for Roosevelt in the 1938 elections, in which the Republicans doubled their representation in both the House and the Senate.

Thus for the first time since 1932 mainstream (i.e., not progressive) Republicans would have significant input in American foreign affairs. The immediate effect of this was a strengthening of the forces opposed to Roosevelt's handling of foreign affairs, though most of the conservatives were far less dogmatic in their attachment to noninterventionism than were their progressive counterparts. The progressives had, after all, been dedicated opponents of collective security, foreign intervention, and Anglo-American cooperation long before the Democrats took control of the White House in 1932 – they had, it will be remembered, fought with equal determination Hoover's forays into 'internationalism' as well. Mainstream Republicans, by contrast, were divided. Midwesterners such as Senators Arthur Vandenberg (R-MI) and Robert A. Taft (R-OH) emerged as vigorous critics of the administration's conduct of foreign affairs, while northeasterners like Henry Cabot Lodge, Jr. (R-MA), Styles Bridges (R-NH) and Warren Austin (R-VT) would end up supporting the Roosevelt international agenda more often than they opposed it. Indeed, the organizations that would lobby most consistently for U.S. aid to Britain after the outbreak of war in Europe – the Century Group, the English-Speaking Union, the Committee to Defend America by Aiding the Allies – were made up mainly of Republicans. The 1938 elections, therefore, while potentially dangerous for Roosevelt domestically, did not prove to be a long-term threat to his foreign policy goals.[28]

It is also important to note that anglophobia was not a particularly strong motive even for those mainstream Republicans who opposed Roosevelt's handling of foreign affairs. There were exceptions, to be sure – Representatives Hamilton Fish (R-NY), Clare Hoffman (R-MI) and George Holden Tinkham (R-MA), for example, had strong anti-British prejudices – but most Republicans were driven far more by distrust of Roosevelt than by any personal animus toward Great Britain. Robert Taft, who in many ways became the spokesman for the anti-interventionist right, repeatedly expressed sympathy for Britain's position between 1938 and 1941. He steadfastly refused to engage in the anti-British rhetoric that would characterize the anti-interventionist movement; his fear was rather that a war might lead to dictatorship at home. As he put it in 1940, war measures would make the president 'a complete dictator over the lives and property of all our citizens.'[29]

Anglophobia, however, remained a visible feature of the noninterventionist left. 1938 saw the formation of the Keep America Out of the War Congress, a New York-based organization made up of liberals, pacifists, and progressives united in their opposition to U.S. involvement abroad. Like the editorials of the *New Republic*, the materials issued by the KAOWC continually emphasized the iniquities of the British Empire. British foreign policy, meanwhile, was blamed for the collapse of Weimar Germany and loyalist Spain. Dorothy Detzer, a prominent peace activist and a founding member of the group, even suggested that members of organizations such as the English-Speaking Union register as foreign agents, since such groups undoubtedly had their 'spiritual headquarters' in England. Other prominent members of the KAOWC included Frederick J. Libby, Norman Thomas, the muckraking journalist John T. Flynn, historian Harry Elmer Barnes, and Oswald Garrison Villard.[30]

Though American opinion of Great Britain hit a low point at the end of 1938, the events of the spring and summer of the following year helped to improve the situation considerably. Hitler's invasion of Czechoslovakia in March cleared up any lingering doubts about Hitler's intentions. While there was virtually no sympathy for the Nazi regime among Americans, there had been a certain willingness to accept his foreign goals as nothing more than a reversal of the unjust Versailles treaty. The annexation of Bohemia and Moravia, however, exposed a desire to dominate, if not the entire world, at least Central Europe, and a willingness to extend his rule over non-German populations. Moreover, Chamberlain's prompt action in guaranteeing the remaining states of eastern Europe was a signal to many Americans that the British had indeed taken the 'good stiff grog' which Roosevelt had prescribed.

Britain's reputation also enjoyed a boost during the New York World's Fair. The British Pavilion became one of the most popular exhibits, attracting over 14 million visitors by the end of the summer. The centerpiece of the pavilion was the 'Hall of Democracy,' dedicated to the foundations of the Anglo-American concept of political liberty, and which included, among other famous objects on display, the original copy of the Magna Carta. Since war had broken out before the close of the fair in September, the British government turned over the priceless document – which was deemed far too valuable to risk to a wartime ocean voyage – to the Library of Congress for safekeeping. This act helped to underline the cultural ties between the two nations while remaining immune to the all-too-common charges of 'British propaganda.'[31]

The most effective step taken by the British Government to improve its public image in the months before the outbreak of war was the visit of the royal couple, King George VI and Queen Elizabeth, in June. Roosevelt had been talking about arranging a visit since the king's coronation in 1937. Since George VI would be the first reigning British sovereign to set foot on American soil, it might help promote greater under-standing between the two countries. Many saw an ulterior motive for the visit. The *Washington Times-Herald* warned that 'it is really Mr. Chamberlain who is visiting us, and let's keep clearly in mind what he wants to sell us.' The *Chicago Tribune* advised the American people to welcome the royal couple with the 'utmost cordiality and respect,' but with no 'fawning.' And in the pages of the *Nation*, Freda Kirchwey argued that a royal visit was insufficient to win over an America chastened by the betrayal at Munich. 'The U.S. should insist on the resignation of Chamberlain and company as the price for American cooperation,' she wrote. 'We know from experience that they would sell out any other country for a liar's promise of immunity for themselves.'[32]

For the most part the visit was a roaring success. There were, of course, some attempts by anglophobes to sour the event. A few days before the arrival of the king and queen, a reputed leader of the Irish Republican Army was arrested by the FBI in Detroit, and nearly seventy-five congressmen, led by James P. McGranery (D-PA), Martin L. Sweeney (D-OH), and Joseph Smith (D-PA) threatened to boycott the sched-uled congressional reception for the royal couple if he were not released. Sweeney went on to embarrass the president by sending a telegram to the royal couple at the British Embassy demanding payment of the war debts. But most Americans welcomed them enthusiastically, much to the chagrin of Hiram Johnson, who called the display 'the most vulgar thing I have seen for many a day.' The young and attractive royal couple charmed the public, showing up in newsreels dining on beer and hot dogs at the president's house in Hyde Park. Even the dour Johnson admitted that the pair 'possess the ordinary virtues we like to see in young people.' Nor were the majority of Americans convinced that the visit was an attempt to bring the United States into an alliance with Great Britain – a poll taken a few months afterward showed that only about 24 percent believed this, while 58 percent said it was 'no more than a token of friendship among English speaking peoples.'[33]

But while the royal visit may have heightened a sense of goodwill toward England, it did not produce any enthusiasm about getting involved in a European war on Britain's behalf.

In March Roosevelt began pressing for a revision of the neutrality laws which would allow belligerents to purchase arms on a cash-and-carry basis, and by late June it had come up for a vote in the House. Hamilton Fish accused the president of 'trying to change a neutral law into an unneutral law,' and of wanting to take sides in an upcoming war. Rep. James C. Oliver (R-ME), meanwhile, claimed the bill was an attempt to lead the United States 'into the snare and the delusion of British political and financial chicanery and treachery.' The bill passed, but only after the inclusion of a killer amendment introduced by John Vorys (R-OH) which maintained the embargo on 'arms and ammunition,' but not on 'implements of war' such as planes. When Roosevelt turned instead to the Senate, he soon found that he lacked sufficient votes even to get the proposal out of the Foreign Relations Committee. But there was little need to worry, Borah assured the president, since he was convinced there would be no war: 'I know it to be a fact as much as I ever will know anything...that Britain is behind Hitler.'[34]

Borah made his prediction on July 18; by September 1 he had been proven wrong. German troops invaded Poland, and Britain and France declared war. For the vast majority of Americans it was not a matter of choosing sides, for the allies were believed to be clearly in the right. At the same time, however, events in Europe were not deemed important enough for the United States to expend its blood and treasure. Thus even though public sympathy lay overwhelmingly with the British cause, a loose coalition of anglophobes, pacifists and conservative Republicans had already formed to maintain a strict American neutrality. The struggle between this coalition and the Roosevelt administration would take center stage in American politics for the next two years.

6 'Ties of Blood and Language'

The results of a revealing poll were published in the January, 1940 issue of *Fortune* magazine. One of the questions asked respondents to choose the statement which best described their feelings toward Great Britain. 9.8 percent agreed with the first answer, 'Great Britain has no greater claim upon our sympathy than any other nation, because she has grown great by employing practically all of the means of aggression, oppression, and secret diplomacy that we criticize in such other nations as Germany' – the position of extreme anglophobes such as Nye, Johnson, Martin Sweeney and Father Coughlin. 25.5 percent chose the second, 'Britain is probably as decent as any nation is likely to be, but our national interests call for going it alone and being on guard against British propaganda,' a statement that would accurately summarize the opinion of most mainstream Republican anti-interventionists such as Taft and Vandenberg. 16.2 percent agreed with the third statement, 'The British probably are no angels, but as a practical matter our vital interests are tied up in the maintenance of the Empire, because her navy is an additional protector of our trade and commercial interests the world over,' a position which best approximated that of President Roosevelt. But the statement which met with more agreement than any other – 38.3 percent – held that 'The British do have a special claim on our sympathies because they are closest to ourselves by ties of blood and language, and because they too are defenders of democracy.' Yet this did not imply that Americans were prepared to go to war; quite the contrary, for even though polls taken in late 1939 showed an overwhelming majority – 83 percent – hoping for an allied victory, an equal percentage opposed sending any U.S. forces abroad to assist Britain and France.[1]

Roosevelt, realizing that the present mood of anglophilia might not last, eagerly called Congress into special session to reconsider neutrality revision. Believing that partisanship had played a significant role in blocking the bill in June, the president backed away from the discretionary power which would have been granted to him under the earlier version. Congress, and not the president, would determine cash-and-carry policy, helping to ease the fears of conservatives of both parties that neutrality revision was merely a disguise for a massive expansion of executive authority. Roosevelt also arranged for prominent Republicans such as Alf Landon, Henry Stimson, William Allen White and Frank Knox to lend their support. Senator George Norris (R-NE), one of the original irreconcilable opponents of the Versailles treaty, spoke for many of his colleagues who believed that, as bad as England was, Hitler 'is so much worse,...that we can reach only one conclusion, and that is, whatever we have a right to do in the premises should be done in favor of England and France, and not in favor of Hitler.' Even the pacifistically-inclined Herbert Hoover went on record as supporting the sale of 'defensive weapons' to the British.[2]

By the time the special session convened in October, Poland had already fallen to its German invaders, giving the new cash-and-carry legislation an enhanced sense of urgency. Informal polling in the Senate showed that the bill would pass by a two-to-one margin, while surveys of public opinion showed nearly 90 percent of Americans favored changing the neutrality laws. Even Borah privately expressed his support for the bill, though he explained that he had to 'make some sort of fight...so as to keep the President from leading us into war.'[3] Anti-interventionists rallied around Senators Borah, Clark, and Nye, who with the support of Father Coughlin and famed aviator Charles A. Lindbergh mounted a spirited opposition to neutrality revision. 'Was the cruel and brutal and revolting creed of Naziism any different at Munich than it was at Warsaw?' Borah asked rhetorically. D. Worth Clark (R-ID) attacked what he called Britain's 'holier-than-thou' posture, calling the British Empire 'the outstanding example of aggression that the world has ever seen.' Sheridan Downey (D-CA), meanwhile, played the nationalist card, reminding his colleagues that 'Great Britain has...denied our sovereignty in the Western Hemisphere more than any other country.' As for Coughlin, the 'radio priest' spearheaded a national campaign which brought over a million telegrams, letters and postcards to congressional offices over the course of three days.[4]

The resistance, however, proved ultimately futile. Republicans split on the issue, with many northeasterners such as Warren Austin and Styles Bridges supporting revision; even Robert Taft refused to oppose the extension of cash-and-carry. Moreover, southern Democrats, who had often joined with Republicans to oppose Roosevelt's domestic agenda, voted as a bloc in favor of the bill. The bill passed in the Senate by a vote of 63 to 30, and then in the House by a comfortable margin of 243–181. Of the House votes, 69 of the 243 were cast by those who had not voted for revision in June. The British government was, of course, quite pleased; as Chamberlain wrote to Roosevelt, the repeal of the arms embargo provided 'profound moral encouragement to us in the struggle upon which we are engaged.'[5]

Anti-interventionists thus lost their first important battle, thanks mainly to public sympathy toward Britain and popular abhorrence of Nazi Germany. They continued to enjoy one advantage, however, and that was the overwhelming aversion of Americans to actual involvement in the war. The trick, then, was to reinforce the public hostility toward intervention without opening up oneself to the charge of being pro-German. One early means of going about this was to charge that the war was not being fought in earnest. Lord Lothian, the British ambassador, remarked that such suspicions would continue among Americans 'so long as Mr. Chamberlain remained Prime Minister,' and that the six months of inactivity that followed the collapse of Poland only strengthened the belief in a 'phoney war.' One powerful advocate of this position was William Borah, who accused the combatants of 'pulling their punches.' The Idaho progressive went on to speculate that Britain and France had only declared war as a face-saving gesture, and would negotiate peace with Hitler after a few months.[6]

Foreign trade soon became another stick with which to beat the English. In order to maintain sufficient gold reserves, one of the first actions taken by the British government was to place prohibitions on the import of 'luxuries and of goods of which there are sufficient home supplies.' These included pottery, glass, cutlery, clocks and watches, clothing and shoes, certain chemicals, soap, office supplies, automobiles, musical instruments, cosmetics, toys and games and tobacco. Since several of these products, especially automobiles and tobacco, were important American exports, there was an immediate protest from the United States. Sen. Rush Holt (D-WV) accused the British of trying to blackmail the United States into repealing the Neutrality Act. Many of those most upset by the restrictions were those who had supported revision of the neutrality laws; the New York Produce Exchange, for example, wrote to Secretary of State Hull that American farmers were 'being penalized for the lifting of the arms embargo.' It also reinforced the desire of many such as Tennessee Democrat Kenneth McKellar that the rest of the Neutrality Act remain in full force. The State Department responded with a vigorous protest, reflecting both Hull's predilection for free trade and his fear of being accused of softness toward the British Empire. The restrictions, Hull wrote, had 'distinctly adverse repercussions' on the American economy, and he warned of growing pressure by businessmen and farmers to terminate the 1938 trade agreement. But although Sir John Simon promised that all restrictions would be strictly temporary, they remained in effect throughout the period of U.S. neutrality.[7]

By far the most popular strategy used by American anglophobes was to show the extent to which the current European war was similar to that of 1914–1918, a war which most Americans continued to believe the United States should have stayed out of. This strategy involved four interrelated elements, the first of which was to document and publicize perceived British violations of the rights of neutrals. On October 7, 1939, the Foreign Office announced that neutral ships carrying mail bound for Europe would be searched for 'contraband or obnoxious documents.' In addition, British authorities in Bermuda began to inspect American planes refueling at that island for mail bound for any nation except Britain and France. By early 1940 this had become a considerable bone of contention between England and the United States. Seizing the opportunity to twist the lion's tail, the *Chicago Tribune* published an eight-column banner headline announcing, 'BRITISH RAID ON MAIL: LETTERS SEIZED AT POINT OF GUN ON U.S. CLIPPER.' In the

Senate, James Mead (D-NY) called upon the British to 'show a more sympathetic consideration' for American interests, and further charged that the Royal Navy had been forcing U.S. ships from neutral sea lanes into belligerent waters in the hope that they would be sunk by German submarines. Bennett Champ Clark (D-MO), meanwhile, introduced legislation prohibiting planes carrying U.S. mail from landing at Bermuda; Ernest Lundeen (R-MN) even suggested seizing the island outright. The response from the State Department reflected comparable outrage (though perhaps not to the extent of Lundeen's). Adolf Berle met with a special British emissary who warned that even if American planes stopped calling at Bermuda they could still be intercepted by British fighters. An indignant Berle accused the Foreign Office of treating the United States 'as though we were a small European nation – say, Czechoslovakia,' and warned that 'the first time a British air squadron shot at an American plane there would be the deuce to pay.' Ambassador Joseph Kennedy, during a brief visit to the United States, conducted an informal poll in his movie theaters. He concluded that nearly 80 percent of all moviegoers were disgusted with British disregard for the rights of neutrals, a finding which he promptly reported upon his return to the Court of St. James. Breckenridge Long also wrote of 'a distinct wave of anti-British feeling,' the result of 'the stupidity of England.'[8]

Another common theme which the anglophobes employed was to deny that the war had anything to do with democracy or democratic values. This was a favored tactic among those on the left wing of the anti-interventionist movement. Oswald Garrison Villard, visiting London shortly after the outbreak of war, wrote in the *Nation* that 'British democracy' was 'vanishing day by day.' Parliament, he claimed, had become nothing more than 'a group which meets once a week to hear a report from the Prime Minister of the progress of the war.' Many others went further. In a KAOWC publication entitled *Keep America Out of War: A Program*, Norman Thomas and Bertram D. Wolfe denied that the British government had any real sympathy toward democratic forms of government, citing its role in the fall of Weimar Germany, Republican Spain, and, of course, Czechoslovakia. Louis Bromfield, in his 1939 book *England:*

A Dying Oligarchy, argued that Britain had never been a democracy, but rather an oligarchy, 'a clique of compromising undecided elderly politicians, decadent and full of cant, as easily terrified by the prospect of a general election as by the face-making of dictators.' This theme was taken up in Congress as well. Gerald Nye contended that 'hundreds of millions of people under the British flag do not know the meaning of the word "democracy."' Robert La Follette, Jr. even called Britain and France 'the illegitimate parents of Nazism.'[9]

For the anti-British elements among the anti-interventionists, once the high-sounding rhetoric about the need to defend democracy had been stripped away the war was laid bare as merely a conflict over imperial possessions. There was, they stressed, a fundamental moral equivalency between Germany's war of conquest and England's efforts to protect her empire, which after all had been won through earlier acts of conquest. As William Lemke put it in a letter to one of his constituents, '[Y]ou could put Hitler, Chamberlain, Churchill, Stalin, Mussolini, Duff Cooper and Daladier all into a big barrel and roll it down a hill and you would always find an agressor [*sic*] with bloody hands on top, no matter how fast the barrel was rolling.' Benjamin C. Marsh, executive secretary of The People's Lobby, called Great Britain 'the mother of aggression,' and ridiculed those Americans who would come to its aid. Hugh S. Johnson, the flamboyant army general who had previously served as director of Roosevelt's National Recovery Administration, wrote that 'Britain is fighting her own war...for continued imperial domination over weaker and exploited, subdued and subject peoples.' For Norman Thomas and Bertram Wolfe, Britain's claim to be resisting German aggression was a masterpiece in hypocrisy: 'Is there in the whole history of Nazi aggression in the building of its continental empire, any more bloody and degrading page than England's Opium War on China? or her war for diamonds and gold upon the South African Boer Republic? or her four centuries of bloody war on Ireland and almost three centuries of war on India?' As H. L. Mencken pointed out, defense of empire might be a 'rational reason' for going to war, 'but it is as devoid of moral content as a theorem in algebra or a college yell.'[10]

But the most common means of evoking memories of 1915–1917 was to warn of the dangers of British propaganda, which was believed to be hard at work in an effort to lure the United States into the war. Anglophobes had a far easier time convincing their fellow Americans of this – a poll taken in October 1939 showed that 40 percent of those surveyed believed that British propaganda had played a significant role in bringing the United States into the First World War. British commentator Alistair Cooke wrote that Americans possessed an 'almost psychotic dread' of British propaganda; Lord Lothian wrote that they were 'terrified' of it. This was, of course, nothing new – British propaganda was believed by some to be behind every initiative that could possibly be construed as pro-English since the Washington Naval Treaties. The argument received a huge boost in 1938, however, from the publication of *Propaganda in the Next War* by former British propagandist Sidney Rogerson. Rogerson claimed that Americans were 'more susceptible than most peoples to mass suggestion'; that despite 'a substratum of suspicion of Great Britain,' British propaganda was 'on firm ground.' Rogerson's book went on to detail the methods which England would employ in the next war, including the exportation of 'our leading literary lights... to put our point of view over the dinner table.' The British government would place special emphasis on film coverage; camera crews would be permitted 'to shoot pictures of air raids, in order that a proper volume of pictorial "horror" will be available in one of the few great countries where "atrocity propaganda" will still be operative.'[11]

Propaganda in the Next War was a godsend for anglophobes; it provided, in Lord Lothian's words, 'an opportune munitions dump' for Britain's enemies in America. It was followed by a whole series of books on the subject of propaganda – *Propaganda for War* by H. C. Peterson, *Atrocity Propaganda* by James Morgan Read, *War Propaganda and the United States* by Harold Lavine and James Wechsler, *The Deadly Parallel* by C. Hartley Grattan, just to name a few. They evidenced varying degrees of scholarship, but all had a common theme – that, according to H. C. Peterson,

The British campaign to induce the United States to come

to their assistance affected every phase of American life; it was propaganda in its broadest meaning.... It was a campaign to create a pro-British attitude of mind among Americans, to get American sympathies and interests so deeply involved in the European war that it would be impossible for this country to remain neutral.[12]

Within months of the outbreak of war anglophobes began to denounce anything which portrayed the British in a positive light (or, to a certain extent, which portrayed the Germans negatively) as mere propaganda. C. Hartley Grattan wrote that 'we can legitimately suspect that British propaganda has been pouring into this country for months.' Rep. Martin Sweeney pressed the Dies Committee in 1940 to look into the activities of 'paid agents of Britain and France in this country, led by the Marquis of Lothian.' Sen. Ernest Lundeen (R-MN), meanwhile, wrote that 'the propaganda of Great Britain is more dangerous than all the propaganda from all the other countries combined.'[13]

Nor was this phenomenon limited to members of Congress. In 1941, the prominent socialist author Theodore Dreiser saw sinister intent in the travels of British citizens such as Noel Coward throughout the country, while columnist Albert Jay Nock cited British propaganda as 'clear proof that we are officially regarded as a nation of manageable half-wits.' An education expert named Porter Sargent gained minor repute for his war on propaganda, which he called 'Britain's best-paying export,' while a 55-year-old electrician named Albert Johnson systematically defaced all books in the New York Public Library that he considered too complimentary to England, 'to help the next reader read properly.' Observing the prevailing degree of suspicion, which often bordered on xenophobia, Alistair Cooke wrote in 1940 that 'speculation and suspicion have turned nervously on any alien resident of the United States who is not a full-blooded Indian.'[14]

The end of the so-called 'phoney war' came in April, 1940, when Hitler's armies invaded Denmark and Norway. Denmark fell in just a few days; Norway held out a bit longer, with the help of British troops, but these were soon dislodged, and Norwegian resistance collapsed by the end of the month. The swiftness of the German victories came as a serious blow to Britain's military reputation in the United States. Roosevelt called the debacle 'outrageous'; proof of the incompetence of the Chamberlain cabinet. Adolf Berle was equally incensed. 'No neutral will rely on British promises again,' he predicted, 'for the British record is pretty nearly perfect.' The *New Republic* felt likewise, devoting an editorial to assaulting all of the major Tory leaders, including Winston Churchill. 'As important to us as is Allied success in the war,' the liberal journal claimed, 'we cannot ensure it as long as the Allies are incompetently led.'[15]

The fall of Norway precipitated the collapse of the Tory cabinet of Chamberlain, which gave way to a new coalition government under Winston Churchill. Churchill did not have a history of popularity among Americans; indeed, he was remembered by many as the chief spokesman for 'Big Navy' forces in Great Britain during the time of the Anglo-American naval rivalry of the late 1920s. Nor was Roosevelt a great admirer of his; when George VI mentioned Churchill as a possible successor to Chamberlain during his visit in 1939, Roosevelt indicated his disapproval. Churchill drank too much, the president noted on a number of occasions, and was 'tight most of the time.' He had also, as a staunch conservative, been fiercely critical of the New Deal. But the new prime minister quickly amassed considerable American support. As an early critic of appeasement, Churchill had won the respect of many liberals, even while they denounced his calls for rearmament. Liberal support became enthusiastic when the Labour party announced its wholehearted participation and support of the Churchill government. 'Destiny has swooped on England like a bombing plane that dives from the clouds,' the *New Republic* gushed. 'The hour called for a captain rather than a premier.' In a mere matter of months, Churchill reputation had gone from that of anti-American reactionary to, in James J. Martin's words, 'a status in English history just a shade below King Arthur.'[16]

But the change of government in London did nothing to stem the German advance on the continent. Wasting no time after the fall of Norway, Hitler unleashed his armies on the Low Countries and France in May. The former were overrun within weeks, and by midsummer France too had succumbed. Great Britain now found itself devoid of allies, facing the might of Nazi Germany on its own. Americans were shocked, and Lord Lothian reported 'a wave of pessimism...to the effect that Great Britain must now be inevitably defeated, and that there is no use in the United States doing any more to help it....' Ambassador Kennedy informed Hull in September of his 'complete lack of confidence in the entire conduct of this war,' adding that the new cabinet had nothing 'to offer in the line of leadership or productive capacity in industry that could be of the slightest value to us.' Roosevelt was almost as pessimistic; for most of the summer, at least, he was convinced that England was doomed and that there was nothing that the United States could do about it. When Interior Secretary Harold Ickes approached him on July 2 regarding the possibility of transferring U.S. destroyers to Britain, the president responded that if Britain were then defeated, 'they might fall into the hands of the Germans and be used against us.' Churchill would later recall that for the six weeks following the collapse of France 'the Americans treated us in that rather distant and sympathetic manner one adopts towards a friend one knows is suffering from cancer.'[17]

Not all Americans, however, looked upon a British defeat with a sense of dismay. Shortly before his death, Borah had mused on the possibility, and concluded, 'Would it be a serious catastrophe if the three hundred and odd million Indiamen were given their freedom? Or, if the possessions scattered all over the earth passed under the control of the people who possess them?' The editors of Catholic World, meanwhile, called the British Empire 'an impossible organization,' adding that its demise was 'inevitable.' In the Senate, Sheridan Downey (D-CA) asked, 'Why not be realists? For years the greatest historians and philosophers of England and of the world have been declaring that the British Empire is crumbling.' Gerald Nye outdid them all: not only did he claim that the empire was doomed, and that its demise ought not cause Americans 'undue alarm,' but he even suggested that a German victory might help U.S. trade 'by removing our chief competitor.'[18]

Roosevelt's most immediate legislative response to Britain's desperate situation was to attempt to rebuild the armed forces, which remained pitifully small in early 1940 – the U.S. Army, in fact, could field fewer than one-third the number of divisions which Belgium had mobilized to meet the German invasion. In the president's view, something had to be done, and done quickly, so he asked Congress to institute the first peacetime conscription program in American history. A bipartisan bill, the Burke-Wadsworth Selective Service Act, came before the Senate in August. Many anti-interventionists suspected the worst. Hiram Johnson, for example, called it the 'most sinister law' which he had encountered in his entire career. William Lemke claimed the bill had 'the support of the British nobility, both domestic and foreign,' while Sen. Dennis Chavez (D-NM) argued that Great Britain posed a far greater threat to American security than did Germany. There were, however, a number of defections from the ranks of the anti-interventionists, self-proclaimed 'nationalists' such as Robert R. Reynolds (D-NC) and Henry Cabot Lodge, Jr. (R-MA), whose belief in a strong American military exceeded their personal hostility toward the president's conduct of foreign affairs. The bill passed the Senate by a lopsided vote of 58 to 31, though only after the narrow defeat of an amendment which would have restricted American armed forces to the western hemisphere.[19]

By mid-August Roosevelt had apparently undergone a change of heart regarding aid to Britain. The ability of the British to withstand sustained aerial bombardment, along with the failure of the Germans to follow up the conquest of France with an invasion of the British Isles, led the president to believe that England might not be such a lost cause after all. He also viewed the British attack in mid-July on the French fleet at Oran as evidence that Churchill was willing to take the offensive when the opportunity presented itself. The president therefore began to look into the legality of Ickes' suggestion that U.S. destroyers be transferred to the British fleet. He was informed that such a transfer would be illegal, but that they might be handed over as part of a trade. A deal was soon worked out – the United States would receive 99-year leases on British bases in Newfoundland, Bermuda, the Bahamas, St. Lucia, Trinidad, and British Guiana. Roosevelt had long been interested in acquiring these bases – he had even brought up the issue during the visit of George VI –

but there was an even more compelling reason to involve the bases in a trade for American ships. A number of prominent anglophobes had for years been demanding that the United States take over Britain's air and naval bases in the western hemisphere as partial payment on England's world war debts. Ernest Lundeen, in fact, suggested that the bases be taken by force, if necessary. In acquiring leases for them, then, Roosevelt was able to protect the transfer of destroyers from the congressional criticism which undoubtedly would have arisen otherwise.[20]

The president turned over the negotiations with Congress to Sen. David I. Walsh (D-MA), chairman of the Naval Affairs Committee and an inveterate anglophobe. In a 'Dear Dave' letter, Roosevelt argued that the United States was actually getting the better of the deal. It was, in his words, of 'utmost importance to our national defense'; the acquisition of off-shore bases more than made up for the loss of the fifty destroyers 'which are on their last legs.' Walsh was apparently convinced, for he quickly composed the legislation authorizing the exchange. When the bill came before Congress, Roosevelt called it 'the most important action in the reinforcement of our national defense that has been taken since the Louisiana Purchase.'[21]

There was, of course, immediate resistance to the proposed transfer by anti-interventionists. Nye called the trade 'a belligerent act making us a party to the war.' Sen. Homer T. Bone (D-WA) compared it to the *Alabama* dispute of the American Civil War, during which Great Britain built commerce raiders for the Confederacy. Others, Lundeen among them, claimed that 99-year leases were not enough. 'We are going to spend millions, perhaps billions of dollars to build airports, naval stations, and military bases...and at the end of 99 years they go back to Great Britain,' Rep. Clare Hoffman (R-MI) remarked. 'What kind of a deal is that?' But there was little doubt that the destroyers-for-bases trade would pass. The bill received the unexpected endorsement of Col. McCormick's *Chicago Tribune*, which had been demanding the acquisition of bases from the British since the 1920s. In addition, the exchange was politically difficult to oppose. A public opinion poll taken on August 17 showed that 62 percent of those surveyed supported it. As one

senator complained in the *New York Post*, '[Y]ou can't attack
a deal like that. If you jump on the destroyer transfer, you're
jumping on the acquisition of defense bases in the Western
Hemisphere. And the voters wouldn't stand for that.
Roosevelt outsmarted all of us when he tied up the two
deals.'[22]

While all of this was going on, America was in the midst of
an election campaign as Roosevelt sought to become the first
president to serve a third term. His opponent was Wendell
Willkie, a moderate Republican (indeed, he had supported
Roosevelt in 1932) from Indiana. His nomination was extremely controversial among some factions of the G.O.P.,
since he was not an anti-interventionist. Lord Lothian wrote
that he was 'personally in favour of doing everything possible
to see that Great Britain did not get beaten in the war.'
Willkie endorsed the Burke-Wadsworth bill and the destroyers-for-bases trade, and even referred to Britain as 'our first
line of defense and our only remaining friend.' This generous attitude, however, began to change late in the campaign.
Though his attacks on waste and fraud in the New Deal were
finding a receptive audience, he continued to lag in the polls.
Therefore, in an attempt to bolster his support among non-
interventionists he began to accuse Roosevelt of wanting to
bring the United States into the war. Willkie claimed that
American boys were 'already almost on the transports' to be
shipped abroad, and declared that if the president were reelected the U.S. would be in the war by the following April.
But while this new line of attack won him increased support
among groups opposed to U.S. involvement, the war issue
helped Roosevelt more than it did Willkie. When asked how
they would vote if they were assured that there would be no
war, those polled chose Willkie over the president by 5.5 percentage points, but when forced to consider the possibility of
American involvement overseas, they preferred Roosevelt by
a margin of 18 percent. As it turned out, the president was reelected by a vote of 27 000 000 to Willkie's 22 000 000. But
while there was considerable rejoicing in London over the
outcome – the *Daily Express* called it 'the best thing that could
happen to Britain' – the election was hardly a nationwide referendum on the war. Significantly, anti-interventionists such
as Burton Wheeler and David Walsh were reelected in their

respective states by larger margins than Roosevelt had received. In Michigan Arthur Vandenberg was overwhelmingly returned to the Senate, and John Thomas of Idaho and C. Wayland Brooks of Illinois both overcame Democratic challenges even though Roosevelt won their states' electoral votes. The only casualty among the noninterventionists in 1940 was Rush Holt of West Virginia, whose loss came during the Democratic primaries. The battle over American involvement, therefore, was far from over.[23]

Yet there is little doubt that by the end of 1940 the anti-interventionist movement was far different from that of the mid- to late-1930s. From the time of the Hoover administration until the elections of 1938, the campaign for strict American neutrality was fought mainly by liberal, progressive, and ethnic anglophobes. In 1940 and 1941, however, the movement had taken on a far more conservative and partisan character. The main reason for this was the defection, almost *en masse*, of the liberals from its ranks. As Selig Adler has written, '[f]aced with the cruel dilemma of risking loathsome war or allowing an abhorrent fascism to envelop the world, they made the choice of the lesser evil.' The fall of France and the subsequent bombings of British cities in the summer of 1940 had a deep effect on the editors of the *New Republic*, and they soon joined those of the *Nation* in supporting full military aid to Great Britain.[24] Even Oswald Garrison Villard, who had been England's foremost liberal critic since the days of the Versailles treaty, was moved by what he saw during his visit to London. Though repeating his belief that the war was 'the result of a contest between idiocy on one hand and insanity on the other,' he went on to say that

> …the faces of those quiet English people continue to come back to me; they are my chief concern. It was not they who set up concentration camps in South Africa; nor was it their grandfathers who instigated the opium war in China….They have their faults, heaven knows; they still have their caste system, their lords and ladies. They have not yet seen to it that full justice is done to Ireland. Still, these are the people whom I would do anything – short of war – to help preserve.[25]

A similar transformation was occurring within the houses of Congress, as Democrats began to abandon their former positions to support the president's foreign policy. The most dramatic shift was among southerners, who for the past few years had been allied with Republicans in opposition to Roosevelt's New Deal programs. Southern support for lifting the arms embargo, and later for lend-lease, has traditionally been attributed to the partiality of the southern elite for British society and culture. Indeed, public opinion polls consistently indicated a greater fondness for England in the South than in other parts of the country. There were no large communities of German-, Irish-, or Italian-Americans south of the Mason-Dixon line, and the British had always been the largest overseas consumer of cotton and tobacco grown there. Nevertheless, in the 1920s all this had not prevented a number of southern politicians, such as Tom Watson, Park Trammell, Kenneth McKellar, and Tom Connally from standing among the Senate's most vehement critics of England. Paul Seabury, in *The Waning of Southern 'Internationalism'* (1957) suggests that there may have been some tacit agreement between southern Democrats and the Roosevelt administration in which the former would agree to support increased aid to the allies if the latter promised to call a halt to further New Deal reforms, especially an anti-lynching bill to which southerners particularly objected. In any case, senators and representatives from the South soon became the most faithful supporters of the president's foreign policy.[26]

At the same time, ethnic group identification was beginning to play less of a role in the formation of anti-interventionist sentiment. A public opinion poll taken in November 1939 showed that 61 percent of Irish-Americans favored an outright repeal of the neutrality legislation. Another survey taken in December 1940 indicated that nearly 45 percent supported increased aid for Britain. As David L. Porter has pointed out, a majority of Irish-American legislators, and around 40 percent of German-American congressmen, voted to lift the arms embargo. For about 10 percent of the Irish in Congress, and 20 percent of the Germans, it had been their first vote in favor of increased overseas involvement. The Irish were motivated not only by their loyalty toward the Democratic party, but also by their fears that a German victory might endanger the religious liberties of Catholics. Germans, meanwhile, came increasingly to believe that Hitler's totalitarianism was a threat to the world, including the German people themselves.[27]

Yet there was another, even more important reason for the decline in ethnic zeal in the battle against American intervention, one that involved a change in the very nature of the ethnic population. The last great wave of immigrants from Central and Eastern Europe had ended with the outbreak of the First World War, and by the late 1930s these foreign-born Americans had not only come of age, but had begun to drift away from their previous affinity with their homelands. While Germany and Italy did enjoy some small degree of support among their respective ethnic groups in the U.S., it was far more muted than German-American support for the Central Powers in World War I. Ties of language and political culture bound second- and third-generation Americans more tightly to Great Britain than to the nations where their parents or grandparents were born, despite the best efforts of the anglophobes to trivialize these ties.

As liberals, ethnics, and southern Democrats defected from the ranks of the noninterventionists, the movement became increasingly associated in the popular mind with Republicanism and conservatism. Those progressives who remained, such as Gerald Nye, Hiram Johnson, and Burton Wheeler, moved noticeably toward the right on domestic issues. The conservatives, as noted in the previous chapter, were not motivated primarily by anti-British prejudices. They interpreted the president's foreign policy less as an effort to shore up the British Empire than as an attempt to use a foreign war as a cover for a massive expansion in the power of government. Nevertheless, they quickly became willing, if not overly enthusiastic, allies of the remaining exponents of anglophobia. Former president Hoover provided some explanation for this several years after the fact: in a meeting with the British ambassador in 1943, Hoover claimed that the British had 'centered their efforts on the left-wing crowd of the New Deal to the exclusion of everybody else.' The efforts of such British academics as Harold Laski to portray England as moving toward socialism, he

argued, led many American conservatives to the conclusion
that Britain perhaps was not worth defending.[28]

The increasingly conservative tone of the anti-interventionist movement, and its relationship to anti-British elements is
most dramatically illustrated in the establishment of the
America First Committee. Founded in Chicago in September
1940 by a number of prominent conservative writers and
businessmen, the AFC rapidly became the foremost antiwar
organization, easily overtaking the older KAOWC in both size
and legislative clout. Its membership included some of the
most famous personalities of the era – Charles Lindbergh,
Laura Ingalls, Henry Ford, Burton K. Wheeler, Gerald Nye,
Alice Roosevelt Longworth, Gen. Hugh S. Johnson, and Gen.
Robert E. Wood, chairman of the board of Sears, Roebuck,
and Company, just to name a few. Since the stated goal of the
organization was to oppose the administration's efforts
toward aiding Great Britain, the AFC was immediately
accused of being anti-British. In actuality, the record is
mixed. One of the group's speakers, Howard G. Swann,
advised against public condemnations of Great Britain,
'because it will win us no new friends. The English haters are
won to us anyway.' Rep. Samuel B. Pettengill, an Indiana
Republican who was one of the organization's most influential advisers, suggested that 'the Committee ought not to be
anti-British or anti-anybody. We are pro-America.' At the
same time, the organization's leaders took pains to avoid
embarrassing association with extreme anti-British and pro-fascist organizations such as Father Coughlin's National
Union for Social Justice, Gerald L.K. Smith's anti-Semitic
Committee of 1 000 000, William Dudley Pelley's Silver
Shirts, or the German-American Bund.[29]

For a while, at least, the America First Committee managed
to avoid being tarred with the same brush as Smith and
Coughlin, but the sheer size of the organization made the
local chapters difficult to control. In October the secretary of
the New York office complained of 'certain individuals who
have attempted to upset the movement by professing to be
very much with us but then advocating measures that are so
extreme that we might be called to account for subversive activities.' Significantly, however, he called this 'a deliberate
attempt, possibly by a British agency, to frame the America

First Committee and discredit them.' Nor can the organization's leadership in Chicago escape blame, for as the battle over intervention became more heated in 1941 the AFC's publications became more blatantly anti-British. One such bulletin argued that England's interests outside Europe went no further than 'the gold, the oil, the rubber, the silver, the diamonds, the rich supplies which her capitalists own there – which belong to the peoples of those countries [in Asia and Africa], but which Britain has stolen.'[30]

There was one other source of anglophobia in pre-Pearl Harbor America, one of foreign origin. By 1941 German propaganda, circulated by paid agents of Berlin, Nazi sympathizers in the U.S., and a few basically well-meaning dupes, had become a common presence in some parts of the country. The official Reich propaganda machine, the German Office of Information, produced pamphlets attempting to justify the actions of the Nazi regime, particularly its invasion of Poland. These had no measurable effect on Americans; even the vast majority of German-Americans believed by 1940 that Hitler's government was beyond the pale. However, there were efforts made through less public channels to disseminate anti-British propaganda in the United States, most of which centered on the experienced propagandist George Sylvester Viereck. Viereck by some estimates received as much as $200 000 from Berlin between September 1939 and the summer of 1941, which he promptly funneled into three operations. The first was the Make Europe Pay War Debts Committee, headed by Ernest Lundeen (who had been on friendly terms with Viereck since 1937) and co-chaired by a number of other prominent anti-interventionists, including Robert Reynolds, Martin Sweeney, and Rush Holt. (Viereck himself had no official role in the organization.) Though in theory the group lobbied for repayment of all war debts, in practice it only seemed to care about Britain's, and the Committee was among the leading voices calling for the seizure of England's possessions in the West Indies.[31]

Secondly, Viereck used German funds to obtain an obscure publishing house called Flanders Hall in Scotch Plains, New Jersey. From early 1940 up to November 1941, when Viereck's role in the operation became publicly known,

Flanders Hall provided a steady stream of anti-British literature, featuring such titles as *One Hundred Families that Rule the
Empire*, *Doublecross in Palestine*, *Seven Periods of Irish History*,
Lord Lothian against Lord Lothian, and *Democracy on the Nile:
How Britain has 'Protected' Egypt*. Most of these works were
written by Germans and German-Americans, but were published under pseudonyms; *Democracy on the Nile*, for example,
was ostensibly written by Sayid Halassie, actually a pseudonym for the rather un-Egyptian Paul Schmitz. One work,
however, entitled *We Must Save the Republic*, was actually
written by a member of Congress, Stephen A. Day (R-IL).
When Flanders Hall was forced to close in late 1941 (a result
of the public revelation that it was being run by a paid
German agent) Viereck was negotiating with Rush Holt for
the publication of his book, *The British Propaganda Network*.[32]

Undoubtedly Viereck's most effective activity, however,
was the use of congressional franking privileges to disseminate anti-British propaganda. Many anti-interventionist
senators and congressmen who railed continuously against
British propaganda showed themselves quite willing to
accept the German variety at face value, and four of them
– Ernest Lundeen, Rush Holt, Hamilton Fish, and Stephen
Day – actually allowed Viereck and his friends to use their
mailing lists and office facilities. At least twenty other legislators regularly entered anti-British articles into the
Congressional Record at the request of Prescott Dennett,
Secretary of the Make Europe Pay War Debts Committee.
These articles were subsequently reprinted and distributed
under the congressional frank.[33]

Under ordinary circumstances, perhaps, little attention
would have been paid to the rather hamfisted methods of
Viereck to attack Great Britain, but circumstances in late
1940 and early 1941 were anything but ordinary, for political debate by this time had become completely polarized
over the issue of 'all-out aid' to England. By the middle of
1940, the British government was warning the U.S. that it
would soon be unable to afford to pay cash for American
exports, and began to ask for the extension of credits. Most
Americans, however, including even Roosevelt and Hull,
found this impossible to believe. What about the vast wealth
to be found throughout the empire? The problem, however,

was not money *per se*, but dollars; despite the restrictions placed on American imports in 1939, the British had run dangerously short by mid-1940. For some unknown reason, the idea that Britain be allowed to pay for American goods in sterling rather than gold was never taken into serious consideration by anyone in the Roosevelt administration. Instead Treasury Secretary Henry Morgenthau suggested the sale of British investments in the United States 'to gain both dollar assets and American goodwill.' This course was rejected in London – it would hardly have made a dent in Britain's dollar crisis in any event – and the British by late 1940 found themselves with almost no American dollars.[34]

All this placed Roosevelt in a precarious position. He was prohibited from extending trade credits to the British, as this would have violated the principle of cash-and-carry. He therefore proposed legislation that would allow him to provide Great Britain directly with American-made arms and ammunition. This idea, dubbed 'lend-lease,' would 'substitute for the dollar sign a gentleman's obligation to repay in kind.' Under the proposal, the president would be empowered to lend armaments to any nation whose survival was deemed by the president to be vital to national security. For Roosevelt this had the added benefit of shifting more of the decision-making process on foreign policy from the legislative to the executive branch. For Hull and the State Department, meanwhile, it was also beneficial in that it could be used as a lever for breaking down the system of imperial preference. One problem remained, however – how to sell what amounted to a gigantic giveaway of American weaponry to an American public which still clung to neutrality. He did this by emphasizing the extent to which U.S. security depended on the survival of England. In his January 6 State of the Union message he unveiled the concept of lend-lease, stressing that 'the best defense of the United States is the security of Great Britain in defending itself.' Four days later the majority leaders of the Senate and House, Alben Barkley (D-KY) and John McCormack (D-MA) introduced the bill in their respective houses. McCormack, however, fearing that tying his name too closely to the bill would hurt his standing among his largely Irish-American constituency, insisted that the bill be called by its number – House Resolution

1776. Significantly, it was not entitled, 'A Bill to Assist Great Britain,' but rather, 'A Bill to Defend the United States.'[35]

It was lend-lease more than any other proposal or event that galvanized the various noninterventionist groups in resistance to Roosevelt's foreign policy. Conservatives saw it as a presidential effort to emasculate Congress; nationalists feared that turning over arms to Great Britain would weaken the military strength of the United States; pacifists believed such an obviously unneutral act would draw the U.S. into war; and anglophobes opposed helping Great Britain on general principle. For three months the America First Committee and the Keep America Out of the War Congress devoted all of their energies to the defeat of Lend-Lease. But since the overwhelming majority of Americans by this time supported aid to Britain, the bill's opponents felt it necessary to offer some sort of substitute. The alternative, sponsored in the House by Hamilton Fish and in the Senate by Robert Taft, was an outright loan of $2 000 000 – despite the fact that this would have violated the neutrality laws. Nevertheless, this gesture does show that anglophobia was not a trait common to all noninterventionists. For example, Arthur Vandenberg (R-MI), who supported the substitute, wrote, 'I believe it is to the advantage of America to have intrepid Britain win.' He claimed to support 'all possible aid to Britain,' as long as it would not weaken the U.S. or bring it into the war. This line of argument was echoed by Taft, Herbert Hoover, and the leadership of the AFC. It is worth noting, however, that support was not unanimous for the loan even among those who also opposed lend-lease; six senators – Nye, D. Worth Clark (R-ID), Homer T. Bone (D-WA), David I. Walsh (D-MA), William Langer (R-ND) and Dennis Chavez (D-NM) – voted against both H.R. 1776 and the Taft-Fish alternative.[36]

But despite the protestations of many anti-interventionists that they wanted to aid the British cause, the voices of the anglophobes were the ones that attracted the most attention in the debate over lend-lease. In the House, communist sympathizer Vito Marcantonio (American Labor-NY) claimed that it was dangerous to send arms to Britain, since 'totalitarian, imperialist England' would inevitably negotiate peace with Hitler. He further suggested that bombers leased to

Britain would 'be used in massacring the Indian tribes [*sic*] who are seeking independence and freedom from British exploitation.' Martin Sweeney argued that Americans should have no more sympathy for 'the selfish imperialistic philosophy of Great Britain' than they did for Nazism. Others, such as John Robsion (R-KY) and Hugh Peterson (D-GA) evoked memories of 1776 and 1812. On the Senate side, Burton Wheeler maintained that lend-lease would go further in defense of Britain than even other members of the British Commonwealth were willing to go. Robert Reynolds suggested renaming the bill, 'A bill for the defense of the British Empire at the expense of the lives of American men and at the expense of the American taxpayer, and for the preservation of the British Empire, without any consideration for the preservation of the United States.' Nye's denunciations of Great Britain, which he called the 'ace aggressor of all time,' went on for a full twelve hours, representing some 20 percent of the entire time that the measure was debated in the Senate.[37]

In retrospect, such remarks worked to the benefit of the administration, since it allowed supporters of lend-lease to characterize their opponents as anti-British, and, by implication, pro-German. Nye in particular was coming to be viewed by many Americans as a dangerous extremist. This view gained credence after the accidental bombing of Dublin by German planes in January 1941; Nye suggested that the raid may actually have been carried out by the British, and then blamed on the Germans in the hope that Ireland could be brought into the war on England's side. It was little more than an offhand remark, and it even reflected a sentiment that was common among the Irish themselves. Nevertheless, the comment generated an amazing storm of hate mail, much of which accused Nye of being a paid agent of Hitler. Moreover, the fact that Nye was a leading speaker for the AFC made it easier to attack that group as anti-British. In any case, enough senators and congressmen were won over to the administration's side that lend-lease passed the House by a vote of 260 to 165, and the Senate by a 60–31 margin. Anti-interventionists, especially the anglophobes among them, were crushed; in the words of Hiram Johnson, 'Like the dog gone back to his vomit, the country has become English again.'[38]

After the passage of lend-lease, no other issue arose which successfully united the noninterventionist movement. Organizations such as the AFC and the KAOWC remained in existence, of course, and continued to attract members, but with the end of the lend-lease debate their goals became less focused. They remained bitter opponents of actual U.S. involvement, and they could cite with satisfaction polls taken in mid- to late-1941 that showed support for intervention dropping still further, but the Roosevelt administration never again gave them a solid issue against which to vent their fury. To be sure, there were some measures – the occupation of Iceland and Greenland, participation in convoys, the arming of merchant ships, etc. – that generated opposition from anti-interventionists. And certainly there were continued attacks on Great Britain, including a much-publicized incident in which the new British Ambassador, Lord Halifax, encountered a mob of egg-throwing old women during a visit to Detroit. Nevertheless, no new presidential initiative arose that galvanized the movement the way that lend-lease had. The battle over intervention had reached an uneasy stalemate, with anti-interventionists unable to undo what had already been done, and the administration unwilling to propose more drastic measures.[39]

Denied a potent legislative issue, some turned their attention back toward the threat of British propaganda. An organization known as Union Now, which advocated union between Great Britain and the United States, became a favorite straw man. The organization, which included some prominent Americans among its membership but which never achieved the status of a mass movement, was attacked as 'subversive' and held up as an example of the British propaganda network in action. Others focused on Hollywood: in a radio address on August 1 Nye denounced the pro-British bias of the movies produced by the eight largest film companies since 1939. He blamed this in part on the number of British actors and writers residing in Hollywood, but he argued that the prime motive was economic – that British audiences had become so important to the success of American-made motion pictures that 'if Britain loses, seven of the eight leading companies will be wiped out.' That same day Nye and Bennett Champ Clark

(D-MO) sponsored a resolution calling for an investigation of propaganda in motion pictures designed 'to influence public sentiment in the direction of participation by the United States in the present European war.'[40]

Nye was indeed on solid ground when he spoke of the motives for Hollywood's pro-British bias. The film industry had studiously avoided any comment on the situation in Europe in the 1930s, fearing that a strong political stand could cost them their audiences in Germany and Italy. This all changed, however, when in an effort to promote the German film industry Hitler in 1938 closed off Central Europe to American movies. Thus denied a large portion of the continental market, American studios began to place more emphasis on selling their films in Britain. The result was a series of pro-British, anti-Nazi films, beginning with *Confessions of a Nazi Spy* in April of 1939.[41]

The investigation, however, soon degenerated into a circus of accusation and counter-accusation. Burton Wheeler, in his capacity as chairman of the Interstate Commerce Committee, formed a subcommittee made up overwhelmingly of anglophobes which inevitably claimed to have found a massive Hollywood conspiracy. The industry, which hired Wendell Willkie as their spokesman, responded by accusing Nye and Wheeler of supporting censorship and of harboring pro-German sympathies. Finally Charles Lindbergh started to blame the Jews for the level of anglophilia in Hollywood, and the entire affair became impossible to take seriously.[42]

Thus the anti-interventionist movement seemed to be spinning its wheels by late 1941, unable to find a viable issue with which to capture the public mind. On December 7 at an AFC rally in Pittsburgh, Nye was commenting on how British propaganda was poisoning relations with Japan when a reporter informed him of the Japanese attack on Pearl Harbor, which had happened just that morning. Though the North Dakota Republican could not resist making the quip that, "It's just what the British planned for us," even he had to admit that America would now have to enter the war as a full participant. Within a few weeks the AFC, as well as the KAOWC, had folded completely. The battle over intervention had finally been decided.[43]

Why were the anti-interventionists unable to block a single

one of Roosevelt's efforts to aid Britain, despite the considerable level of distrust toward Great Britain that had existed in the U.S. prior to the outbreak of war? The easy answer, of course, is that Americans still felt a certain affinity for British culture and society, despite any political qualms they might have had regarding the Foreign Office or the Empire. In 1939 Frank C. Hanighen, himself no friend of Britain, wrote about the nature of Anglo-American understanding. For the British, Hanighen claimed, the understanding was political in nature, while Americans saw it as primarily cultural. For example, when British public figures visited the U.S., they tended to go on speaking tours; American leaders, by contrast, visited Stratford-on-Avon or the town where their ancestors came from. The popular author Margaret Halsey put it in a somewhat different way. In a 1938 account of her travels in England (entitled *With Malice Toward Some*), she compared England to 'a stupid but exquisitely beautiful wife. Whenever you have definitely made up your mind to send her to a home for morons, she turns her heart-stopping profile and you are unstrung and victimized again.' This attitude may have given British statesmen fits when in the 1930s they tried in vain to extract some sort of political commitment from the United States, but it worked to Britain's advantage in 1940–1941, at a time when American help mattered most. Anglophobes such as Nye and Wheeler may have been sanguine regarding the possible defeat of England, but the vast majority of Americans were not. For all the distrust of British foreign policy, all the ridicule of the English upper classes, and all the hand-wringing over the plight of India, the thought of Nazi soldiers goose-stepping through the streets of London was not one that the American people relished.[44]

Another reason for the noninterventionists' failure, less critical but still significant, was the inability of the various organizations which made up the movement to cooperate effectively. The AFC and the KAOWC made some effort to work together, but their political differences prevented any serious joint action. And while there was a certain level of cooperation among extremist groups, both of the mainstream organizations were (quite understandably) unwilling to associate themselves with them.[45]

But there was a still deeper source of disharmony within

the ranks of the movement, one which internally divided the AFC as well as the entire noninterventionist coalition. While many different factors led individuals to oppose Roosevelt's foreign policy, most tended to fall either into the category of 'realist' or 'idealist.' Those under the former heading believed, generally, that the United States had certain interests beyond its borders, and that when necessary active steps had to be taken to defend them. Members of this group tended to support measures designed to promote U.S. military strength, including conscription, the acquisition of offshore bases, and the arming of merchant vessels. Colonel McCormick of the *Chicago Tribune*, Senators Robert Reynolds, Ernest Lundeen, and Arthur Vandenberg, and Generals Robert E. Wood and Hugh S. Johnson could all be appropriately placed in this category.

The idealists, by contrast, were those who feared above all that war, or even preparations for war, would somehow corrupt or contaminate American institutions. Members of this group include conservatives such as Taft, who feared the destruction of the free enterprise system, progressives such as Wheeler and historian Charles A. Beard, who saw war as destructive of social reform, and even radicals such as Gerald L.K. Smith, who felt that overseas intervention might expose Americans to dangerous foreign, communist and Jewish influences.

Idealists and realists were able to make common cause only against lend-lease, and of course even then their united ranks were insufficient to resist the administration's will. On other issues, from the arms embargo to conscription to the destroyers-for-bases deal to the arming of merchant ships, there was no common ground for the two groups. Realists believed such steps were desirable, even necessary; idealists remained opposed, but they were completely isolated.

Both realists and idealists, it should be noted, were capable of strident anglophobia. Realists were inclined to see Great Britain as no less a potential enemy than Germany or Japan; these were the ones, after all, demanding seizure of British possessions in the Western Hemisphere. Idealists, meanwhile, suspected that the British were secretly pulling the strings of the State Department.

The division between realists and idealists was not limited

to the anti-interventionist movement. Within the ranks of the interventionist forces there were realists such as Adolf Berle, who saw the war as an opportunity for the United States to emerge as a truly global power, as well as liberal idealists who envisioned a global crusade against fascism. And for all the charges of 'pro-British' hurled against them by their opponents, there was considerable potential for anglophobia among the interventionists as well. As will be seen in the final two chapters, realists wanted an Anglo-American alliance, but one in which the British were clearly the junior partners.[46] And though liberal idealists were effusive in their praise of the British war effort in 1941, their support did not come without strings attached. As James J. Martin points out in *American Liberalism and World Politics*, liberals hoped to defend a certain kind of England, one dominated by the Labour party and committed to social equality at home and decolonization abroad. Therefore, even though England and the United States now found themselves on the same side of a global war for the second time in a generation, this did not mean that American anglophobia would disappear, but merely that it would change. The nature of this change, and the effect that it would have on Anglo-American relations and American politics in the 1940s, is the subject of the final two chapters.[47]

7 'India and the Boer War, And All That'

In early January 1942, only a month after the bombing of Pearl Harbor, Franklin Roosevelt discussed at length the attitude of Americans toward the British Empire. 'It's in the American tradition,' he said, 'this distrust, this dislike and even hatred of Britain – the Revolution, you know, and 1812; and India and the Boer War, and all that.' Lord Halifax sounded a similar note in a letter to the Foreign Office when he warned that, as an empire, 'we owe the USA and the world a justification of ourselves in these respects. Something of this sentiment is undoubtedly almost universal among Americans, though it varies in intensity. It is a barrier to mutual confidence and holds plain danger for future Anglo-American collaboration on terms which we would consider acceptable.' The sentiment to which the ambassador referred was one which would find expression on many occasions between 1942 and 1945: that even though England and the United States might find themselves on the same side in the fight against the Axis, this did not imply that there was a genuine unity of aims between the two nations. Moreover, when and if conflict arose between the interests of the United States and those of the British Empire, Americans made it more than clear that it was the aspirations of the former that would prevail.[1]

During the first weeks after Pearl Harbor, however, there was little evidence of this sort of thinking; these were, in the words of Lord Halifax, 'honeymoon days' for Anglo-American relations. A whole series of permanent commissions and boards were set up to handle the conduct of the war, and hordes of British officials crossed the Atlantic, forming what historian John Baylis has called 'a sort of lesser Whitehall overseas.' Churchill himself visited Washington, signing a variety of agreements with Roosevelt and speaking before a joint session of Congress, where he was given a welcome which 'recalled the triumphal visits of Lafayette.'

149

Not everyone was pleased by this, of course; Hiram Johnson, ever the arch-nationalist, complained that '[t]he English have taken practical control of our government.... We are now followers of Winston Churchill.'[2]

By the end of January, however, it was already clear that the honeymoon was coming to an end, and in early February Halifax wrote that British prestige in America was in the midst of one of its 'recurrent periods of slump' – a slump which would last for at least the next two years. Now that the United States was an active participant in the war, Halifax explained, it was more difficult to rally American sympathies to Britain's plight. Indeed, inasmuch as the attack on American forces came from Japan instead of Germany, public attention now shifted from Europe to Asia, where the Chinese were regarded as the real heroes. Moreover, many Americans had apparently expected that the entry of the United States into the war would immediately turn the fortunes of war in favor of the Allies. If this was the case, their hopes would be quickly disappointed, for the six-month period after Pearl Harbor brought Axis victories on all fronts, and most of these came at British expense. In Europe, the German pocket battleships *Scharnhorst* and *Gneisenau* eluded the Royal Navy and slipped from the port of Brest to prey on Allied convoys in the North Atlantic; in the Pacific theater, the British fortress of Singapore fell to the Japanese, and the warships *Prince of Wales* and *Repulse* were sunk by Japanese planes; in North Africa Axis divisions under the command of Erwin Rommel captured the fortress of Tobruk and threatened the entire Middle East.[3]

This string of British defeats hastily revived America's traditional anti-English prejudices, and, as Halifax reported, anti-interventionists 'crawled out of the woodwork' to call for an 'American' war, emphasizing the Pacific theater, and fought for American ends. A public opinion poll, meanwhile, showed that in the rural midwest nearly half of those who claimed to be dissatisfied with the conduct of the war felt that the British were to blame. Nor was this sentiment limited to America's heartland: according to a senior official of the State Department, there was 'a growing feeling in Washington that the British are absolutely incapable of exercising command or using equipment.' Even as committed an anglophile as

Henry Stimson concluded that 'if this war is to be won, it's got to be won by the full strength of the virile, energetic, initiative-loving, inventive Americans.' British performance, he claimed, was the result of 'decadence – a magnificent people, but they have lost their initiative.'[4]

Stimson was certainly not alone; as an official of the Foreign Office reported, Americans increasingly viewed the British not only as 'Imperialists, but bungling Imperialists.' Public opinion polls showed that only seven percent of those surveyed believed that Britain was pulling its weight in the alliance. One poll taken after the fall of Tobruk asked why the British were not winning; among the responses were, 'Too much wine, chess games and noble blood in the leadership'; 'Too much tea-drinking and not enough fighting'; 'The British should take more generals from the ranks and fewer from the ruling classes.' Liberals in particular saw Britain's empire and class system as the main causes of its discomfiture. The editors of *Collier's* blamed the fall of Singapore on the 'old-school-tie boys' in London, as well as the 'Colonel Blimps who still clutter up her army.' The editors of *Catholic World* heartily agreed, calling British generals in Asia 'a collection of duds, blimps, and fossils.' With America safely in the war, the *New Republic* began to return to the anti-British positions it had maintained before 1940. In March Bruce Bliven complained that 'there are still too many unreconstructed Tories in high places in Britain,' men who 'refuse to admit that this is a war for the democratic way of life and not merely one for the privileges of their own class.' Four months later, the liberal journal blamed the fall of Tobruk on the British army's 'social rigidity which has kept the best British military ability from coming to the top.'[5]

The British disasters in Asia especially served to focus American attention on India, which many believed was vulnerable to a Japanese invasion. As early as May 1941 Adolf Berle warned that native opposition to the continuing British presence might encourage pro-Japanese sympathies on the subcontinent; after all, as he put it in February 1942, 'Why should India defend a freedom she hasn't got?' The fall of Singapore during that same month lent considerable urgency to the issue; Roosevelt concluded that the 'British defense [of India] will not have sufficiently enthusiastic support from the people of India themselves.' Under pressure from the Senate Foreign Relations Committee, which argued that American aid to Britain justified some say by the U.S. in Anglo-Indian relations, the president tapped Louis Johnson, former Assistant Secretary of War, to be his personal representative at the ongoing Anglo-Indian negotiations in New Delhi. Based on Johnson's reports, Roosevelt cabled Churchill that 'American public opinion' blamed British intransigence for the failure to reach an agreement. By late May Johnson had concluded that the British would rather lose India to the Japanese than make any concessions, on the assumption that India 'will be returned to them after the war with the *status quo ante* prevailing.'[6]

Though the president regularly cited 'American public opinion' as an expression of his own views, this did not mean that the public remained indifferent to the situation in India. Polls taken in the summer of 1942, in fact, showed that 43 percent of Americans surveyed believed that Britain should grant India 'complete independence,' and that nearly half of these felt that the British should do so immediately. India also quickly returned to the pages of the liberal journals. 'A war to save freedom from the threat of totalitarian slavery,' wrote Charles Clayton Morrison in *Christian Century*, 'has been turned by Mr. Churchill into a struggle to preserve imperialism from the menace of democratic self-rule.' In the *New Republic*, meanwhile, Michael Straight complained, 'As progressives, who struggled to join Britain in this war, we are able to assert that the Indian policy of the British government...has been devastating for the United Nations.'[7]

Nor was India the only object of American attention; the whole British Empire remained a decidedly unpopular institution. A public opinion poll taken in June 1942 showed that nearly six out of ten Americans surveyed believed that the British were 'oppressors' who exploited their imperial possessions. In August former presidential candidate Wendell Willkie made a trip around the world as Roosevelt's personal representative; upon his return he published *One World*, which called for American opposition to all forms of imperialism, British as well as Axis. In discussing his visit to Egypt, for example, he claimed that the British presence was characteristic of 'Rudyard Kipling, untainted even with the

liberalism of Cecil Rhodes.' Roosevelt himself felt likewise; on
a brief refueling stop in Gambia on the way to Casablanca the
president was shocked by the condition of those living under
British rule. 'Those people are treated worse than the live-
stock,' he raged to his son, Elliott, 'Their cattle live longer.'[8]
    Yet surprisingly little of this sentiment found its way onto
the floors of the House and Senate. In fact, aside from some
bitter comments by a few congressional renegades such as
Democratic Louisiana Senator Allen Ellender, who complained about 'the apparent apathy of British military
leadership and its inability to cope with the Axis,' almost no
attempt was made to generate political capital from the
United Kingdom's predicament. Far more was said in
England's defense; Rep. Charles Faddis (D-PA) attributed
public anglophobia to 'clever Axis propaganda' which aimed
at undermining Allied unity. When veteran anti-interventionist and anglophobe Sen. Robert R. Reynolds (D-NC)
called upon Great Britain to give independence to India, his
suggestion was met with howls of protest from Republicans
and Democrats alike. Sen. Styles Bridges (R-NH) insisted that
telling the British to give up India was 'rather overstepping
the bounds of propriety,' while others accused Reynolds of
trying to promote Allied disunity.[9]
    Perhaps the most amazing example of magnanimity
toward the British came from Gerald Nye, who only one year
earlier had accused the British of sinking the American ship
Robin Moor and then blaming it on Germany to whip up
public sentiment in favor of war. Now, however, he came to
the defense of his old *bête noire* in response to an editorial
which appeared in Henry Luce's *Life* magazine in October.
Entitled, 'An Open Letter to the People of England,' it
assured the British that Americans were '*not* fighting…to
hold the British Empire together. We don't like to put the
matter so bluntly, but we don't want you to have any illusions.' This article, as well as Willkie's anti-imperialist
musings, aroused an enraged response from Nye. Calling
the Luce editorial 'an act fraught with more trouble than all
that the fifth columnists in the land afford,' he attacked those
who 'would now jeopardize our own security by damning
our allies,' and concluded by calling for 'a united front on the
part of the Allied cause.'[10]

What was the reason for such generosity toward the British, especially from those who had been her most vocal critics before Pearl Harbor? The answer lies in the fact that in 1942 those who had led the crusade against intervention in 1940 and 1941 believed themselves to be vulnerable in the upcoming elections. Strong forces within both the Democratic and Republican parties were working to oust 'isolationists' in the primaries; Republicans in New York, for example, mobilized a 'Stop Fish' campaign to defeat Hamilton Fish, who had not only been an outspoken opponent of Lend-Lease but a G.O.P. stalwart since the early 1920s. The *New Republic* published a pre-election supplement entitled, 'A Congress to Win the War,' which singled out certain 'obstructionists' by name for defeat. Anti-interventionists were widely believed to have been on the wrong side of the foreign policy debate, so in general they tended to remain silent on such issues in the months prior to the elections. Nor was electoral defeat their only worry; anti-interventionists in 1942 had to worry about the possibility of federal indictment as well. A public scandal ensued when it was found that several pro-fascist organizations operating in the U.S. were sending out mailings in envelopes bearing the frank of some 25 senators and congressmen, all of whom had been critical of the Roosevelt administration's support for Great Britain. A number of these, including Hamilton Fish and Clare Hoffman, were eventually called upon to appear before grand juries. These proceedings produced a chilling effect not only among former anti-interventionists, but also among those who had favored increased aid to Britain in 1940–41 – they were reluctant to criticize the British for fear of being associated with the discredited philosophy of 'isolationism.'[11]

But this more charitable attitude of Congress toward Great Britain was not destined to survive. Despite the best efforts of the Roosevelt administration and the *New Republic*, nearly all of the prewar anti-interventionists (though Martin Sweeney was a notable exception) were returned to office, while one supporter of Roosevelt's foreign policy, the venerable George Norris of Nebraska, was defeated by a conservative Republican, Kenneth Wherry. The significance of these results was not lost on Lord Halifax. Even though public hostility toward the British was in decline, due in large part to the Allied victories in North Africa, Congress was likely to move in the opposite direction. In his weekly report to the Foreign Office, the ambassador noted that the 'personnel of the new Congress is somewhat less friendly to Britain than its predecessor,' and that they could be expected to accuse FDR of being 'too tender to [the] interests of that feudal institution, the British Empire.'[12]

But Congress was not the only institution which hoped to assume a tougher stance toward the British by late 1942; high-ranking U.S. policymakers and military leaders were becoming increasingly annoyed by what they believed to be foot-dragging on the part of their British counterparts. Of particular concern was Churchill's persistent opposition to the opening of a second front in France. An invasion was necessary, U.S. leaders argued, both to reduce the pressure on the Soviets and to assure the American people that some progress was being made toward the defeat of Germany. The British alternative, which involved operations on the periphery of Europe combined with bombing raids against Germany itself, was dismissed by General Albert Wedemeyer and Admiral William Leahy as 'absolutely unsound,' and designed to do nothing more than 'to maintain the integrity of the British Empire.' By the middle of 1942 the debate had become so intense that the Joint Chiefs of Staff formally suggested that the Pacific be made the primary theater of operations for the American armed forces.[13]

This, of course, would be a drastic step. The United States had committed itself early in 1941 to a strategy of 'Germany First'; that is, the armed forces would assume a defensive posture in the Pacific while the real effort was directed toward the defeat of Germany. The attack on Pearl Harbor, however, made this strategy difficult to put into practice, since the American public tended to view Japan as the more serious threat. As Stimson pointed out to Churchill in mid-1942, 'only by an intellectual effort' had the public 'been convinced that Germany was their most dangerous enemy and should be disposed of before Japan;...the enemy whom the American people really hated, if they hated anyone, was Japan which had dealt them the foul blow.' Yet these efforts were never more than partially successful. A Gallup Poll conducted in February 1943, for example, showed that a solid majority of Americans continued to regard the Japanese as the 'chief enemy.' Many in the military felt likewise; Admiral Ernest King, Chief of Naval Operations, continually pressed for a diversion of resources to the Pacific theater, since he saw no real role for the navy in Europe. And when General Joseph Stilwell learned of the 'Germany First' plan, he complained that 'the Limeys have sold Roosevelt a bill of goods.... [Churchill] and his staff officers have the President's ear, while we have the hind tit.'[14]

By mid-1943 King had made some important allies in Congress. The main source of 'Pacific-first' sentiment in the Senate was Albert B. 'Happy' Chandler, a Kentucky Democrat, a prewar interventionist, and a powerful opponent of the administration in domestic affairs. In the wake of the German surrender in Tunisia in May, 1943, Chandler argued that, since any immediate Nazi threat to Britain had been eliminated, the U.S. ought to make the Pacific conflict its primary theater of operations. Having recently returned from an inspection trip to Alaska, he expressed concern for the safety of the Aleutian Islands, and charged that the Roosevelt administration did not appreciate the dangers of Japanese penetration into Alaska and the Pacific Coast. Chandler was soon joined by two other former interventionists, Styles Bridges (R-NH) and Millard Tydings (D-MD), as well as two veterans of the anti-interventionist cause, Burton K. Wheeler and Henrik Shipstead (R-MN). Though U.S. policy remained committed in theory to the defeat of Germany first, the administration could not remain deaf to the public and congressional outcry. Planes, equipment and landing craft began to be shifted to the Pacific, prompting Churchill to remark bitterly, 'Just because the Americans can't have a massacre in France this year, they want to sulk and bathe in the Pacific.' By the end of 1943 there were actually more Americans employed in the war against Japan than there were engaged in the fight against Germany.[15]

Closely associated with the call for 'Pacific-first' was criticism of Britain's contribution in Asia. Of primary concern to Americans was the reopening of the Burma Road as a source of supply for the embattled Chinese. When the British showed little enthusiasm for such a course they were accused of making an insufficient effort in that area, and of being interested only in trying to regain their former territories in Burma and Malaya. Indeed, the acronym for the joint Southeast Asia Command (SEAC) was soon nicknamed 'Save England's Asian Colonies' by resentful Americans, and even Roosevelt expressed doubt that the British were particularly interested in defeating Japan. Within SEAC, an intense personal hostility developed between the British commander, Lord Louis Mountbatten, and his American deputy commander, General Joseph W. 'Vinegar Joe' Stilwell. Stilwell in his diary repeatedly referred to his superior as 'childish Louis' and 'Glamor Boy,' who could not resist 'playing the "Empah" Game.' Army Air Corps Chief of Staff Henry H. 'Hap' Arnold, meanwhile, concluded that the Asian theater had become a dumping ground for British officers 'who had more or less outlived their usefulness in other theaters.' Admiral King found similar fault with British naval officers in the Pacific, and he consistently opposed joint operations between British and American naval units.[16]

Such attitudes provided vital ammunition for 'Pacific-firsters' in Congress. On the Senate floor, Chandler charged that despite a ten-to-one superiority in troop strength along the India/Burma front, 'so little energy has been put into the campaign that the British Army is now back where it started on the border of India.' Wheeler claimed to be 'shocked' by British reluctance to advance, while Shipstead declared that he could 'not see how Great Britain could render a greater aid to Japan than doing what she is doing now.' More than one member of Congress professed to believe that British 'lethargy' was consciously motivated by imperial policy; Rep. Calvin D. Johnson (R-IL), for example, insisted that the British did not want to take the offensive in Burma for fear of insurrection in India, and maintained that they refused assistance from the Chinese on that front lest such an act 'give China a stake that must be considered at the peace table.' So pervasive was this sentiment becoming that Churchill himself saw fit to address the controversy in a speech before a joint session of Congress. He assured the assembled group that Britain was committed to waging an 'unflinching and relentless' war against Japan, and that it was only 'what your American military men call the science of logistics' that had prevented the British Army from advancing over the rugged

Burmese terrain. This had the effect of quieting the issue, though only temporarily.[17]

What accounts for this increased willingness of Congress to find fault with the British contribution to the war effort? Some of the criticism, to be sure, came from former anti-interventionists emboldened by the results of the 1942 elections. Yet the noninterventionists were far less inclined to take the initiative in attacking the British during 1943 and 1944, for a new group had emerged which was willing to do it for them. These new critics of England were not 'isolationists,' but rather a coalition of moderate Republicans and conservative Democrats espousing a new variety of American nationalism. This breed of nationalism insisted that since the United States was contributing the most to the war effort in terms of money and resources, it was necessary to ensure that America's 'vital interests' were protected.[18]

A key element in the rising American nationalism of 1943 was an emphasis on ensuring American security and prosperity in the postwar world. In September and October five Senators – Chandler, Ralph Owen Brewster (R-ME), Henry Cabot Lodge, Jr. (R-MA), James M. Mead (D-NY), and Richard B. Russell (D-GA) – made a trip around the world to visit the various battlefronts. Though none of the five had any particular reputation for anglophobia before their journey, they came back, in the words of one Senator, with enough anti-British stories 'to supply the *Chicago Tribune* for a year.' Lodge asserted that 'it is common sense to recognize' that the British were pursuing selfish aims. They described in detail how British officials and businessmen ('a bunch of cunning and scheming brutes,' opined Brewster) routinely frustrated the efforts of naive and inexperienced American officials. Russell, meanwhile, spoke of the 'indescribable poverty' and 'unspeakable suffering' brought on by British policy in India.[19]

One tangible result of the five senators' tour was a heightened sense of skepticism regarding Lend-Lease. Suspicion that American funds were being used for nonessential purposes was not exactly new (Rep. William Lemke claimed in March that 'not ten per cent of Congress approves [of] all that has been going on under lend-lease,' while Hamilton Fish complained that the money was going 'into a bottomless pit.'), but the reports brought back from the battlefronts brought this sentiment to new heights. Russell charged that the British were giving American war *matériel* to the Turkish army as 'effective propaganda to gain the goodwill of the 250 000 000 Mohammedans of the world.' In a similar vein, Allen Ellender (D-LA) accused the British government of selling nonmilitary Lend-Lease items to wholesalers in London and pocketing the proceeds. Hugh Butler (R-NE) called for a full-scale congressional investigation of what he termed 'the most colossal dole of all time.' A subcommittee of the Senate Appropriations Committee was hastily formed for this purpose, and it included in its membership Nye, Tydings, and the anglophobic Illinois Republican C. Wayland 'Curley' Brooks.[20]

Another facet of the new American nationalism was a renewed demand that the British turn over bases in the Western Hemisphere and Asia to the United States, in partial repayment of Lend-Lease aid. Tydings, Russell, and several others professed to be dissatisfied with the 99-year leases for bases which had been turned over to the U.S. in 1940 in return for 50 old destroyers. Comparing the acquisitions to the purchases of the Louisiana Territory and Alaska, they claimed that a 99-year lease was of little value. 'This is not any 99-year country!' Russell announced. A longtime advocate of this position was Sen. Robert R. Reynolds, who sought to create a 'band of steel around our portion of North America' by obtaining 'in fee simple' British Guiana, British Honduras, Jamaica, Bermuda, Nassau, and Bimini. Sen. Kenneth D. McKellar (D-TN) became so associated with the demand for British territory that Lord Vansittart, former permanent under-secretary at the British Foreign Office, coined the verb 'to mckellar,' which he defined as 'to aspire laughably to what does not belong to you.' In Spring of 1944 a three-man sub-committee of the House Naval Affairs Commitee returned from a tour of the South Atlantic naval bases leased from the British, having concluded that it would be a grave mistake for the United States ever to abandon them. When Churchill seemed disinclined to make an outright gift of the bases, Hamilton Fish was outraged by his apparent ingratitude, given that the U.S. had 'saved England and the British Empire in their darkest moment from invasion and destruction.'[21]

What inspired this great outpouring of American nation-alism? The answer has very much to do with the political scene in the wake of the 1942 elections. Buoyed by their gains in Congress, the Republican Party had set its sights on the White House in 1944, but realized that it could not hope to win the presidency unless the cleft in the party over foreign policy could be bridged. A fragmented party had doomed Wendell Willkie to defeat in 1940, so the 1944 plat-form had to include a statement on foreign affairs that could be made acceptable to prewar 'isolationists' and interven-tionists alike. The Mackinac Declaration, drafted jointly by Warren Austin of Vermont and Arthur Vandenberg, was their solution. Combining calls for 'prosecution of the war by a united Nation to conclusive victory' and 'responsible participation...in post-war cooperative organization' with admonitions that 'Constitutionalism should be adhered to in determining the substance of our policies,' the Mackinac statement was satisfactory to all but the most extreme non-interventionists.[22]

Yet while the Mackinac Declaration might have made it possible to reunite the disparate wings of the G.O.P., it could not by itself carry the party to victory over a popular wartime president. Calls for a 'nationalistic' foreign policy, one which required a hardheaded view of the world and a paramount concern for the preservation of U.S. interests, was to become the weapon of choice for Republicans and anti-Roosevelt Democrats in 1944. Rep. Claire Booth Luce (R-CT) outlined her brand of nationalism in June, 1943 by distinguishing it from the internationalism of Woodrow Wilson and Franklin Roosevelt. Internationalism, she contended, was 'simply the adoption *in extremis* of another nation's foreign policy.' An internationalist was nothing more than 'a renegade isola-tionist,' since neither the internationalist nor the isolationist 'has honestly thought through his own country's true inter-ests.' Rep. Melvin Maas (R-MN), another outspoken advocate of this approach, summarized his foreign policy views in this way: 'By all means, let us have world cooper-ation. Let the world cooperate from now on with the United States.'[23]

The attitude of the American nationalists regarding Great Britain was complex. On the one hand, they continued to exploit such traditional themes as the British obsession with empire and the image of the 'slick' foreign diplomat. Yet their anglophobia was significantly different from that practiced by the anti-interventionists and liberals. Britain, in the nationalist view, was not to be faulted for playing 'power politics' and pursuing national self-interest, for this was expected and acceptable behavior for a great power. The British Empire, however, had become decadent, having lost not only the military means but also the moral authority to lead the world. The United States, they believed, was destined to fill this role, and must not shrink from copying British tactics in so doing. Thus when senators such as Brewster, Chandler, and Lodge warned about the activities of British diplomats and businessmen around the world, they did so not to call attention to any supposed English perfidy, but rather to illustrate the need for an American presence strong enough to compete with British interests.[24]

The use of nationalism as a domestic political tactic, meanwhile, became more pronounced with the approach of the 1944 elections. As Halifax put it, Republicans such as Brewster and Lodge were 'competing against the Middle Western isolationists for leadership in Republican politics,' but in order to do so, they had to show that they were capable of attacking the administration 'on internationalist grounds more effective than the *Chicago Tribune* type of tirade.' Thus as early as Fall, 1943 the ambassador reported to the Foreign Office that Roosevelt's opponents in both parties were 'looking for an anti-British issue' to use against the administration. When, in the wake of the Quebec Conference, rumors circulated that the Army Chief of Staff, General George C. Marshall, was to lead the Anglo-American forces in Europe, some saw the sinister hand of 'perfidious Albion' at work. These suspicions found their most persistent voice in Rep. Jessie Sumner (R-IL), a woman described by Halifax as 'a shrewish Anglophobe disciple of [the] *Chicago Tribune*.' She expressed her contention that the British sought to kick Marshall upstairs 'because he stands up for our American rights.' Furthermore, she accused them of trying to remove Admiral Leahy (who had criticized the British in the Pacific) and to prevent MacArthur from being promoted, both at the behest of Lord Mountbatten, commander of SEAC. Sumner, and others like her, viewed this as part of an ongoing British campaign to control the U.S. armed forces: '[W]henever they find an officer who stands up for American rights they get some American officer they can handle to ask that the officer they cannot handle be put somewhere that looks like a promotion, or sent to South America, or given a vacation.'[25]

Opponents of Roosevelt remained especially alert for signs of British interference in the upcoming elections; when Churchill reportedly claimed that it would be 'a tragic catastrophe' if FDR were defeated in 1944, Gerald Nye (whose own Senate seat was considered among the most vulnerable) expressed his resentment at 'the insistent manner in which those of other lands...are nosing into American politics.' Reports circulated in early 1944 that the English were handing out campaign literature for Roosevelt to American servicemen stationed in the United Kingdom, evoking vehement protests from Clare Hoffman and Sen. Harry Flood Byrd (D-VA).[26]

The Tyler Kent affair provided Roosevelt's opponents with another opportunity to portray the president as a stooge of the British. Tyler Kent, a clerk in the U.S. embassy in London, had embarked on a lucrative career of deciphering and then selling secret diplomatic correspondence to the German and Soviet governments. Kent was arrested by the British authorities in 1940 after having decoded vital correspondence between Roosevelt and Churchill, and was held in an English prison until his deportation in 1945. However, while Kent was in prison, his mother sought the assistance of certain members of the U.S. Senate. Noting that some of the intercepted Roosevelt–Churchill cables contained potentially damaging information (many hinted at U.S. entry into the war at a time when Roosevelt was saying publicly that he would not ask American mothers to send their sons off to fight 'in any foreign wars.') Kent decided to portray himself as an American hero, working to uncover a dastardly plot to involve the United States in an 'entangling alliance.' Kent's plight attracted the attention of Burton Wheeler, who professed outrage that an American had been incarcerated by the British, and that Roosevelt had known of, and indeed approved of, the whole affair. On June 19, 1944 – less than five weeks before the opening of the Democratic National

Convention – Wheeler took the floor of the Senate. 'What would happen,' he asked rhetorically, 'if we should arrest a member of the British Embassy here and endeavour to try him in an American secret court?' Wheeler suggested the existence of a massive cover-up, and was joined by fellow Democrat David I. Walsh of Massachusetts, as well as Republicans Nye, Shipstead, and Brewster. The accusations, however, would not stick. Congressional supporters of Roosevelt, led by the Chairman of the Senate Foreign Relations Committee, Tom Connally (D-TX) pointed out that Kent had clearly violated British law in decoding and stealing confidential dispatches, and many conservative Republicans refused to press the attack when his links with Soviet Russia were revealed.[27]

As it turned out, Republican strategy for 1944 did not prevent the reelection of Franklin Roosevelt over Thomas E. Dewey. Moreover, professions of loyalty to a new nationalist creed did not save a significant number of prewar non-interventionists from electoral defeat. Among the casualties of 1944 in the House were Hamilton Fish and Illinois Republican Stephen A. Day, while Gerald Nye lost his seat in the Senate. Historian Robert A. Divine has called the results 'a clear-cut mandate' for internationalism.[28]

Why did the Republicans' appeal to American nationalism fail? One important reason was that public opinion had by mid-1943 rallied behind the British as the tide of war turned clearly against the Axis. In April Halifax wrote that 'British military prestige is at its highest,' and noted that 'critical feeling…has entered a passive phase.' In May the *American Mercury* denounced 'romantic liberals' who espoused the breakup of the British Empire; in September the *Saturday Evening Post* published an article entitled, 'The British Get Out of the Doghouse.' By late summer a public opinion poll showed that 61 percent of the respondents favored a 'permanent military alliance' with Britain after the war. Indeed, Dewey himself claimed to support such an alliance at Mackinac, which did nothing to ingratiate himself with the more anti-British elements of the G.O.P.[29]

But like the 'honeymoon' of early 1942, this period of public anglophilia was short-lived, and the pro-British consensus of mid- to late-1943 was already showing signs of fraying before the elections. One such sign was the hostility generated among American Jews toward British prohibitions on Jewish emigration to Palestine. This policy had first been announced in a White Paper of April 1939, to take effect in five years. There were, to be sure, bitter attacks by American Zionists on the White Paper when it was originally released, but criticism was somewhat muted by the fact that Great Britain was recognized by most Jews as the nation most likely to fight Hitler. Nor were Jews moved when a number of prominent anti-interventionists attempted to use the issue to stir up anti-British sentiment in the U.S. By 1944, however, it had become possible for the Zionist community to vent their anger over the White Paper without appearing to give aid and comfort to Nazi Germany. They were encouraged in this by the Republicans, who saw in Zionism an opportunity to win Jews away from the Roosevelt coalition. A resolution was introduced in Congress calling for 'free entry of Jews' into Palestine, but this failed when the Army's Chief of Staff, Gen. George C. Marshall, informed the Senate Foreign Relations Committee that this would hurt the war effort in the Middle East. By mid-October, however, both parties had pledged their opposition to the White Paper.[30]

There were also by late 1944 renewed concerns about the British commitment to the war in Asia. In 1943 Roosevelt had dispatched William Phillips, a career diplomat and reputed anglophile, to New Delhi as his personal representative. Within a few months Phillips wrote a letter to the president in which he claimed that not only were the British unwilling to do anything to alleviate the tense situation in India, but that the United States could expect no more than 'token assistance' from Great Britain in the war against Japan. Over a year later, in August 1944, the letter was leaked to the *Washington Post*. The Foreign Office asked the administration to distance itself from Phillips' views, but Hull, recognizing the importance of not backing down to British requests during an election year, refused to do so.[31]

By the end of 1944 the belief that the British were not pulling their weight in Asia had become almost universal. Much attention was given to the fact that American and Chinese forces under Stilwell had made far more progress on the Burmese front than Mountbatten's much larger

Anglo-Indian army; Former Secretary of War Gen. Patrick J. Hurley went so far as to call the performance of the British in Burma 'one of the deplorable chapters in the history of a great Empire.' Of particular concern was whether the British would even continue fighting after Germany were defeated; Hull warned in a September 24 memorandum to the president that 'any indication that British participation in the Far Eastern struggle is at a rate below their utmost capabilities' would result in an 'immediate and hostile public reaction in the United States.'[32]

Yet neither Palestine nor the sluggishness of British forces in Asia were enough to generate widespread anglophobia. Outside the Jewish community there was little interest in the Palestinian question, and the Burmese front was not considered a particularly important one for most Americans. Nevertheless, in what Halifax termed 'a classic illustration of the emotional instability of American opinion,' sentiment in both Houses of Congress within a month of the election turned to 'an orgy of "twisting the lion's tail"...more enthusiastic and sustained than on any occasion since the United States entered the war.'[33]

The immediate cause of this wave of anglophobia lay in two Anglo-American disputes concerning southern Europe. The first involved Italy, where a new government was forming in which Count Carlo Sforza, a veteran anti-fascist and opponent of the Italian monarchy, appeared likely to emerge as prime minister or foreign secretary. When the British Foreign Office, believing Sforza to be a troublemaker, announced that the United Kingdom would refuse to recognize any new government which included the Count, American opinion was incensed. Sforza had traveled widely in the United States, and was popular among influential circles in New York and Washington. Indeed, as Halifax pointed out, Sforza 'symbolizes Italian democracy to the American public, which has heard of scarcely any other anti-Fascist Italian....' Many in Congress, especially those with substantial Italian-American constituencies, accused Churchill of blocking Sforza's appointment solely because of his anti-monarchical beliefs, and protested that Britain was trying to 'keep Italy under an iron heel.'[34]

At the same time, British forces were becoming increasingly

involved in the Greek civil war, in which they were backing a conservative monarchical regime against a leftist insurgency. While the Foreign Office claimed to be protecting the legitimate government of Greece from a communist-led guerrilla force, to Americans it appeared that London was merely protecting its imperial interests in the eastern Mediterranean, and defending the institution of monarchy (as many Americans believed to be the case in Italy). This view grew stronger when an American columnist obtained and published a secret cable in which Churchill had instructed the British commander in Athens to behave 'as if you were in a conquered city where a local rebellion is in progress.' On the floor of the Senate, Allen Ellender accused the British of 'taking the lead in causing disunity among the Allies' by 'seeking to...form blocs of nations here and there all over the world so as to help her to maintain her pre-war world-wide domination.' Others began to hint darkly at some massive 'Mediterranean strategy' masterminded by Churchill. So sharply did American opinion turn against England that Halifax wrote the Foreign Office that it was 'open season against British foreign policy.'[35]

But for Halifax the most noteworthy aspect of this latest round of anglophobia was that so much of it came 'not from our traditional enemies but from our disillusioned friends,' that is, from liberal supporters of Roosevelt who had been in the forefront of the interventionist movement before Pearl Harbor. The liberal weekly *PM*, for example, contrasted Britain's 'stakes of power' in Italy with America's 'stakes of peace.' Charles Clayton Morrison lamented in *Christian Century* that '[M]en who have proved their readiness to die for freedom are dying – for what? For British policy in the Mediterranean!' In the House, John Coffee (D-WA) defended the Greek rebels, insisting that no more than 10 percent of its leadership was communist. Besides, he argued, 'Greek Communists are not similar to American Communists but more like our Democrats or even Republicans.' Emanuel Celler (D-NY) spoke of the 'horrible spectacle' of 'American tanks being used against Greek resistance patriots,' and concluded that 'We must have it out with England now.' In the Senate, such liberal stalwarts as Claude Pepper (D-FL) and Glen Taylor (D-ID) charged that London was subjecting

Greece to a 'selfish clique of rulers' and 'a dissolute puppet king' for no other reason than 'to protect British investments.'[36]

To the remaining anti-interventionists in Congress such criticism was a welcome surprise, and they immediately leaped at the chance to say, 'I told you so.' Halifax noted that the Greek and Italian situations had given the enemies of England a new lease on life: 'The old-fashioned isolationists, the America-Firsters, the new-fangled economic imperialists, the anti-British hyphenates, all came happily into the open again.' Sen. C. Wayland Brooks (R-IL) warned that the British were attempting 'to establish puppet governments in Italy, Greece, Belgium and France,' while Sen. Hiram Johnson, in one of his last speeches on the Senate floor (he would die in August 1945), insisted that the Greeks should not be 'shot down like dogs' for wanting to choose their own type of government. The internationalist Sen. Joseph H. Ball (R-MN) dejectedly observed that, for the first time, he and Burton Wheeler found themselves on the same side of an issue.[37]

Anti-British sentiment was evident outside Washington as well. The American press was almost unanimous in its denunciations of English policy in Italy and Greece, and a State Department survey taken in late December found that 54 percent of those Americans dissatisfied with cooperation among the allies blamed Britain (only 18 percent blamed Russia). 71 percent, furthermore, believed Britain was interfering in the affairs of smaller European nations. Another poll conducted in early 1945 showed that 9 percent of the American public thought that there might be a war between the U.S. and Great Britain in the next 50 years, whereas only 8 percent thought there might be another war with Japan.[38]

This wave of criticism had become so intense by the end of 1944 that the British press, which had until this time remained silent on the subject, struck back. On December 30 the influential *Economist* published an editorial entitled 'Noble Negatives,' which charged that Americans 'have twisted the lion's tail once too often.' It pointed out that the same country which practiced cash-and-carry during the Battle of Britain was now substituting 'lofty moral generalities' for a genuine foreign policy. The article finally

suggested that the price paid for Anglo-American collaboration was 'too high for what we are likely to get,' and warned
that each 'spasm' of anti-British sentiment in the U.S. made
the average Englishman 'one degree more cynical about
America's real intentions of active collaboration, and one
degree more ready to believe that the only reliable helping
hand is in Soviet Russia.'[39]

Why had American liberals in Congress, after years of
rushing to defend the United Kingdom from isolationist and
nationalist criticism, suddenly jumped onto the anti-British
bandwagon? Perhaps it is more fitting to ask why they waited
so long. After all, such liberal journals as the *Nation* and the
New Republic had been chastising Britain, and its Prime
Minister in particular, since 1942. In fact, at about the same
time that the *New Republic* was targeting anglophobic congressional 'obstructionists' for electoral defeat, its editor,
Bruce Bliven, was attacking Churchill for fighting 'a white
British Tories' war.' Unlike Bliven and other sources of
liberal opinion, however, those within Congress had to worry
about the next election. Men like Pepper of Florida and
Taylor of Idaho were careful not to identify themselves with
anglophobic elements at a time when Roosevelt was closely
associated with the pro-British cause, and therefore possibly
vulnerable in the 1944 election. But in December, with FDR
safely elected to a fourth term and a number of his
staunchest opponents on their way out of the legislature, the
liberals could feel free to speak their minds.

Moreover, the Roosevelt administration during this
period showed an increasing tendency to criticize British imperialism. The president reportedly reacted to British
actions in Greece with outrage. 'How the British can dare
such a thing!' he complained to his son. 'The lengths to
which they will go to hang on to the past!' One State
Department official, no doubt speaking for many of his colleagues, called British policy 'unnecessarily stupid,' and
accused the Foreign Office of 'playing her old game of
power politics with inadequate means.' Admiral King took
it upon himself to prohibit American ships from carrying
British supplies to Greece. Edward Stettinius, who succeeded Cordell Hull as Secretary of State in November, publicly
rebuked the British for their actions in Italy and Greece in

a statement issued on December 5, gaining him applause from both parties.[40]

December 1944 marked the high point of wartime anglophobia in the United States, but this latest wave quickly petered out when news of the German counteroffensive in the Ardennes reached Washington. According to Halifax, this had the effect of 'a cold douche upon an inflamed situation.' Ever since D-Day a quick victory had been expected, but now there was a perceived need for the Allies to work together more closely until the end of the war. In Congress, Sen. J. William Fulbright (D-AR) professed to be in agreement with the *Economist*'s critique of U.S. policy. Joseph H. Ball wrote in the *New York Times Magazine* that Americans ought to 'look inward' before criticizing British policy. Even Sen. Alexander Wiley (R-WI), who had gained a reputation for anti-interventionism before the war, warned his colleagues that it was time to 'quit indulging in the folly of ally-baiting.' American anglophobia fell to a new low, and would remain insignificant until the end of the war in Europe. A telling indicator was a poll taken in April 1945 which showed that 52 percent of those surveyed believed that the U.S. and Great Britain should sign a permanent military alliance after the war. When asked what the U.S. had to fear most from Great Britain, the response 'nothing' received more votes than any other.[41]

It is clear, then, that the nature of anglophobia underwent a profound change between 1941 and 1945. Before Pearl Harbor, the only anti-British voices heard in the public arena were those of the most extreme anti-interventionists. By the end of 1943, however, anti-interventionism was for all practical purposes dead. Evidence of this is to be found in the fact that the Connally Resolution, pledging U.S. involvement in some form of international organization after the war, passed the Senate in November of that year by a vote of 85 to 5.[42] Anglophobia at the end of the war came instead from two wildly divergent forces. 'Nationalists,' comprising mainly southern Democrats and northeastern (pre-Pearl Harbor interventionist) Republicans, saw the United States as the leading power of the postwar world, and they expected Great Britain to follow the American lead in all important matters. With the end of the war in sight, they believed (in Owen Brewster's words) that, '[a]s the world's Number One nation,

it's time to begin to look out for Number One.' Liberal internationalists, on the other hand, imagined a world in which
the guiding hand of the United Nations replaced the old
'balance-of-power' notions of the past; Britain had a role to
play in the new world order, but only if it abandoned its pre-
tensions to empire. These two opposing paradigms would
dominate American thinking on foreign affairs in the immediate postwar era, and neither one necessarily dictated a
policy that would be pleasing to the Foreign Office.[43]

The wartime alliance between the United States and Great
Britain was extremely close – closer perhaps than any military relationship in history. Yet it was, first and foremost, a
military arrangement, and no matter how intimate it became,
it could not guarantee that there would be a continuation of
cooperation after the guns stopped firing. American distrust
of the British remained strong in 1945 – almost as strong as it
had been in 1938 – and it would ultimately require the perceived common threat of Soviet expansionism to create
genuine harmony between the English-speaking nations.
The final decline of anglophobia in American politics, then, is
the subject of the final chapter.

8 'Who Shall Lead the World?'

An article in the December 1945 issue of *Catholic World*, asked the pointed question, 'Who shall lead the world?' For its author, James M. Gillis, the answer was clear – not Great Britain. 'Britain's reputation is that of the hypocrite, the nation whose high-hatted diplomats play low-browed politics – gracing their actions with the appearance of gentility and aristocratic distinction.' After reciting the roll call of nations wronged by British diplomacy through history, the editorial concluded that '[n]ot one of them would receive with anything but scorn the suggestion that Britain be their moral leader.' It was a stunning piece of anti-British rhetoric, the sort which was so commonly expounded around the time of Munich. But by the end of 1945 even Lord Halifax was prepared to accept the fact that Great Britain would never be well-liked by Americans. As he wrote in his report for the fourth quarter of that year, 'the only solid basis of Anglo-American relations is not liking but esteem.... Provided Britain continues to be vigorous in action and leadership; progressive in social and political evolution; and pursues enlightened policies both towards other countries and in relation to the Empire; there seems good reason to believe that American esteem for her will be steadily maintained.'[1]

Yet the American mood was often difficult to count on. As the war reached its conclusion public opinion polls showed that only 6 percent believed that foreign affairs were of pressing concern, even though substantial majorities wanted continued U.S. involvement in world affairs. Though Americans had clearly rejected isolation, they refused to condone an alliance with Great Britain or any other European nation. As Cushing Strout has argued, 'It was as if they had recognized the involvement of the New World in the world at large without recognizing any change in their relationships with the specific countries of the Old World.'[2]

Britons were also concerned about the recent change of

leadership in Washington. Roosevelt, who had come to personify (if not always accurately) cordial Anglo-American relations in the British public mind, died unexpectedly in April 1945, and his successor, vice-president Harry S. Truman, was somewhat of an unknown quantity. Before being chosen as Roosevelt's running mate in 1944, Truman had served as senator from Missouri, a state whose politicians were not known for having particular fondness for the British – Missouri had produced, after all, such notorious anglophobes as James Reed, Bennett Champ Clark, and Representative Dewey Short. Moreover, unlike his predecessor, Truman had few social or intellectual connections to the so-called 'Eastern establishment,' which had long supported closer relations between the English-speaking powers. And while he himself was not ill-disposed toward Great Britain, in his early days as president he appeared eager to keep the United States separate from the Anglo-Soviet feud which was brewing at the time. In any case, the Foreign Office expected little of the new president; soon after he took office, one British official wrote, 'One can only hope that the dignity of his new office will reveal in him unsuspected qualities which will render him equal to his enormous responsibilities.'[3]

But if Truman's attitude toward the British remained somewhat cloudy, the feelings of most American policymakers were all too clear. The United States had won the war, and was now the most powerful nation in the world. Great Britain, if it were to enjoy American friendship, protection, and aid, would have to defer to American wishes. Such attitudes had certainly begun to manifest themselves long before the end of the war, particularly in reference to the question of the atomic bomb. Scientific exchanges of atomic research began as early as 1940, but as work moved from beyond the purely theoretical stage the leaders of the American team began to doubt the wisdom of continued British involvement. By mid-1942 James B. Conant, head of research, claimed to see 'no reason for a joint enterprise as far as development and manufacture is concerned.' The British, he argued, were only interested in using American-financed atomic technology for industrial purposes after the war. Conant was supported in this by Secretary of War Stimson, who believed that shutting out the British was perfectly acceptable given that '[w]e were doing nine-tenths of the work.'[4]

By the end of 1942, then, British researchers found themselves virtually cut off from important atomic information, but this situation lasted only a few months. After seven months of badgering, in early spring 1943 Churchill convinced Roosevelt that the partnership had to be restored, since otherwise Great Britain would be forced to divert money and manpower from the war effort in order to pursue its own atomic energy program. The revived partnership manifested itself in the Quebec Agreement, a secret arrangement signed on August 19, 1943. Aside from promising that the atomic bomb would never be used by either side against the other, it established that neither would use it against a third party without the other's consent. Roosevelt signed the agreement against the advice of his advisors; as the Manhattan Project's director, General Leslie Groves, later complained, Roosevelt had listened exclusively to British advisors at Quebec, and had failed to consult with any Americans.[5]

After the bombing of Hiroshima, of course, the existence of the atomic bomb became public knowledge, and Congress and public opinion were now forces which had to be taken into account. It became clear almost immediately after the end of the war that British assistance was no longer welcome, and the flow of atomic information slowed to a trickle. When a team of British diplomats arrived in November to renegotiate the Quebec Agreement, they found themselves face to face with an American team which included General Groves and Vannevar Bush, both of whom had fought to limit British access to American technology in 1942. Groves demanded placement of all of the British Commonwealth's atomic raw materials at U.S. disposal as the price for continued collaboration, a demand which the British refused. In the end nothing more was produced by the meeting than a 'memorandum of intention' which was so ambiguous in its wording that it proved to have no value whatsoever to the British.[6]

The resolve of American policymakers to maintain an atomic monopoly was further stiffened by the arrest of Dr. Alan Nunn May in early 1946. A member of the British atomic research team, May was found to have transmitted in-formation on the design and construction of atomic piles to the Soviet Union. The fact that he had been cleared for such top secret work by British Intelligence helped to encourage the notion that continued collaboration, even with the nation's closest ally, was an intolerable security risk. Congress soon responded by passing the McMahon Act (sponsored by Sen. Brien McMahon [D-CT]), which in addition to placing control of atomic technology in the hands of an Atomic Energy Commission, made it a federal crime to export 'any fissionable material' or 'directly or indirectly engage in the production of any fissionable material' outside of the United States. Though it did not mention Great Britain specifically, the McMahon Act had the practical effect of cutting off all ex-change of atomic technology between Britain and the United States, and it led the British to launch a program to develop their own atomic weapons.[7]

The increasing willingness of the U.S. government to treat the British as subordinates could also be found in the American demand for overseas base rights. As the Japanese were slowly driven from their strongpoints in the Pacific, the inevitable question emerged as to what should be done with these newly conquered islands. The Foreign Office sug-gested a mandate system similar to that employed after the First World War, but this immediately came under fire in the American press as a scheme to expand the British Empire in the Far East. A group of senators, meanwhile, demanded that islands occupied by U.S. forces remain under American dominion. As Sen. Patrick McCarran (D-NV) put it, 'I'm a hell-tootin' American from out West, and I'm for keepin' the mandates under the Stars and Stripes.' After years of de-nouncing British imperialism, it now seemed to Halifax that Americans wanted an empire of their own.[8]

The desire for Pacific bases grew with the surrender of Japan. In August a subcommittee of the House Naval Affairs Committee issued a report contending that since the United States had 'restored peace in the Pacific almost single-hand-edly,' it ought to be granted 'the authority and the means' to keep order in the region. To that end the subcommittee named a series of territories which would either have to be acquired from Japan or from other countries. In November the State Department became involved, sending to the British Embassy a list of locations in which the U.S. sought 'long-term base rights,' adding that the British were expected to 'support and assist' the Americans in negotiations to receive them. The countries from which rights were being demanded included Iceland, Portugal (in the Azores and Cape Verde Islands), France (Espiritu Santo), Australia, and New Zealand (various Pacific Islands). Moreover, the communiqué made it clear that the U.S. expected to maintain the bases which it constructed during the war in Egypt, India, and Burma. Finally, the State Department demanded exclusive base rights on the islands of Canton, Christmas, and Funafuti, all of which were subjects of disputed U.S. and British claims. When the Foreign Office suggested that this was the sort of thing that should wait for the convocation of the United Nations, Secretary of State James Byrnes protested that 'hundreds of details and thousands of procedural questions' would create an intolerable delay.[9]

In the following February the U.S. began to back away from the previous list, admitting that the American people would be unwilling to pay to maintain so many bases, but that Christmas Island and Canton remained vital to national security. Byrnes called on Britain to 'recognize unconditionally' U.S. sovereignty over these islands, and to divide the other contested islands equally. This was necessary, the secretary of state argued, in order to maintain a 'genuine good relationship at this critical period.' There were, he warned, still forces in Congress hostile to Great Britain, and refusal to cooperate in the Pacific would help their cause immeasurably.[10]

Byrnes was not being deceitful – anglophobia did indeed remain a potent force in Congress, and for that matter among important sectors of public opinion as well, and with the end of the war in Europe these groups showed an increased willingness to make their feelings known. One of the most immediate causes of this were the results of the parliamentary elections of July 1945. In a stunning victory, the socialist Labour party ousted the Churchill coalition cabinet, and by the end of the year the Labourites had embarked on an ambitious program of nationalization and social services. Though American liberals were overjoyed by the change of government, many moderates and conservatives viewed it as a dangerous flirtation with communism. The new Britain, they argued, now embodied what historian Justus Doenecke has called 'the twin perils of the decaying continent – the traditional imperialist plutocracy and a new collectivist despotism.' American officials friendly to Britain urged that a Labour cabinet minister make a speech 'reciting once more the limits of Britain's socialization program and emphasizing the large scope for private enterprise which still remains' in order to calm public concerns. Meanwhile, the new British ambassador, Lord Inverchapel, urged Foreign Secretary Ernest Bevin to restate his 'detestation of communism in order to quieten [*sic*] the voices of those (some even in high places) who suggest that we are being pushed steadily towards it.'[11]

There was also continued American pressure for Indian independence, especially after reports began to circulate to the effect that American policy in the region was beginning to be viewed as identical to that of the British. In one of his first acts as president, Truman gave SEAC responsibility for the liberation of Southeast Asia and the Dutch East Indies, thus giving his tacit approval to the reestablishment of European colonies in that region. This did not sit well with American liberals, who now led the chorus of charges that the administration was trying to 'pull the British chestnuts out of the fire.' In a speech before the Senate on May 31, Robert La Follette, Jr. claimed that the reluctance of the British to abandon their empire 'deserves the greatest censure....I am no more prepared to commit the United States to enforcing British rule over India, Burma, or Malta than I am to commit my country to enforcing Russian dominion' over eastern Europe. In the September issue of *Catholic World*, meanwhile, Francis McCullagh accused the Foreign Office of wanting to partition India as they had done Ireland.[12]

But concerns over India amounted to little compared with the anger generated by British policy in Palestine. A British journalist traveling in the U.S. at the time wrote that he found 'widespread antagonism' toward his country 'in practically every stratum of society.' Democrats and Republicans, both eager to win Jewish support, attempted to outdo each other in their denunciations of the White Paper of 1939. Britain's policy of blocking Jewish immigration to Palestine was, according to Congressman Emanuel Celler (D-NY) 'in violation of all moral and legal precepts.' Despite the fact that American Jews had been the most loyal supporters of the British cause before and during the war, he continued, Britain chose to 'appease' the Arabs by issuing the White Paper. One of his Republican colleagues, Rep. George Bender of Ohio, accused the British of 'seeking to terrorize the Jewish community of Palestine and the world' in a 'desperate effort to bolster a shaking empire.' The situation was the same in the Senate. Sen. Henry M. 'Scoop' Jackson (D-WA) called the British presence in Palestine 'an arbitrary tyrannical power ruling by force alone.' La Follette, meanwhile, called it 'a rule of force only, a rule of bayonets.'[13]

Nor was the Truman administration eager to come to Britain's defense. Most of the State Department, as well as the Joint Chiefs, advised the president to support British policy in the Middle East, fearing (with uncanny prescience) that the United States would be inevitably drawn into the region if the British were to withdraw. Nevertheless, domestic political considerations were given precedence. Truman simply could not afford to alienate American Jews, a crucial part of the Democratic coalition, when the 1946 midterm elections were only a few months away.[14] He therefore announced publicly his support for the revocation of the White Paper, to the fury of Foreign Minister Ernest Bevin, who claimed that the president's decision was motivated by the fact that Americans 'did not want too many Jews in New York.'[15]

Another point of contention between Americans and the Foreign Office arose during a speech by Churchill in Fulton, Missouri, on March 5, 1946, in which the former prime minister claimed that the Soviets had drawn an 'iron curtain' across the heart of Europe.[16] Only a closely-knit Anglo-American partnership, he argued, could resist Stalin's ambitions. Some conservative anticommunists welcomed Churchill's frank remarks about the Soviet threat; these, however, were in a minority. To most others, especially liberals, the former prime minister appeared to be calling for an Anglo-American alliance directed against the U.S.S.R. The editorial pages of such newspapers as the *New York Herald Tribune*, the *New York Post*, the *Chicago Sun*, the *Atlanta Constitution*, and the *Boston Globe* accused him of promoting anti-Soviet hysteria; the editors of the *Nation* claimed that his speech had 'added a sizable measure of poison to the already deteriorating relations between Russia and the Western Powers.' Manhattan's pro-Soviet *PM*, meanwhile, called the speech 'an ideological declaration of war against Russia.' In the Senate, Claude Pepper (D-FL) warned the United States to avoid becoming the 'guarantor of British imperialism'; he and Glen Taylor (D-ID) issued a joint statement charging Churchill with being unable to see beyond 'the roll of the drums and the flutter of the flag of Empire.' Even Eleanor Roosevelt, the late president's widow, made a point of criticizing the former prime minister's vision of an English-speaking alliance for not including 'the far greater number of people who are not English-speaking.'[17]

The liberals were soon joined in their assault by many of the former anti-interventionists, who were quick to reject any proposal that resembled an 'entangling alliance.' The *Chicago Tribune* accused Churchill of attempting to chain America to an 'old and evil empire' that had imposed 'slavery' over three-fifths of the world's surface. As in the past, Americans, the paper went on to warn, 'would be asked to furnish 90 percent of the fighting power and 80 percent of the money in any British alliance to maintain British tyranny in the world.' Senator Arthur Capper (R-KS), meanwhile, called his suggestion 'a bid for us to furnish forces to help hold Gibraltar, Malta, Suez, Singapore, India and all the British colonial possessions.' Rep. John Vorys (R-OH), in the tradition of William Borah in the League of Nations debates, reminded his colleagues that in any Anglo-American arrangement, the United States would have only one vote compared to to the British Commonwealth's six.[18]

The hostile reaction of the liberals and former non-interventionists might have been expected, but the spontaneous expressions of disdain from grass-roots America were not. Letters and telegrams poured into the White House from across the country. A Seattle resident complained that 'Britain has subsidized not only the pot-bellied reactionary rulers of India but every bloodthirsty puppet ruler in the Middle East.' Another correspondent charged that 'Churchill is ready to destroy us all in order that his own brand of tyranny may prevail.' Yet another asked, 'Does criticizm [sic] of Russia negate the fact that millions of Britain's colonials are living in slavery?' The former prime minister's remarks continued to haunt him through the rest of his visit to the U.S. – when he spoke in New York City on March 15, for example, his hotel was surrounded by protesters chanting 'Winnie, Winnie, go away, UNO is here to stay!' and 'Don't be a ninny for imperialist Winnie!' As the *Wall Street Journal* pointed out, 'the country's reaction to Mr. Churchill's Fulton speech must be convincing proof that the United States wants no alliance or anything that resembles an alliance with any other nation.'[19]

Finally, economic nationalists displayed concern about Britain's trade policies in the immediate postwar period. An article in the *Atlantic* entitled 'British Trade and American Policy,' made repeated reference to the 'hesitant altruism' of the U.S. as opposed to the 'realistic' strategies pursued by the British. Its author, Raymond P. Baldwin, argued that ever since the tide had turned decisively against the Axis, the British gradually became more concerned with furthering their own postwar trade than they did with actually winning the war. Anglophobes in Congress eagerly repeated this charge. Representative Daniel A. Reed (D-NY), for example, charged that by means of the 'imperial preference plan,' Britain monopolized world trade 'by bringing a population of 394 235 338 within the orbit of her exclusive trade.' John Vorys, meanwhile, compared British trade policy to the 'economic warfare' of the Barbary pirates. On the other side of the Capitol, Senator Edward H. Moore (D-OK) assailed what he called Britain's 'international banditry,' while Wayne L. Morse (D-OR) referred to English policy as 'international war against the United States.' At the same time, C. Wayland Brooks added, American markets would be flooded with products made in the British Empire, where employers could 'pay from 15 cents to $1 a day to their labor.'[20]

Unfortunately for the British, all this pent-up discontent was being unleashed at precisely the same time that England was trying to secure a huge loan from the United States for the purpose of postwar recovery. On August 21, 1945

Truman abruptly terminated lend-lease, claiming that it was meant to be nothing more than strictly a wartime measure. Though popular at home, Truman's decision was greeted with shock and indignation in London, which had become dangerously dependent on American economic aid. Now the British faced the unenviable task of rebuilding with gold reserves of less than one billion pounds sterling (Britain's gold reserve had stood in 1939 at roughly 650 billion pounds). Less than one month later a delegation headed by John Maynard Keynes arrived in Washington to negotiate a loan of $6 billion. Sympathetic to Britain's plight, yet realizing the state of congressional opinion, the administration agreed in early December to a loan of $3.75 billion, but only on the condition that steps be taken to dissolve the imperial preference system and to allow American goods to compete on equal terms within the Commonwealth.[21]

Yet even this watered down version of the loan faced an uphill fight in Congress, where anglophobia had returned to full bloom. As Halifax wrote, 'Congress is in a bad temper and we can certainly assume much more delay than we had bargained for.' Public opinion surveys taken at the end of 1945 showed only about 30 percent in favor of the loan, and only one in eight believed that it would ever be repaid. Some professed to be amazed at the sheer gall of the request. In a speech in Cincinnati, Rep. Gerald W. Landis (R-IN) repeated the charges of British wealth that characterized so much of the Lend-Lease debate. 'They now own 1 500 000 shares in United States industries. They have unmined gold reserves of $24 500 000 000, unmined diamond reserves of $8 800 000 000, and $14 000 000 000 in foreign investments. Let her use these assets before coming over here with cup in hand.' William Lemke called Great Britain 'the most arrogant beggar of all time.' An editorial cartoon in the *Chicago Tribune* showed a caricature of John Bull standing at America's back door saying, 'Spare a morsel for a poor, weak, sick, hungry, starvin' man, [but] make it sirloin, medium rare...and if it isn't done just right, I won't eat it! No use beggin' me!'[22]

Many conservatives of both parties opposed the loan on the grounds that it would be used to bring private industries under government control. Rep. Raymond E. Willis (R-IN), for example, claimed the loan would do nothing more than 'to bolster a shaky Socialist regime,' while Rep. Harold Knutson (R-MN) called on the British to 'look to Moscow for such financing.' Zionists and liberals, meanwhile, feared that the loan might be spent in local wars against nationalist movements in India, Palestine, and elsewhere in the empire. In granting the loan, as Rep. Adam Clayton Powell (D-NY) argued, Americans would be 'placing our approval on hypocrisy, imperialism, colonialism and broken pledges.' 'Our Thunderbolts, our tanks, and our machine guns were used to maim and strafe innocent citizens in Dutch Indonesia, in French Indochina, and supposedly independent Siam,' charged Emanuel Celler. 'The moneys [from the loan] can be used to enable Britain to continue to tear-gas and V-bomb her way into Palestine villages and settlements, there, again, to kill innocent men, women, and children.' Economic nationalists joined the fight as well, contending that despite their promises the British had no intention of doing away with imperial preference. Under such circumstances, they argued, 'cheap socialist-produced goods' would soon flood American markets.[23]

Other objections ranged from the serious to the downright silly. Some protested that the loan might needlessly provoke the Soviet Union: Rep. Karl Mundt (R-SD), for example, labeled the measure 'Russia-baiting dollar diplomacy and monetary imperialism' which would threaten the peace and undermine the United Nations by 'dividing the world into armed camps.' On the other hand Kenneth McKellar, in a performance reminiscent of his Big-Navy days, wrote to the president asking whether the British might use the loan 'to build a stronger navy than we will have.' Sen. William Langer (R-ND) objected to the credit on the grounds that Keynes had once been disrespectful toward Woodrow Wilson. Rep. Dewey Short (R-MO) chose the populist route, remarking that 'So long as...they have crown jewels,...as long as they wear ermine and emeralds in London,...I am not going to vote one dollar to take food out of the mouths of my own people.'[24]

Indeed, had the loan agreement been voted on in December 1945, or even in the first several months of 1946, it is unlikely that it would have passed. However, Congress chose to debate the issue at leisure – it was not voted on in the Senate until May, and the final vote in the House did not come until mid-July. Halifax complained bitterly about the 'interminable quantity of talk, a great deal malevolent, and nearly all ignorant,' but the delay actually proved beneficial to the British cause, for it gave the loan's American supporters far more time to win new converts. The liberal editors of the *Nation* and the *New Republic* began pressing for passage of the agreement as early as October 1945 – nearly two months before even the administration had approved it. Accusing the loan's opponents of 'exploiting widespread public ignorance of the realities of international economics,' it gently chastised those who claimed it would go to support British imperialism. 'Our own views on British imperialism are a matter of record,' the editors of the *Nation* stated, 'but we do not believe that the way to combat it is to deny assistance to the British people at this time.' Indeed, the *New Republic* added, it was arch-imperialists such as Lord Beaverbrook who opposed the loan, fearing that the end of imperial preference would lead to the dissolution of the empire. 'If the agreement is defeated,' the journal's editors warned, 'Britain must strengthen her economic control, and therefore her political control,' of its colonial possessions.[25]

Particular attention was given to American Zionists. The *New Republic*, while displaying sympathy with Jewish frustration 'over the blundering, tactless, weak and often brutal dallying of the British....in Palestine,' insisted that without the loan the situation would become even worse. The editors of the *Nation*, meanwhile, asked rhetorically whether failure to pass the loan agreement would 'bring one Jewish D.P. one foot nearer the promised land?' Both journals pleaded with their Zionist readers not to give aid and comfort to the 'isolationists,' their former enemies, by opposing the loan.[26]

Though conservatives were more united in their opposition to the loan than their liberal colleagues, there were some significant defections. The editorial board of the *Saturday Evening Post*, a bulwark of the American Right since the 1920s, defended the loan as a means of breaking down imperial preference and strengthening moderate elements within the British Labour party. Others felt that it was necessary for England and the United States to present a solid front against the Soviet Union. In the Senate, for example, the two ranking Republican members of the Foreign Relations Committee, Robert Taft and Arthur Vandenberg, eventually came around to support the measure. Taft, while claiming to 'think very little of the economic arguments' for it, confided to his longtime friend Herbert Hoover that the failure of Congress to pass the agreement would create 'a serious divergence of policy between this country and Great Britain.' In a similar vein, Vandenberg wrote in his diary in December 1945, 'I have a feeling that we ought to "go along" with this loan for the sake of some nebulous affinity which the English-speaking world must maintain in mutual self-defense. But I also confess my feeling that about 90 percent of my constituency will be unimpressed by this ideology.' By spring the 'nebulous affinity' overcame his political instincts, and on April 22 he announced his support for the loan agreement.[27]

In the end, enough converts were made, both on the Left and the Right, to pass the agreement with widespread bi-partisan support. In the Senate, nearly half the Republicans joined nearly two-thirds of the Democrats in passing the bill. And while only about a third of House Republicans sup-ported the agreement, Democratic Majority Leader John McCormack (D-MA) mustered more than enough votes to cover the margin. The British loan, which had seemed an impossibility in late 1945, was an established fact by the middle of 1946.[28]

The turnabout of public and congressional opinion on the loan, however, was only one manifestation of a much larger trend which was occurring during the period 1946–1948 – namely, the decline of anglophobia as a tool of American pol-itics. The first hints of this decline came in 1940 and 1941, when the Irish-American and German-American communi-ties played no more than a secondary role in the anti-interventionist coalition. The war served to dampen further the hatred of ethnic America for Great Britain, espe-cially among Irish-Americans. The steadfast refusal of the government of Eire to enter the war on the side of the allies was a decision which even America's sons of Erin found dis-maying. After the war, when the Irish government tried to enlist American support for its attempt to force Britain to give up Northern Ireland, it received a rather tepid response. According to the American Minister in Dublin, even Irish-Americans resented 'the effort to inject this issue into American politics.' A member of the British Embassy staff reported that 'The Irish seem to be flogging a horse which if not dead, is at least in a state of suspended animation.' Irish neutrality, he claimed, 'rankles in even Irish-American breasts and has been a great handicap to exploitation of anti-British feeling by Irish extremists.' Indeed, the only expression of support in Congress came from Rep. Thomas J. Lane (D-MA), the voice of the Boston Irish. Lane made a brief speech citing America's traditional support for those 'who wish to throw off the yoke of imperialism,' but in the end he was unwilling to suggest anything more than a series of Anglo-American conferences to discuss the issue, since, as he claimed, 'Unilateral action never solves any political problem.'[29]

Liberal anglophobia took somewhat longer to die, mainly because it continued to have strong support within the administration. Joseph Davies, former envoy to the Soviets and author of the controversial book *Mission to Moscow*, assumed that America's postwar role would be to serve as a mediator in the inevitable struggle between Soviet security and the British desire to preserve the empire. After a visit to London in May 1945, Davies reported to Truman that Churchill was 'first, last, and all the time,' a great Englishman, and that he cared more about preserving England's position in Europe than he did about maintaining the peace. Another inveterate anglophobe of the Left was Henry Wallace, Roosevelt's former vice president who now served as Truman's Secretary of Agriculture. Wallace publicly described Churchill's speech in Fulton, Missouri, as 'shocking,' and stated his opposition to an Anglo-American alliance on the grounds that 'it was not a primary objective of the United States to save the British Empire.' Like Davies, he saw the U.S. as an intermediary between Britain and Russia, 'not as a defender of England.'[30]

Midwestern Progressive anglophobia, meanwhile, did not disappear; progressivism itself, however, did. As a political movement in the Upper Midwest it had been steadily dying since the late 1930s, when most of its leaders broke with Roosevelt over his foreign policy and his attempt to pack the

Supreme Court. Thereafter they began to disappear in favor of a new generation of Republican politicians who might be called 'populist conservatives.' Men such as Senators John Bricker (R-OH) and Kenneth Wherry (R-NE), and Representatives Karl Stefan (R-NE), Reid F. Murray (R-WI) and Karl Mundt (R-SD) combined traditional conservative attacks on the New Deal with populist rhetoric against elites; while the old progressives directed their anger toward Wall Street bankers and railroad monopolies, populist conservatives took aim at international bankers, university professors, government bureaucrats, and alleged 'foreign agents' in America. By the end of the war most of the old progressives – Borah, Johnson, Norris, Nye, etc. – were either dead or had lost bids for reelection. Their final humiliation came in the election of 1946, when Wheeler, Henrik Shipstead (R-MN), and Robert La Follette, Jr., were all defeated by challengers within their own respective parties; La Follette, significantly, lost to Joseph R. McCarthy. The conservative populists, it should be noted, were by no means pro-British – indeed, they had been among the most dedicated opponents of the British loan – but when compared to the Soviet Union they unquestionably viewed London as the lesser of two evils.[31]

One senator, however, continued the tradition of progressive anglophobia. The son of German immigrants and a graduate of Columbia University Law School, William Langer (R-ND) was first elected to the Senate in 1940, but only after the war did he become vocal in his opposition to Great Britain. On December 4, 1945, he gave a long speech before the Brooklyn Academy of Music entitled, 'England – Enemy of Liberty,' in which he called for 'another revolutionary war to regain our independence from Great Britain.' As one of only two senators to have opposed U.S. involvement in the United Nations, Langer called the U.N. 'a British scheme to keep half the world in subjection.' Langer had a long-standing feud with Winston Churchill, claiming repeatedly, beginning in 1946, that the former prime minister had fought alongside the Spanish in Cuba during the Spanish-American War.[32]

Yet such accusations were becoming increasingly rare in postwar America. An important reason for this was that beginning in 1946 Great Britain rapidly began to divest itself of its overseas colonies. Burma was promised independence in December 1946, while India received a similar pledge in February 1947. By the end of that year the British had announced their intention to extricate themselves from both the civil war in Greece and the turmoil in Palestine. These decisions, of course, arose only partly due to pressure from the U.S.; Great Britain could simply no longer afford to maintain its extensive global commitments. But the effect of decolonization on American public opinion was undeniable. In a column in the *New York Times* on January 29, 1947, Marquis Childs announced that it was 'time to stop talking about "imperialism" as though Gunga Din were still carrying gin slings to the complacent British Raj. While the shreds of that old order cling on, the empire system is actually a part of history.' Even the *Chicago Tribune* started to back off from its criticisms of the British Empire; when later asked about this, Col. McCormick responded that 'the British Empire was no longer important enough' to require his attention. Indeed, given the bloodshed which immediately followed the British withdrawal from India, some U.S. editors began to question whether British imperialism had ever been all that bad in the first place.[33]

Another reason for the decline of public anglophobia had nothing whatsoever to do with British policy. In mid-1945, a majority of Americans surveyed in a public opinion poll claimed to have faith that the Soviet Union would cooperate with the United States in the postwar world; it was, in fact, the great fear of Wallace and his fellow liberals that Britain would try to lure America into an anti-Soviet alliance. In February 1946, however – less than a year later – the percentage of Americans who believed that the USSR would cooperate had dropped by half. By 1948 the Soviets had consolidated their hold over nearly all of eastern Europe, were clearly supporting a left-wing guerrilla movement in Greece, were pressuring Turkey and Iran for concessions, and were channeling funds to communist parties in western Europe. Most Americans had become convinced by this time that Stalin's regime posed a genuine long-term threat not only to world peace, but to American security.[34]

In such an uncertain international climate, sniping at the nation's closest friend was a luxury which few believed the

U.S. could afford. Communism, and not imperialism, had become the chief concern. As one American diplomat asked, 'When perhaps the inevitable struggle came between Russia and ourselves, the question would be, who are our friends[?]...Would we have the support of Great Britain if we had undermined her [colonial] position?' Admiral Leahy felt likewise, warning Secretary of State Byrnes in March 1946 that the 'defeat or disintegration of the British Empire would eliminate from Eurasia the last bulwark of resistance between the United States and Soviet expansion. Even the popular press seemed to agree; *Time* magazine, one of Henry Luce's publications, actually expressed sympathy for British policies in the Mediterranean, where only a few months ago it had seen only the dead hand of imperialism. And when, in March 1947, the president announced his desire to assume Britain's role in supporting the anti-communist regime in Greece, public fear of the Soviet menace made persuading Congress all the easier. By 1948 this fear had become so widespread that when Henry Wallace launched an independent campaign for the presidency on a pro-Soviet, anti-British theme, he found no significant support for his message from any sector of public opinion.[35]

But there were, of course, limits to the Anglo-American partnership, and one of these became evident in August 1947. Prime Minister Attlee, in an apparent attempt to break the deadlock over the exchange of atomic technology, made public the terms of the heretofore secret Quebec Agreement of 1943. The response was not exactly as Attlee had expected – rather than demanding that the administration live up to the terms of Quebec, important senators and congressmen expressed outrage that such an agreement could ever have been signed. Of particular concern was the pledge that neither side would use atomic weapons without the other's consent, as well as the provision that all uranium produced in the Belgian Congo (the only known source of the element at the time) would be shared equally between the two powers. Arthur Vandenberg, now chairman of the Senate Foreign Relations Committee, called the agreement's terms 'astounding' and 'unthinkable.' Sen. Bourke Hickenlooper (R-IA), meanwhile, spelled out his view of the Anglo-American relationship by saying, 'If our country is expected

to…pull British chestnuts out of the fire, then I think we
should have all of the implements of strength readily and se-
curely available to us.' Both men demanded that the Quebec
Agreement be immediately rescinded, and promised to block
'any future aid to Britain' as long as the issue remained un-
resolved. After a few months of negotiation, the State
Department assured them that 'the obnoxious agreement'
would be canceled, and the crisis passed. The whole affair,
however, helped to define the nature of the postwar partnership between the English-speaking nations: the United
States pledged to defend Britain and its possessions against
attack, and in return the British were expected to keep quiet
and do as they were told.[36]

By 1948, then, anglophobia, a salient feature of American
political life since the founding of the republic, had passed
into the pages of history. There were, to be sure, some out-
bursts of anti-British rhetoric in following years: when
Churchill visited the United States in 1952, for example, Sen.
William Langer asked that two lanterns be hung in the Old
North Church in Boston. But Langer by this time had
become something of an anachronism. His antics during
Churchill's visit generated a good deal of hate mail from his
own constituents, and thereafter even he stopped 'twisting
the lion's tail.' As the Cold War intensified between the U.S.
and the Soviet Union, a bipartisan consensus emerged on
foreign policy, one which considered Great Britain, if a distinctly junior partner, a partner nonetheless. As accusations
that the British were controlling American foreign policy
faded into obscurity, the centuries-old conflict of 'Old World'
versus 'New World' began to collapse. Pundits began to
speak of 'Atlanticism,' defining the struggle as one between
the 'First World' and the 'Second World,' or 'East' and
'West,' with the West clearly including not only Great Britain
but western Europe as well. In 1947 the Senate passed the
Marshall Plan, in which billions of American dollars poured
into Britain and Europe to aid in postwar reconstruction.
Two years later the North Atlantic Treaty Alliance was ratified, and the United States became involved in its first
'entangling alliance.'[37]

Disputes and misunderstandings between the two countries would, of course, continue throughout the Cold War,

but from the late 1940s onward such difficulties were increasingly matters purely to be dealt with between the State Department and the Foreign Office. Gone were the days when any difference between the English-speaking powers immediately became a subject for congressional debate. No longer was there a receptive public audience for anti-British rhetoric; indeed, in the ultra-patriotic world of the United States in the 1950s attacks on the nation's most important foreign ally might even be construed as un-American.[38] The 'special relationship,' the goal longed for by anglophiles and denounced by anglophobes since the turn of the century, had finally become a reality.

Conclusion

In a speech in early 1947, Lord Halifax told the story of a European-born American who asked a senator who had just finished an anti-British diatribe why, if the senator was of purely British blood, he was anti-British while the European-born American was pro-British.

'Ah,' replied the senator, 'but I have something that you have not got.... The memory of the redcoats.'[1]

The anecdote rather neatly illustrates the driving force behind American anglophobia. The experience of the revolutionary war remained a crucial element of the country's national mythology, comparable to the Hundred Years' War for the French or the Franco-Prussian War for Germans. As the foregoing chapters have shown, anti-British sentiment was employed by a wide range of interest groups and organizations for a huge variety of purposes. What, for example, could the cries of 'perfidious Albion' made by the conservative Big Navy Party in 1927 and liberal protests against Winston Churchill in 1946 possibly have in common? The answer involves the national myth, and the belief of both groups that Americans were prepared to believe the worst when it came to Great Britain and the British Empire.

To a considerable extent this attitude stemmed from simple parochialism, a widespread ignorance of foreign peoples and cultures, combined with a strong tendency to judge other societies according to strictly American standards. And American standards, of course, were determined largely by the precepts of the national myth. There was little genuine effort to examine the deeper issues involved in the Irish or, later, the Indian situation, no attempt made to understand why Great Britain continued to insist on the need for a navy larger than that of the U.S., no investigation of the real causes of appeasement, no serious consideration of the difficulties faced by British forces in Asia....the list goes on and on. Instead, the national myth was ready with a simple answer to every question. Why the insistence on a larger navy? To strangle American trade and violate the rights of

190

neutrals in wartime, of course. British presence in Ireland, India, Egypt, etc.? That stemmed from a desire to enslave foreign peoples in order to sustain the English upper classes. Appeasement? A cynical attempt to protect the empire, and to use Hitler to destroy the Soviet regime. Military defeats in North Africa and Asia? The result of a military dominated by members of the decadent British aristocracy. Stereotypes and historic prejudice, not rational regard of American interests, motivated a great deal of U.S. policy toward Great Britain throughout the period considered here.

Where did the American national myth come from, and why did it continue to hold such appeal for Americans in the twentieth century? Anthony D. Smith, in his seminal works on the origins of nationalism, makes special mention of the development of political identity in colonies that share a common culture with the mother country. In such cases some sort of 'counter-culture' had to be developed which would give some unity to the various factions who had engaged in rebellion against the colonial power, and who afterward hoped to form a single nation. In the case of Britain's American colonies, this counter-culture became based on 'common speech, the literacy of their middle classes, a common settler life-style and separate political institutions' from those of England. Thus in the early days of the republic there evolved a whole mythology, replete with heroes (George Washington, Thomas Jefferson, Thomas Paine), villains (Benedict Arnold, the redcoats, Lord North, and, of course, the omnipresent George III), and dramatic events (Lexington and Concord, the signing of the Declaration of Independence, Bunker Hill, Valley Forge, Yorktown). These elements, according to Smith's analysis, formed the only glue capable of uniting the commercial, proto-industrial economy of the North and the slaveowning, plantation economy of the South in a single political entity. It is, then, little wonder that such legends died hard in the American popular imagination.[2]

Moreover, the national myth was continually being strengthened by foreign immigrants. The Anglo-Saxon 'nationalists' who in the early part of the twentieth century railed against immigration as a dilution of American culture would have found this surprising, but the themes of the revolution struck a receptive chord in those fleeing economic, political, or religious persecution abroad. The myth served a dual role. For the foreign-born, allegiance to America's founding principles, and to the revolutionary events behind them, was a means of asserting their own loyalty to a sceptical (and increasingly hostile) native population. But it served another purpose as well; for German- and Irish-Americans in the 1920s and 1930s, as well as for Greek-Americans and American Jews in the mid-1940s, the national myth corresponded well with the (largely anti-British) aspirations of their countrymen in Germany, Ireland, Greece, or Palestine. This reaction, which Anthony Smith calls 'vicarious nationalism,' helped to compensate for the partial loss of their own ethnic heritage which occurred in their assimilation into American culture.[3]

The national myth as applied to the first half of the twentieth century had both an international and a domestic component. In international affairs, it encouraged in Americans a belief in the inherent evil of power politics as practiced by the British. As Henry Kissinger has pointed out, most Americans found it disconcerting that British leaders 'should be primarily concerned with British national interests – something that the statesmen of any other country would have treated as the most natural thing in the world.' To most Americans, moral principles, and not national interests, were the only justification for foreign intervention. This prevailing attitude manifested itself in a grave misinterpretation of Washington's Farewell Address, one which placed great emphasis on the first president's supposed admonitions regarding 'entangling alliances,' while overlooking his words about 'excessive dislike' of certain foreign nations.[4] And it certainly showed itself in the popular image of the slick, bespatted and monocled British diplomat that was so common during the interwar and immediate post-World War II periods. American negotiators, this legend maintained, were no match for their counterparts from across the Atlantic; as the Lieutenant Governor of New York claimed in 1944, 'Every time the American eagle sits in diplomatic conference in Europe, he comes back plucked to the pinfeathers.' This hostility to power politics, obviously, did not always manifest itself in the same way – some, like Woodrow Wilson, believed that an open, straightforward, 'American'-style diplomacy could reform the world, while others such as William Borah insisted that Europe was beyond redemption – but both shared the same basic principle.[5]

The domestic component of the national myth involved a strong sense of hostility toward elites. Even though the revolution and the early republic were led by men of wealth and social standing, the legend of the ragtag army of citizen-soldiers taking up their muskets to resist the well-trained, well-equipped legions of British royalty had a powerful hold on the American mind. While to some extent a certain degree of anglophobia could be found among almost all Americans, it is significant that during the period under consideration the most vehement expressions of anti-British rhetoric came from those who believed themselves to be on the 'outside' of the country's political, social, and cultural elite. The denunciations of British policy so commonly made by Irish- and German-Americans, northern liberals and socialists, southern populists, and midwestern progressives were directed as much toward Wall Street and Big Business as they were at the British.[6] Conversely, membership in pro-English organizations such as the English-Speaking Union, the Century Group, and Union Now was drawn almost exclusively from the upper echelons of American society. Politicians, of course, realized this fact and readily exploited it. When, for example, Herbert Hoover was attacked for his presumed indifference to the plight of American workers and farmers, his political opponents took pains to juxtapose this against his supposedly pro-British leanings in foreign policy. In the mid-1930s, Franklin Roosevelt coupled his assault on 'economic royalists' at home with a foreign policy which, at best, kept England at arm's length. And when, in the late 1930s, Roosevelt began to move closer to Great Britain, he opened himself up to attack from a new generation of conservative populists who targeted the 'Harvard elites' and Rhodes Scholars who staffed his administration and were allegedly receiving their marching orders from London.

Why, then, did anglophobia continue to play such a prominent role in American politics in the twentieth century? Perhaps, given the power of the national myth, the more appropriate question is why it ever disappeared. After all, both of its components continued to operate long after politicians stopped blaming Great Britain for the country's ills. The American distrust of power politics still manifests itself in a need to justify on moral terms every exertion of armed force abroad, as seen in the Korean and Vietnam wars, as well as in the Persian Gulf conflict of 1990–91. And the Democratic Party's successful portrayal in 1992 of George Bush as a man who cared more about foreign countries than he did about the suffering of the masses at home could well have been taken straight from Franklin Roosevelt's campaign handbook for 1932.

It would appear, then, that while the world has unquestionably changed, the way that Americans perceive the world remains largely the same. As columnist Charles Krauthammer wrote in the *New Republic* in late 1988, 'Nations need enemies. Take away one, and they find another.... Parties and countries need mobilizing symbols of 'otherness' to energize the nation and to give it purpose.'[7] In the late 1940s it became ridiculous to imagine that Great Britain posed any sort of threat to the United States, so fear and hatred of Great Britain simply gave way to paranoia about the Russian Bear and the Red Menace, which yielded in the 1980s to fears of Japanese domination of international trade, and in the 1990s to the specter of Islamic fundamentalism in the Middle East. Washington's advice regarding 'excessive dislike' of foreign nations remains, alas, unfortunately unheeded to this day.

Notes

INTRODUCTION

1. Felix Gilbert, *To the Farewell Address: Ideas of Early American Foreign Policy* (Princeton, 1961), pp. 144–7; Melvin Small, *Democracy and Diplomacy: The Impact of Domestic Politics on U.S. Foreign Policy, 1789–1994* (Baltimore, 1996), p. 2.
2. Cushing Strout, *The American Image of the Old World* (New York, 1963).
3. The classic treatment of the improvement in Anglo-American relations is Bradford Perkins, *The Great Rapprochement: England and the United States, 1895–1914* (New York, 1969). See also Walter LaFeber, *The New Empire: An Interpretation of American Expansion, 1860–1898* (Ithaca, NY, 1963), pp. 62–101, and Michael H. Hunt, *Ideology and U.S. Foreign Policy* (New Haven, CT, 1987), pp. 77–80, 133–4.
4. The conduct of the British in the war seems to have especially impressed Lodge. 'Nothing could be finer,' he wrote in 1915, 'than the way in which the aristocracy of England has sacrificed itself nor the way in which the workingmen of England have gone to the front.' William C. Widenor, *Henry Cabot Lodge and the Search for an American Foreign Policy* (Berkeley, CA, 1980), p. 218.
5. Dennis J. McCarthy, 'The British,' in Joseph P. O'Grady (ed.), *The Immigrants' Influence on Wilson's Peace Policies* (Lexington, KY, 1967), pp. 102–3; Selig Adler, *The Isolationist Impulse: Its Twentieth Century Reaction* (New York, 1957), p. 76.
6. Henry Seidel Canby, 'Anglomania,' *Harper's* (November 21, 1921): 713.
7. 'The Source of Anti-Britishism,' *New Republic* 52 (November 16, 1927): 325–6.
8. Samuel Lubell, *The Future of American Politics* (New York, 1948), p. 143; Manfred Jonas, *Isolationism in America, 1935–1941* (Ithaca, 1966), p. 184. B. J. C. McKercher has done an admirable job of dealing with American anglophobia in the 1920s, but his analysis remains limited to that period, and moreover focuses mainly on British diplomacy. See B. J. C. McKercher, *The Second Baldwin Government and the United States* (Cambridge, 1984), and *Esme Howard: A Diplomatic Biography* (Cambridge, 1989).
9. Lloyd E. Ambrosius, *Woodrow Wilson and the American Diplomatic Tradition: The Treaty Fight in Perspective* (Cambridge, 1987), pp. 94–6. One Democratic Senator, Thomas J. Walsh of Montana, claimed that it was this that doomed the treaty from the start; though he believed that Lodge's opposition to the League was based on 'personal antagonism to the President,' he nevertheless lamented that the Massachusetts Republican and his allies could have been won over

'unquestionably...had even a modicum of diplomacy been ob-
served.' Walsh to C. B. Nolan, September 18, 1919, Thomas J.
Walsh Papers, Box 4, American Historical Survey, University of
Illinois Library, Urbana, Illinois.

10. Widenor, *Henry Cabot Lodge*, p. 303.

11. Joseph P. O'Grady, 'The Irish,' in O'Grady, *Immigrants' Influence*, pp.
71–9; Adler, *Isolationist Impulse*, pp. 77–80; Ambrosius, *Woodrow
Wilson*, pp. 168–9; Widenor, *Henry Cabot Lodge*, p. 47; Again in this
instance Thomas J. Walsh found fault in the president's handling of
the negotiations. The Montana Democrat wrote in September 1919
that Wilson's 'treatment of the Irish question to me is inexplicable,'
since '[w]ithout the Irish in this country, the democratic party as a
fighting force would be a negligible quantity.' Walsh concluded morosely that the president had passed up 'the greatest opportunity
ever accorded to a man to achieve distinction....' Walsh to C. B.
Nolan 3 September 1919, Thomas J. Walsh Papers, Box 4,
University of Illinois Library, Urbana, Illinois.

12. Austin J. App, 'The Germans,' in O'Grady, *Immigrants' Influence*, pp.
39–40; Adler, *Isolationist Impulse*, pp. 84–6; Louis L. Gerson, *The
Hyphenate in Recent American Politics and Diplomacy* (Lawrence, KS,
1964), p. 101.

13. Ibid., p. 81. Thomas J. Knock, *To End All Wars: Woodrow Wilson and
the Quest for a New World Order* (New York, 1992), pp. 128–41, 157–60,
252–6. See also Stuart I. Rochester, *American Liberal Disillusionment in
the Wake of World War I* (University Park, PA, 1977), p. 91.

14. Widenor, *Henry Cabot Lodge*, p. 127. As Secretary of State John Hay
complained, 'Whatever we do, [Democratic candidate William
Jennings] Bryan will attack us as a slave of Great Britain. All their
state conventions put on an anti-English plank in their platforms to
curry favor with the Irish (whom they want to keep) and the
Germans whom they want to seduce. It is too disgusting to have to
deal with such sordid lies.' Small, *Democracy and Diplomacy*, p.32.

15. One prominent conservative Republican, the New York lawyer
Henry A. Wise, actually apologized to the British ambassador for the
anti-British rhetoric which he knew would be employed by his colleagues in the G.O.P. However regrettable this might be, Wise
claimed, 'it would be necessary to attack all who stood with
[Wilson]..., [even] the British Government.' Neville K. Meaney,
'The American Attitude Towards the British Empire from 1919 to
1922 – A Study in the Diplomatic Relations of the English-Speaking
Nations,' (Ph.D. diss., Duke University, 1958), p. 269.

16. H.C. Allen, *Great Britain and the United States: A History of Anglo-
American Relations, 1783–1952* (London, 1954), pp. 718–20;
O'Grady, 'The Irish,' p. 77; Strout, *American Image*, p. 168; Thomas
N. Guinsberg, *The Pursuit of Isolationism in the United States Senate from
Versailles to Pearl Harbor* (New York, 1982), pp. 30–1; Meaney,
'American Attitude,' pp. 264–8; Ambrosius, *Woodrow Wilson*, p. 90;
Richard Coke Lower, *A Bloc of One: The Political Career of Hiram W.
Johnson* (Stanford, 1993), p. 128.

17. Even this may require some qualification – Robert David Johnson has argued that the so-called 'Peace Progressives,' such as Borah, La Follette, Norris, and Asle Gronna (R-ND) were not so 'isolationist' as has been previously assumed. According to Johnson, these senators did envision a role for the United States in world affairs, but only in association with 'weaker states and peoples' and in opposition to British and French imperialism. Viewed in this way, it would appear that they objected only to Wilson's choice of associates, and not to the general principle of overseas involvement. See Johnson, *The Peace Progressives and American Foreign Relations* (Cambridge, 1995), p. 3.

18. It should also be noted that, as Thomas Guinsberg points out, fewer than one-third of the irreconcilables came from states in which Irish- or German-Americans made up more than fifteen percent of the population. Most senators from states where immigrant votes truly mattered (mainly the northeast) merely expressed reservations to the treaty – they did not seek to throw it out altogether. Guinsberg, *Pursuit of Isolationism*, p. 36.

19. In an attempt to avoid being associated with any particular party, the committee endorsed James A. Reed for the Democrats, Eugene V. Debs for the Socialists, and the anti-British newspaper mogul William Randolph Hearst as an Independent. Niel M. Johnson, *George Sylvester Viereck: German-American Propagandist* (Urbana, IL, 1972), pp. 84–5.

20. Johnson, *George Sylvester Viereck*, p. 86.

21. Howard A. DeWitt, 'The "New" Harding and American Foreign Policy: Warren G. Harding, Hiram W. Johnson, and Pragmatic Diplomacy,' *Ohio History* 86 (Spring 1977): 96–114; Benjamin D. Rhodes, 'Harding v. Cox: The "Ohio" Election of 1920 as Viewed from the British Embassy at Washington,' *Northwest Ohio Quarterly* 55 (Winter 1982–83): 17–24.

22. Viereck responded to Roosevelt's accusations with an indignant telegram in which he accused the future president of being a 'dupe of British propagandists.' It was not the last time that FDR would face this charge. Johnson, *Viereck*, p. 87.

23. John B. Huff, 'The Italians,' in O'Grady, *Immigrants' Influence*, pp. 136–7.

24. Ambrosius, *Woodrow Wilson*, p. 248.

25. Gerson, *Hyphenate*, p. 106.

CHAPTER 1 'THE MOST IMPERIALISTIC NATION ON EARTH'

1. Widenor, *Henry Cabot Lodge*, pp. 37–9.

2. Ibid., p. 304.

3. John M. Carroll, 'Henry Cabot Lodge's Contributions to the Shaping of Republican European Diplomacy, 1920–1924,' *Capitol Studies* 3 (Fall 1975): 153–65; *Congressional Record*, 67th Cong., 2d. Sess., 62 (16 March 1922): 3956.

4. 'Citizenship and Residency' Subject File, Special Collections, Hoover Library; Lower, *Bloc of One*, pp. 151–2.
5. Michael J. Hogan, *Informal Entente: The Private Structure of Cooperation in Anglo-American Economic Diplomacy, 1918–1928* (Columbia, MO, 1977).
6. Frank Costigliola, *Awkward Dominion: American Political, Economic, and Cultural Relations with Europe, 1919–1933* (Ithaca, 1984): 142.
7. Elting E. Morison, *Admiral Sims and the Modern American Navy* (Boston, 1942), pp. 482–3.
8. By the time Sims returned to Washington, the storm had blown over. Navy Secretary Edwin Denby gave him a mild reprimand for expressing an opinion on international topics while in a foreign country, and Harding never even brought up the issue when Sims paid him a visit later that same day. Morison, *Admiral Sims*, pp. 483–5; Walsh to Rev. M. J. Foley, 11 June 1921, Walsh-Erickson MSS, Box 295, Library of Congress Manuscript Collections, Washington, D.C.
9. Petition of the American Association for the Recognition of the Irish Republic [n.d., 1921], William E. Borah MSS, Box 116, Library of Congress Manuscript Division, Washington, D.C.
10. *Congressional Record*, 67th Cong., 2d Sess., 61 (26 April 1921): 646; F. M. Carroll, 'The American Committee for Relief in Ireland, 1920–22,' *Irish Historical Studies* 23 (May 1982): 30–49.
11. Ibid., pp. 40–4.
12. *Congressional Record*, 67th Cong., 2d Sess., 61 (21 June 1921): 2803; John S. Galbraith, 'The United States, Britain, and the Creation of the Irish Free State,' *South Atlantic Quarterly* 48 (October 1949): 566–74.
13. *Literary Digest*, 17 December 1921, p. 5.
14. Manoranjan Jha, 'Britain and the Pro-India Activities in the U.S.A.,' *Political Science Review* 12 (Spring 1973): 1–34.
15. *Literary Digest*, 14 January 1922, p. 12.
16. Thomas H. Buckley, *The United States and the Washington Conference, 1921–1922* (Knoxville, TN, 1970), p. 23.
17. Harold and Margaret Sprout, *Toward a New Order of Sea Power: American Naval Policy and the World Scene, 1918–1922* (Princeton, NJ, 1940), pp. 68–70, 77–85.
18. Ibid., pp. 106–7; Widenor, *Henry Cabot Lodge*, p. 143; John D. Hicks, *Republican Ascendancy, 1921–1933* (New York, 1960), p. 33.
19. John Chalmers Vinson, *The Parchment Peace: The United States Senate and the Washington Conference, 1921–1922* (Athens, GA, 1955), pp. 62, 102–3.
20. Daniel F. Cohalan to Borah, 27 January 1921, Borah to Cohalan, 29 January 1921, Borah MSS, Box 206; Robert James Maddox, *William E. Borah and American Foreign Policy* (Baton Rouge, 1969), p. 88; LeRoy Ashby, *The Spearless Leader: Senator Borah and the Progressive Movement in the 1920s* (Urbana, IL, 1972), pp. 105–6; Robert Maddox, 'Borah and the Battleships,' *Idaho Yesterdays* 9 (Summer 1965): 20–27.

21. D. Cameron Watt, *Succeeding John Bull: America in Britain's Place, 1900–1975* (Cambridge, 1984), p. 42; Costigliola, *Awkward Dominion*, p. 83.

22. Ibid., Vinson, *Parchment Peace*, p. 90; *Congressional Record*, 67th Cong., 1st Sess., 61 (25 May 1921): 1757.

23. Memorandum of Conversation between Hughes and Geddes, 23 June 1921, *Foreign Relations of the United States*, 1921, v.2, pp. 314–16.

24. Sprout, *Toward a New Order*, p. 129; Ambassador George Harvey to Hughes, 8 July 1921, *FRUS*, 1921, v.1, p. 20.

25. One of the principal architects of the Four Power Pact on the American side, Elihu Root, favored the consultative agreement because he believed it would force Great Britain to seek American support for any action the Foreign Office should wish to pursue in Asia. This insistence on safeguards against possible British aggression shows that even many of those who, like Root, considered themselves pro-British did not completely trust the diplomats of Whitehall. See Watt, *Succeeding John Bull*, pp. 44–5.

26. Borah to Jordan, 27 October 1921, Borah MSS, Box 202.

27. Resolution of Friends of Irish Freedom, 5 December 1921, Borah MSS, Box 110; *Congressional Record*, 67th Cong., 2d Sess., (13 March 1922): 3779; ibid., 62 (14 March 1922): 3851; ibid., (16 March 1922): 3945; ibid., (22 March 1922): 4228, 4256; ibid., (23 March 1922): 4339; Borah to White, 4 January 1922, Borah MSS, Box 112.

28. *Congressional Record*, 67th Cong., 2d Sess., 62 (16 March 1922): 3945.

29. *Congressional Record*, 67th Cong., 1st Sess., 61 (28 June 1921): 3153; ibid., 67th Cong., 2d Sess., 62 (17 March 1922): 4016; ibid., (22 March 1922): 4234; Statement by La Follette, 21 October 1921, La Follette MSS, Box B183, Library of Congress Manuscript Division, Washington, D.C.

30. George L. Grassmuck, *Sectional Biases in Congress on Foreign Policy* (Johns Hopkins University Studies in Historical and Political Science, Series LXVIII, No. 3, 1951), p. 62.

31. 'The British Empire at the Conference,' *New Republic* 29 (7 December 1921): 44–6; Costigliola, *Awkward Dominion*, p. 86; Grassmuck, *Sectional Biases*, p. 67; Buckley, *U.S. and the Washington Conference*, pp. 183–4; La Follette, who was also on record as being opposed to the treaties, was absent on the day of the final vote.

32. Johnson to sons, 26 March 1922, in Robert E. Burke (ed.), *The Diary Letters of Hiram Johnson* (New York, 1983), vol.4.

33. James Harold Mannock, 'Anglo-American Relations, 1921–1928,' (Ph.D. diss., Princeton University, 1962) p. 122; Melvyn Leffler, 'The Origins of Republican War Debt Policy, 1921–1923: A Case Study in the Applicability of the Open Door Interpretation.' *Journal of American History* 59 (December 1972): 585–601; *Literary Digest*, 19 February 1921.

34. Hicks, *Republican Ascendancy*, pp. 137–9.

35. Costigliola, *Awkward Dominion*, p. 81; Mannock, 'Anglo-American Relations,' p. 136.

36. Hicks, *Republican Ascendancy*. Ironically, Britain's most formidable

opponent on the Debt Commission was none other than Herbert Hoover, whom Geddes believed was 'not only anti-British but also anti-European.' While Hoover was in favor of considering each individual settlement on a capacity-to-pay basis, he was determined that England not get off as easily as many others. So eager was Hoover to avoid being viewed as pro-British that he canceled a planned address before the American Bankers' Association after several of its leading members advocated cancelation. See Roberta Allbert Dayer, 'The British War Debts to the United States and the Anglo-Japanese Alliance, 1920–1923,' *Pacific Historical Review* 45 (November 1976): 569–95, and Benjamin D. Rhodes, 'Herbert Hoover and the War Debts, 1919–1933,' *Prologue* 6 (Summer 1974): 130–44.

37.   Lower, *Bloc of One*, pp. 176–7; Robert Dean Pope, 'Senatorial Baron: The Long Political Career of Kenneth D. McKellar' (Ph.D. diss., Yale University, 1976), pp. 194–5; *Congressional Record*, 67th Cong., 4th Sess., 64 (1, 16 February 1923): 2825–30, 3759; Ralph M. Tanner, 'James Thomas Heflin: United States Senator, 1920–1931' (Ph.D. diss., University of Alabama, 1967), pp. 103–4. See also William George Pullen, 'World War Debts and United States Foreign Policy' (Ph.D. diss., Harvard University, 1972).

38.   *Congressional Record*, 67th Cong., 4th Sess., 64 (29 January 1923): 2669.

39.   Ibid., Pope, 'Senatorial Baron,' pp. 194–5; *New York Times*, 2 February 1923; Pullen, 'World War Debts,' pp. 95–7; *Congressional Record*, 67th Cong., 4th Sess., 64 (15, 16 February 1923): 3671, 3742; Johnson, *Peace Progressives*, pp. 158–60.

40.   *New York Times*, 14 April 1921; *Congressional Record*, 67th Cong., 2d Sess., 62 (9 August 1922): 11593–6; Lawrence Spinelli, *Dry Diplomacy: The United States, Great Britain and Prohibition* (Wilmington, DE, 1989), pp. 18–19.

41.   Ibid., pp. 7–8; H. G. Chilton to Hughes, 10 July 1923, Hughes to Chilton, 16 July 1923, *FRUS*, 1923, v.1, pp. 163–70.

42.   Spinelli, *Dry Diplomacy*, pp. 18–19.

43.   Hughes to Post Wheeler, 25 August 1923, Chilton to Hughes, 17 September 1923, *FRUS*, 1923, v.1, pp. 172–79, 188–91; Spinelli, *Dry Diplomacy*, pp. 31, 81. Typical of the opposition's arguments was the charge, made by Henry St. George Tucker (D-VA) that the treaty would allow 'John Bull' to get away with violating the Volstead Act, while some 'North Carolina mountaineer' would go to jail for carrying 'a half pint of moonshine,...sealed it may be.' *Congressional Record*, 68th Cong., 1st Sess., 65 (19 April 1924): 6723.

44.   *Congressional Record*, 67th Cong., 1st Sess., 61 (6 June, 1 August 1921): 2156, 4511; Alan Edmond Kent, 'Portrait in Isolationism: The La Follettes and Foreign Policy' (Ph.D. diss., University of Wisconsin, 1956), p. 70.

45.   Spinelli, *Dry Diplomacy*, pp. 35–6; *Congressional Record*, 67th Cong., 4th Sess., 64 (12 December 1922): 282; ibid., (23 February 1923): 4347.

46.   Norris to S. K. Warrick, 26 February 1923, Norris MSS, Box 41;

Congressional Record, 67th Cong., 4th Sess., 64 (15 December 1922): 417; Spinelli, *Dry Diplomacy*, p. 46; Those who had supported the measure blamed its defeat on British propaganda in the American press. Sen. Joseph E. Ransdell (D-Louisiana) claimed that 'British capital controls the policy of many great American journals.' In April the National Merchant Marine Association (of which Ransdell was president) issued a press release showing how English newspapers had rejoiced upon hearing news of the subsidy's defeat. *Congressional Record*, 67th Cong., 4th Sess., 64 (18 December 1922): 603–5; Press Release of National Merchant Marine Association, 2 April 1923, Borah MSS, Box 144.

47. B. J. C. McKercher, *The Second Baldwin Government and the United States, 1924–1929: Attitudes and Diplomacy* (Cambridge, 1984), pp. 50–1; Benjamin D. Rhodes, 'British Diplomacy and the Silent Oracle of Vermont, 1923–1929,' *Vermont History* 50 (Spring 1982): 69–79.

48. *Literary Digest*, 17 November 1923; 'Does Cooperation with Britain Mean Intervention?' *New Republic* 35 (14 November 1923): 296–8; A. G. Gardiner, 'England and America: Their Misunderstandings and Their Opportunity,' *Harper's* 149 (July 1924): 145–52.

49. H. C. Allen, *Great Britain and the United States: A History of Anglo-American Relations, 1783–1952* (London, 1954), pp. 138–9.

50. John Lukacs, *Outgrowing Democracy* (New York, 1984), p. 228; David Allen Richards, 'The Abortive Entente: The American Popular Mind and the Idea of Anglo-American Cooperation to Keep the Peace, 1921–1931.' Ph.D. diss., Florida State University, 1976), pp. 136–40; *Literary Digest*, 9 June 1923; 'American Language,' *Collier's* (23 January 1926): 20.

51. 'Language by Legislation,' *Nation* 116 (11 April 1923): 408. The *Nation*'s editors mocked this idea, suggesting that Congress 'set up that Academy of the American Language that the Honorable McCormick has doped out. Make Mencken president of the outfit, put George Ade, Ring Lardner, Warren Harding, and Billy Sunday on the executive committee, and tell them to go to it.'

52. Warren I. Cohen, *The American Revisionists: The Lessons of Intervention in World War I* (Chicago, 1967), pp. 33–4.

53. Selig Adler, 'War-Guilt and American Disillusionment,' *Journal of Modern History* 23 (March 1951): 14–15. *Congressional Record*, 68th Cong., 1st Sess., 65 (18 December 1923): 355–97; ibid., (25 February 1924): 3064.

54. Hiram Johnson to Archibald Johnson, 28 April 1922, in Burke (ed.), *Diary Letters*, v.4.

55. Richards, 'The Abortive Entente,' pp. 89–92; McSweeney to Borah, 11 April 1922, Borah MSS, Box 110; *Literary Digest*, 31 December 1921.

56. Richards, 'Abortive Entente,' pp. 86–8, 92; Hicks, *Ascendancy*, p. 183.

CHAPTER 2 'THE ENGLISH NAVY HAS GONE MAD'

1. Mannock, 'Anglo-American Relations,' pp. 45–6; B. J. C. McKercher, *Esme Howard: A Diplomatic Biography* (Cambridge, 1989), pp. 288–90.
2. La Vern J. Rippley, *The German-Americans* (Boston, 1976), pp. 192–3.
3. B. J. C. McKercher, *The Second Baldwin Government and the United States, 1924–1929: Attitudes and diplomacy* (Cambridge, 1984), pp. 43–4, 52–3.
4. 'Borah Twists the Lion's Tail,' *Literary Digest* 89 (10 April 1926), p. 13; R. Douglas Hurt, 'The Settlement of Anglo-American Claims Resulting from World War I,' *American Neptune* 34 (July 1974): 155–73; *Congressional Record*, 69th Cong., 1st Sess., 67 (15 June 1926), p. 11267.
5. Houghton to Kellogg, 3 November 1925, *FRUS*, 1926, v.2, pp. 214–15; Howard to Kellogg, 16 March 1926, *FRUS*, 1926, v.2, pp. 220–1; Spencer Phenix to Kellogg, 9 November 1926, *FRUS*, 1926, v.2, pp. 250–87; Hurt, 'Settlement of Anglo-American Claims,' pp. 167–8; 'Those Neutral Rights,' *Nation* 124 (15 June 1927), p. 659.
6. Michael J. Hogan, *Informal Entente: The Private Structure of Cooperation in Anglo-American Economic Diplomacy, 1918–1928* (Columbia, MO, 1977), pp. 192–3; *Congressional Record*, 67th Cong., 4th Sess., 64 (9 January 1923): 1450.
7. Frank Robert Chalk, 'The United States and the International Struggle for Rubber, 1914–1941' (Ph.D. diss., University of Wisconsin, 1970), p. 48; *Congressional Record*, 67th Cong., 4th Sess., 64 (18 December 1922, 24 February 1923): 605, 4521.
8. Ibid., 69th Cong., 1st Sess., 67 (19, 21 December 1925): 1106, 1267, 1270.
9. Chalk, 'Struggle for Rubber,' p. 108.
10. Ludwell Denny, *America Conquers Britain* (New York, 1930), p. 206; Richards, 'The Abortive Entente,' pp. 204–7; Chalk, 'Struggle for Rubber,' p. 109; *Congressional Record*, 69th Cong., 1st Sess., 67 (15 March 1926): 3766.
11. Ibid., 67 (6,7 January 1926): 1603–5, 1644; Chalk, 'Struggle for Rubber,' p. 110. The argument that tire manufacturers were using the Stevenson Plan as an excuse to raise prices was a gross misrepresentation – according to Joseph Brandes, the profit rates of the five leading rubber manufacturers in America were below ten percent; in 1926 Firestone's profit rate, the highest in the country, was only 5.3 percent. Joseph Brandes, *Herbert Hoover and Economic Diplomacy: Department of Commerce Policy, 1921–1928* (Pittsburgh, PA, 1962), pp. 125–6.
12. Thomas Herbert Bernhard Dressler, 'The Foreign Policies of American Individualism: Herbert Hoover, Reluctant Internationalist' (Ph.D. diss., Brown University, 1973), p. 70; 'Reefing in Rubber,' *Saturday Evening Post* (5 June 1926): 150; 'End of British Rubber Control,' *Literary Digest* 96 (21 April 1928): 10.
13. Gerald E. Wheeler, *Prelude to Pearl Harbor: The United States Navy and the Far East, 1921–1931* (Columbia, MO), p. 131; Mannock, 'Anglo-

American Relations,' pp. 54–6.

14. *Congressional Record*, 68th Cong., 2d Sess., 66 (7 December 1924, January 16, 1925): 133, 1963; *Washington Post*, 7 December 1924.

15. *Congressional Record*, 69th Cong., 2d Sess., 68 (5 January 1927): 1125; Johnson to Hiram Johnson, Jr., 11 February 1927, in Burke (ed.), *Diary Letters*, v.4.

16. Clipping from *Scientific American*, Borah MSS, Box 256; Armin Rappaport, *The Navy League of the United States* (Detroit, 1962), pp. 89–90. The position of some naval officers was summed up in a speech given in late February 1925 by Rear Admiral William W. Phelps, a member of the United States Navy General Board, in which he asserted that the 'possibility of serious differences between Great Britain regarding shipping policies could only be prevented by a strong United States Navy.' This statement by a high-ranking officer caused considerable embarrassment for the State Department, which quickly released a statement 'that no serious problem has arisen in Anglo-American relations and...that existing problems do not threaten serious complications.' McKercher, *Esme Howard*, pp. 288–90.

17. The British ambassador, Sir Esme Howard, identified Simonds as 'the most able and insidious worker for the Big Navy cause.' McKercher, *Second Baldwin Government*, pp. 86–7; McKercher, *Esme Howard*, p. 337.

18. George Sylvester Viereck, 'Shall Uncle Sam Commit National Suicide?' *American Monthly* (January 1925), p. 341.

19. *New York Times*, 25 December 1926; Mannock, 'Anglo-American Relations,' p. 245; McKercher, *Second Baldwin Government*, p. 60.

20. Hicks, *Republican Ascendancy*, pp. 146–7; Donald R. McCoy, *Calvin Coolidge: The Quiet President* (New York, 1967), p. 363; McKercher, *Second Baldwin Government*, pp. 55–6; Costigliola, *Awkward Dominion*, p. 188.

21. Raymond G. O'Connor, *Perilous Equilibrium: The United States and the London Naval Conference of 1930* (Lawrence, KS, 1962), p. 13; Richards, 'Abortive Entente,' pp. 164–5; Hugh Fullerton, 'The Coming Naval Disarmament Conference and What We Won't Get Out of It,' *Liberty* (30 April 1927), p. 39.

22. *Congressional Record*, 69th Cong., 2d Sess., 68 (21 January 1927): 2060; Hiram Johnson to Hiram Johnson, Jr., 11 February 1927, in Burke (ed), *Diary Letters*, v.4; *Congressional Record*, 69th Cong., 2d Sess., 68 (28 January 1927): 2430.

23. Mannock, 'Anglo-American Relations,' p. 245; McKercher, *Second Baldwin Government*, p. 56.

24. Norman Gibbs, 'The Naval Conferences of the Interwar Years: A Study in Anglo-American Relations,' *Naval War College Review* 30 (Summer 1977): 50–63; Robert William Dubay, 'The Geneva Naval Conference of 1927: A Study of Battleship Diplomacy,' *Southern Quarterly* 8 (January 1970): 177–99; David Carlton, 'Great Britain and the Coolidge Naval Disarmament Conference of 1927,' *Political Science Quarterly* 83 (December 1968): 373–98; Ernest R. Andrade,

'The Cruiser Controversy in Naval Limitations Negotiations, 1922-1936,' *Military Affairs* 48 (July 1984): 113–20; Kellogg to Gibson, 19 July 1927, *FRUS*, 1927, v.1, pp. 116–17; Kellogg to Coolidge, 22 July 1927, ibid., pp. 124–7.

25.   This argument is best detailed in Christina Newton's 'Anglo-American Relations and Bureaucratic Tensions, 1927–1930' (Ph.D. diss., University of Illinois, 1975), but may be found in many standard works of the period, including Hicks, *Republican Ascendancy*, p. 148.

26.   Carlton, 'Great Britain and the Coolidge Naval Disarmament Conference,' p. 576; Dubay, 'Geneva Naval Conference of 1927,' p. 198. The Geneva correspondent of the *New York Times*, Wythe Williams, later claimed to have been reminded by his editor that he was reporting a disarmament conference and not a battlefield. Watt, *Succeeding John Bull*, pp. 58–9.

27.   Gibbs, 'Naval Conferences of the Interwar Years,' p. 53.

28.   Kellogg to Coolidge, 22 July 1927, *FRUS*, v.1, pp. 124–7; Kellogg to Coolidge, 10 August 1927, ibid., pp. 157–9.

29.   *Literary Digest* 94 (20 August 1927): 8–9; ibid., 97 (7 April 1928): 10; *The Independent* 119 (13 August 1927): 152.

30.   Address on Effects of the Geneva Naval Conference, 1927, Thomas J. Walsh MSS, Box 5; *Congressional Record*, 70th Cong., 2d Sess., 70 (15 December 1928): 755; 'The Menace of Anglo-American Naval Rivalry,' *Literary Digest* 100 (5 January 1929): 5–7.

31.   Mannock, 'Anglo-American Relations,' pp. 284–5; Wheeler, *Prelude to Pearl Harbor*, pp. 150–2; Christopher Hall, *Britain, America and Arms Control, 1921–37* (London, 1987), p. 54.

32.   Ibid., Lower, *A Bloc of One*, pp. 197–8.

33.   McKercher, *Esme Howard*, p. 331; Hall, *Britain, America, and Arms Control*, pp. 57–8; Rappaport, *Navy League of the United States*, p. 120.

34.   Though some leaders of the peace movement criticized Coolidge for this navalist stance, others defended him. Salmon Levinson, for instance, told the president's detractors that 'they had better direct their fight against the British Tories that [*sic*] had irritated and insulted the President and thwarted all his moves for limitation of naval armaments, rather than fight the man who was our greatest power in securing the consummation of the [Kellogg-Briand] peace treaty.' McCoy, *Calvin Coolidge*, pp. 375–7.

35.   Wheeler, *Prelude to Pearl Harbor*, pp. 154–5; Mannock, 'Anglo-American Relations,' pp. 290–1; Houghton to Kellogg, 12 September 1928, *FRUS*, 1928, v.1, pp. 278–9; Newton, 'Anglo-American Relations and Bureaucratic Tensions,' pp. 154–5.

36.   Wheeler, *Prelude to Pearl Harbor*, p. 155; *Congressional Record*, 70th Cong., 2d Sess., 70 (16 January 1929), p. 1758.

37.   'War with Britain not "Unthinkable",' *Literary Digest* 100 (9 February 1929): 5–7; Hall, *Britain, America and Arms Control*, p. 54; William R. Braisted, 'On the American Red and Red-Orange Plans, 1919–1939,' in Gerald Jordan (ed.), *Naval Warfare in the Twentieth Century, 1900–1945: Essays in honour of Arthur Marder* (London,

1977), pp. 167–85; *Congressional Record*, 70th Cong., 2d Sess., 70 (2 February 1929): 2692; ibid., (30 January 1929): 2464.

38. 'Admiral Plunkett's War with England,' *Literary Digest* 96 (11 February 1928): 7–9; *Congressional Record*, 70th Cong., 2d Sess., 70 (21 February 1929): 3980; Ludwell Denny, *America Conquers Britain: A Record of Economic War* (London, 1930), p. 407; See also David A. Richards, 'America Conquers Britain: Anglo-American Conflict in the Popular Media During the 1920s,' *Journal of American Culture* 3 (Spring 1980): 95–103.

39. Clipping by Frank Simonds, 'Freedom of Seas Seen as Real Naval Issue,' 1928, Box 794, Borah MSS; Borchard to Borah, 29 November 1927, ibid.; William E. Borah, 'Freedom of the Seas,' *Current History* 29 (March 1929): 922–7; *Congressional Record*, 70th Cong., 2d Sess., 70 (12 December 1928): 482; ibid., (24 January 1929): 2179–85; ibid., (28 January 1929): 2337; ibid., (5 February 1929): 2838.

40. John Chalmers Vinson, *William E. Borah and the Outlawry of War* (Athens, GA, 1957), pp. 151–2; Houghton to Kellogg, 25 May 1928, *FRUS*, v.1, pp. 72–4; *Congressional Record*, 70th Cong., 2d Sess., 70 (7 January 1929): 1282; Borah to Salmon O. Levinson, 2 August 1928, Box 290, Borah Papers, Library of Congress Manuscript Division, Washington, D.C.; Johnson to Archibald Johnson, 2 January 1928, in Burke (ed.) *Diary Letters*, v.4.

41. *Congressional Record*, 70th Cong., 2d Sess., 70 (7 January 1929): 1282; Ibid., (9 January 1929): 1406; Press Release, 3 January 1929, Box 61, John J. Blaine MSS, Wisconsin State Historical Society, Madison, WI; Guinsberg, *Pursuit of Isolationism*, p. 124; Johnson, *Peace Progressives*, pp. 178–9.

42. Hogan, *Informal Entente*, p. 219.

43. Wheeler, *Prelude to Pearl Harbor*, pp. 122–9; Rappaport, *Navy League*, pp. 113–14; McKercher, *Esme Howard*, p. 290.

44. Frank Simonds, *The ABC's of War Debts, and the Seven Popular Delusions About Them* (New York, 1933); William Howard Gardiner, 'Naval Parity? The Outlook after Geneva,' *Harper's* 156 (January 1928): 211–19; *Congressional Record*, 70th Cong., 2d Sess., 70 (16 January 1929): 1758; Frank Simonds, *Can America Stay at Home?* (New York, 1932).

45. Richards, 'Abortive Entente,' pp. 92–114; Frederick Bausman, 'Under Which Flag?' *American Mercury* 12 (October 1927): 195–203.

46. Richards, 'Abortive Entente,' pp. 92–114; Lloyd Wendt and Herman Kogan, *Big Bill of Chicago* (Indianapolis, 1953), pp. 248–61; Paul M. Green and Melvin G. Holli, 'Big Bill Thompson: The "Model" Politician,' in Green and Holli (eds.), *The Mayors: The Chicago Political Tradition* (Carbondale, IL, 1987), pp. 61–81.

47. Wendt and Kogan, *Big Bill of Chicago*, p. 285; Holli, 'Big Bill Thompson,' p. 78.

48. Benjamin D. Rhodes, 'Anglophobia in Chicago: Mayor William Hale Thompson's 1927 Campaign Against King George V,' *Illinois Quarterly* 39 (Summer 1977): 5–14; Wendt and Kogan, *Big Bill of*

Chicago, pp. 286–8, 295–302.

49. Rhodes, 'Anglophobia in Chicago,' pp. 9–10; Wendt and Kogan, *Big Bill of Chicago*, pp. 289–91; William Hale Thompson, 'Patriots and Propagandists,' *Forum* 79 (April 1928): 503–15.
50. 'Beware the Flag Flappers,' *Collier's* (26 November 1927): 50; Thomas A. Bailey, *The Man in the Street: The Impact of Public Opinion on Foreign Policy* (New York, 1948), pp. 22–3; Joseph Gies, *The Colonel of Chicago* (New York, 1979), pp. 115–16; 'King George Defied by "Big Bill"', *Literary Digest* 95 (5 November 1927): 5–8.
51. Garet Garrett, 'A Primer of Propaganda,' *Saturday Evening Post* (15 January 1927): 4; Holli, 'Big Bill Thompson,' p. 61.
52. Richards, 'Abortive Entente,' p. 172; Blaine to Gustav Haas, 19 September 1928, Blaine MSS, Box 61; Patrick G. O'Brien, 'Senator John J. Blaine: An Independent Progressive During "Normalcy",' *Wisconsin Magazine of History* 60 (Autumn 1976): 25–41; Assorted clippings, Special Collections, Herbert Hoover Presidential Library, West Branch, IA.
53. Edmond D. Coblenz (ed.), *William Randolph Hearst: A Portrait in His Own Words* (New York, 1952), p. 92; Jerome E. Edwards, *The Foreign Policy of Col. McCormick's Tribune, 1929–1941* (Reno, NV, 1971), pp. 74–5.

CHAPTER 3 'AN ALIEN ADMINISTRATION'

1. Dressler, 'Foreign Policies,' p. 13; Newton, 'Anglo-American Relations,' p. 165; Costigliola, *Awkward Dominion*, p. 144.
2. McKercher, *Second Baldwin Government*, pp. 193–4; Newton, 'Anglo-American Relations,' p. 165.
3. *New York Times*, 9 September 1929; Hall, *Britain, America and Arms Control*, pp. 75–6.
4. *New York Times*, 11 September 1929; Hall, *Britain, America and Arms Control*, pp. 75–6.
5. Ibid.
6. Dawes to Stimson, 16 September 1929, *FRUS*, 1929, v.1, pp. 232–4; Hoover to Stimson, 17 September 1929, ibid., pp. 240–3.
7. MacDonald to Dawes, 24 September 1929, ibid., pp. 253–6; 'England and America,' *New Republic* 60 (9 October 1929): 186–8.
8. Newton, 'Anglo-American Relations,' pp. 211–14; David Dimbleby and David Reynolds, *An Ocean Apart: The Relationship between Britain and America in the Twentieth Century* (New York, 1988), p. 91; *New York Times*, 13 October 1929. Even some of the old irreconcilables were enthusiastic in their praise for MacDonald. George Norris, for example, interpreted the Labour politician's rise to power as a repudiation of Versailles and of Britain's 'unjust and indefensible treatment of Russia.' According to Robert David Johnson, this is evidence that England, unlike France, was redeemable in the eyes of the 'peace progressives,' as long as it was governed by Labourites committed to a program of social reform at home and decoloniza-

tion abroad. This is a theme which would be taken up by the mainstream of American liberalism in the months preceding U.S. entry into World War II. Johnson, *Peace Progressives*, pp. 154–5.

9. Costigliola, *Awkward Dominion*, p. 228.

10. Raymond G. O'Connor, 'The "Yardstick" and Naval Disarmament in the 1920s.' *Mississippi Valley Historical Review* 45 (December 1958): 441–63; Costigliola, *Awkward Dominion*, p. 228.

11. O'Connor, *Perilous Equilibrium*; Hicks, *Republican Ascendancy*, pp. 242–3; Robert H. Ferrell, *American Diplomacy in the Great Depression: Hoover-Stimson Foreign Policy, 1929–1933* (New Haven, 1957), pp. 102–3; Stimson to Acting Secretary of State Cotton, 23 February 1930, *FRUS*, 1930, v.1, pp. 28–9.

12. *Chicago Tribune*, 20 December 1929, 10 February 1930; Edwards, *Col. McCormick's Tribune*, p. 53; Stimson to Dawes, 20 May 1930, *FRUS*, 1930, v.1, p. 126; Johnson to C. K. McClatchy, in Burke (ed.), *Diary Letters*, v.5; *Congressional Record*, 71st Cong., 2d Sess., 72 (15 February 1930): 3712; ibid., (28 February 1930): 4454; Resolution by the American Association for the Recognition of the Irish Republic, 13 July 1930, Kenneth D. McKellar MSS, Memphis Public Library, Memphis, TN.

13. McKercher, *Esme Howard*, p. 347; Wheeler, *Prelude to Pearl Harbor*, pp. 178–9; Borah to John Maher, 19 May 1930, Box 310, Borah MSS; McKellar to H. A. Strong, 18 July 1930, Box 198, McKellar MSS.

14. *Congressional Record*, 71st Cong., Special Session, 73 (10 July 1930): 69; ibid., (16 July 1930): 184; ibid., (18 July 1930): 243; ibid., (15 July 1930): 167; ibid., (11 July 1930): 102; (18 July 1930): 302.

15. Ibid., (10 July 1930): 76; ibid., (16 July 1930): 184; ibid., (16 July 1930): 197; ibid., (17 July 1930): 214; Press statement by Blaine, Box 63, Blaine MSS.

16. Johnson to sons, 21 July 1930, in Burke (ed.), *Diary Letters*, v.5; McKellar to John A. Chambliss, 24 September 1930, Box 207, McKellar MSS.

17. *Congressional Record*, 72d Cong., 1st Sess., 75 (6 May 1932): 9467; ibid., (2 May 1932): 9364.

18. Ibid., (6 May 1932): 9708; Mellon to Stimson, 25 October 1932, *FRUS*, 1932, v.1, pp. 536–9.

19. Cohen, *American Revisionists*, pp. 92–4; C. Hartley Grattan, *Why We Fought* (New York, 1929), p. 71; H. L. Mencken, 'Editorial,' *American Mercury* 8 (June 1926): 155–7; 'The British-American Alliance,' *Nation* 124 (30 March 1927): 332.

20. Watt, *Succeeding John Bull*, p. 73; Dimbleby and Reynolds, *An Ocean Apart*, p. 103. The Depression, indeed, strengthened American desire to have nothing whatever to do with the rest of the world and concentrate on domestic recovery. Congressmen George Holden Tinkham (R-MA) and Adolph Sabath (D-IL), for example, suggested that the U.S. refuse to attend any more international conferences in the name of economy in government; as they pointed out, American participation in such conferences had cost the taxpayers a

total of $4 574 986 since 1918. *Congressional Record*, 72d Cong., 1st Sess., 75 (2 June 1932): 11868.

21. Armin Rappaport, *Henry L. Stimson and Japan* (Chicago, 1963); Ferrell, *Great Depression*, pp. 157–9; Christopher Thorne, *The Limits of Foreign Policy: The West, The League and the Far Eastern Crisis of 1931–1933* (New York, 1972).

22. Michael Holcomb, 'Sir John Simon's War with Henry L. Stimson: A Footnote to Anglo-American Relations in the 1930s,' in Clifford L. Egan and Alexander W. Knott (eds.), *Essays in Twentieth Century American Diplomatic History Dedicated to Professor Daniel M. Smith* (Washington, D.C., 1982), pp. 90–110; Memorandum by Stimson, 25 February 1932, *FRUS*, 1932, v.2, pp. 440–1; Prentiss B. Gilbert to Stimson, 29 October 1932, ibid., v.4, pp. 317–22.

23. Ferrell, *Great Depression*, pp. 159–60. Indeed, when the Senate was considering Roosevelt's nomination of Stimson as Secretary of War in 1940, the former Secretary of State came under intense fire from many anti-interventionists for having called for Anglo-Amercian co-operation in 1932. *Congressional Record*, 76th Cong., 3rd Sess., 86 (9 July 1940): 8955.

24. Hiram Johnson to Hiram Johnson, Jr., 13 February 1932, in Burke (ed.), *Diary Letters*, v.5; Holcomb, 'Sir John Simon's War,' p. 92.

25. Dressler, 'Foreign Policies,' pp. 156–7; Atherton to Stimson, 18 June 1931, *FRUS*, 1931, v.1, pp. 24–6.

26. Memorandum of Trans-Atlantic Telephone Conversation between MacDonald and Stimson,19 June 1931, ibid., pp. 29–30; Stimson to Edge, 20 June 1931, ibid., pp. 33–5; Edge to Stimson, 17 December 1931, ibid., pp. 246–7. Many senators, even though they supported the moratorium, expressed reservations about it. Nebraska progressive George Norris voiced his suspicions that 'the suggestion is not President Hoover's but Great Britain's,' while both of Wisconsin's senators, Robert La Follette, Jr., and John J. Blaine, expressed their fears that the moratorium might be viewed 'as an entering wedge for debt cancellation.' Norris to John A. Simpson, 30 June 1931, Box 34, Norris MSS; La Follette to Hoover, 24 June 1931, Box C9, La Follette Family MSS; Press Release, Box 63, Blaine MSS.

27. *Chicago Tribune*, December 20, 1931; Edwards, *Col. McCormick's Tribune*, p. 67; *Congressional Record*, 72d Cong., 1st Sess., 75 (22 December 1931): 1104, 1113; Memorandum by Stimson of Conversation with Lindsay, 24 December 1931, *FRUS*, 1931, v.1, pp. 249–50.

28. Benjamin D. Rhodes, 'British Diplomacy and the Congressional Circus, 1929–1939,' *South Atlantic Quarterly* 82 (Summer 1983): 300–13.

29. Memoranda of Press Conferences, 10 August 1931, and 20 April 1932, William R. Castle Papers, Herbert Hoover Presidential Library, West Branch, IA; Castle to Mellon, 30 April 1932, *FRUS*, 1932, v.1, p. 624; *Congressional Record*, 72d Cong., 1st Sess., 75 (17 March 1932): 6291; Costigliola, *Awkward Dominion*, p. 253. A disgusted Lindsay complained that 'Congress has given an exhibition of

irresponsibility, buffoonery and ineptitude that could hardly be paralleled in the Haitian legislature.' Rhodes, 'British Diplomacy,' pp. 304–5.

30. *Congressional Record*, 72d Cong., 1st Sess., 75 (19 April 1932): 8490; *Chicago Tribune*, 27 November 1932; Stimson to Lindsay, 7 December 1932, *FRUS*, 1932, v.1, pp. 771–5; Costigliola, *Awkward Dominion*, p. 253.

31. John Thomas Anderson, 'Senator Burton K. Wheeler and United States Foreign Relations,' Ph.D. diss., University of Virginia, 1982; Frederick Marks notes that during the campaign, as in the early days of his administration, Roosevelt went out of his way to emphasize his desire to stay out of the affairs of Europe. See Frederick W. Marks III, 'Franklin Roosevelt's Diplomatic Debut: The Myth of the Hundred Days,' *South Atlantic Quarterly* 84 (Summer 1985): 245–63.

32. Press Statement by Henry J. Allen, Director of Publicity, Republican National Committee, 3 October 1932, Special Collections, Herbert Hoover Presidential Library, West Branch, IA; John Hamill, *The Strange Career of Mr. Hoover Under Two Flags* (New York, 1931); Raymond Moley, *After Seven Years* (New York, 1939), p. 71; Benjamin D. Rhodes, 'Sir Ronald Lindsay and the British View from Washington, 1930–1939,' in Egan and Knott, *Essays in Twentieth Century American Diplomatic History*, pp. 62–89.

33. Benjamin D. Rhodes, 'The Election of 1932 as Viewed from the British Embassy at Washington,' *Presidential Studies Quarterly* 13 (Summer 1983): 453–7.

34. *Congressional Record*, 72d Cong., 2d Sess., 76 (3 February 1933): 3337; ibid., (22 February 1933): 4762.

CHAPTER 4 'TAIL TO THE BRITISH KITE'

1. Castle address to Women's National Republican Club, 21 January 1933, Castle MSS.

2. Frederick W. Marks III, *Wind Over Sand: The Diplomacy of Franklin Roosevelt* (Athens, GA, 1988), pp. 127–8; J. M. Blum quoted in James R. Leutze, *Bargaining for Supremacy: Anglo-American Naval Cooperation, 1937–1941* (Chapel Hill, NC, 1977), pp. 4–6; David Reynolds, *The Creation of the Anglo-American Alliance, 1937–1941: A Study in Competitive Co-operation* (London, 1981), pp. 23–5; Robert Dallek, *Franklin D. Roosevelt and American Foreign Policy* (Oxford, 1979), p. 152.

3. Rhodes, 'Sir Ronald Lindsay,' p. 71; Johnson, *Peace Progressives*, pp. 247–8; Hiram Johnson to Archibald Johnson, 21 January 1933, in Burke (ed.), *Diary Letters*, v.5. At least part of the motive behind Roosevelt's offer to make Johnson Interior Secretary was a desire to remove the old irreconcilable from the Senate, where he was likely to cause trouble. See J. Chal Vinson, 'War Debts and Peace Legislation: The Johnson Act of 1934,' *Mid-America* 50 (July 1968): 206–22.

210 *Notes*

4. Memorandum of Conversation between Stimson and Lindsay, 11 December 1932, *FRUS*, 1932, v.1, pp. 775–8; Ferrell, *Great Depression*, p. 236; Rhodes, 'Sir Ronald Lindsay,' p. 72.
5. *Congressional Record*, 72d Cong., 2d Sess., 76 (11 February 1933): 3850; ibid., 73rd Cong., 1st Sess., 77 (13 June 1933): 5887; ibid., (1 June 1933): 4750. Apparently the suggestion of Johnson came from Raymond Moley, who wanted someone on the delegation who could be counted on to stand up to the British. Once again, Johnson refused, since he would be subordinate to the chairman of the delegation, Cordell Hull, whom Johnson considered 'an extremely weak but extremely obstinate individual, wholly internationalist.' Johnson to sons, 26 May 1933, in Burke (ed.), *Diary Letters*, v.5.
6. Memorandum by Acting Secretary of State William Phillips, 13 June 1933, *FRUS*, 1933, v.1, pp. 826–47; *Congressional Record*, 73rd Cong., 1st Sess., 77 (14 June 1933): 6000; ibid., 73rd Cong., 2d Sess., 78 (7 May 1934): 8192.
7. Vinson, 'War Debts and Peace Legislation,' p. 206; Memorandum by Hull, 5 February 1934, *FRUS*, 1934, v.1, p. 527; Lower, *Bloc of One*, pp. 272–5; Hull to Roosevelt, 12 April 1934, *FRUS*, 1934, v.1, p. 527; Memorandum by Under Secretary of State William Phillips, 11 May 1934, ibid., pp. 535–6.
8. Hull to FDR, 29 May 1935, Memorandum by Hull, 5 August 1935, *FRUS*, 1935, v.1, pp. 378–82; Vinson, 'War Debts and Peace Legislation,' pp. 220–2; Lower, *Bloc of One*, pp. 275–6.
9. Leutze, *Bargaining for Supremacy*, pp. 5–6; Robert H. Levine, *The Politics of American Naval Rearmament, 1930–1938* (New York, 1988), pp. 488–90; Hall, *Britain, America and Arms Control*, pp. 134, 144; Memorandum by Davis, 22 September 1933, *FRUS*, 1933, v.1, pp. 211–17; British Embassy to State Department, 14 September 1933, ibid., pp. 380–95; State Department to British Embassy, 22 September 1933, ibid.
10. *Congressional Record*, 73rd Cong., 2d Sess., 78 (30 January 1934): 1591–614; ibid., 74th Cong., 2d Sess., 80 (7 May 1936): 6815. Roosevelt's commitment to the navy won him praise from many pro-Navy Republicans. Fred Britten proclaimed that 'Franklin Roosevelt did more... with the scratch of a pen for the American Navy... than has been done by all the rest of them put together in the past fourteen years,' while Robert E. Wood, president of Sears and Roebuck (and later chairman of the America First Committee) wrote the president that naval rearmament was one of the greatest achievements of his administration. *Congressional Record*, 73rd Cong., 2d Sess., 78 (22 January 1934): 1104; Wood to Roosevelt, 14 October 1936, Robert E. Wood MSS, Herbert Hoover Presidential Library, West Branch, IA.
11. Dallek, *FDR and American Foreign Policy*, p. 85; Cohen, *American Revisionists*, pp. 135–6; H. C. Engelbrecht and F. C. Hanighen, *Merchants of Death* (New York, 1934).
12. Dimbleby and Reynolds, *An Ocean Apart*, p. 113; Wayne S. Cole, *Gerald P. Nye and American Foreign Relations* (Minneapolis, 1962);

Memorandum by Joseph C. Green, 20 March 1935, *FRUS*, 1935, v.1, pp. 360–6; Marks, 'Franklin Roosevelt's Diplomatic Debut,' pp. 252–3.

13. Memorandum by Joseph C. Green, 18 March 1935, *FRUS*, 1935, v.1, pp. 360–6; Lindsay to Hull, 20 March 1935, ibid.; Hull to Lindsay, 19 April 1935, ibid.; Rhodes, 'British Diplomacy,' p. 308.

14. Johnson to Hiram Johnson, Jr., 18 January 1936, in Burke (ed.), *Diary Letters* , v.6; *Congressional Record*, 74th Cong., 2d Sess., 80 (16 January 1936): 501–6; Report of the Nye Committee, Gerald P. Nye MSS.

15. Marks, 'Franklin Roosevelt's Diplomatic Debut,' p. 253; Robert A. Divine, *The Illusion of Neutrality* (Chicago, 1962), pp. 145–6.

16. Dallek, *FDR and American Foreign Policy*, p. 106.

17. Hiram Johnson to Hiram Johnson, Jr., 18 January 1936, in Burke (ed.), *Diary Letters*, v.6; Marian C. McKenna, *Borah* (Ann Arbor, MI, 1961), pp. 345–6; Divine, *Illusion of Neutrality*, pp. 147–8; Borah to Charles P. Jervey, 14 January 1936, Borah MSS, Box 468; Edwin M. Borchard to Charles Callan Tansill, 20 November 1936, Charles Callan Tansill MSS, Herbert Hoover Presidential Library, West Branch, IA; Edwin Borchard and William Potter Lage, *Neutrality for the United States* (New Haven, CT, 1937).

18. Nye to Key Pittman, 10 July 1935, Nye MSS; Johnson to Hiram Johnson, Jr., 18 January 1936, in Burke (ed.), *Diary Letters*, v.6; Lower, *Bloc of One*, pp. 311–12.

19. Bruce Russett, *Community and Contention: Britain and America in the Twentieth Century* (Cambridge, MA, 1963), p. 117; Ronald H. Bayor, *Neighbors in Conflict: The Irish, Germans, Jews, and Italians of New York City, 1929–1941* (Baltimore, 1978), pp. 79–80; David H. Bennett, *Demagogues in the Depression: American Radicals and the Union Party, 1932–1936* (New Brunswick, NJ, 1969), pp. 75–6; *Congressional Record*, 74th Cong., 2d Sess., 80 (29 January 1936): 1145.

20. Rippley, *The German-Americans*, pp. 198–201; Bayor, *Neighbors in Conflict*, p. 118.

21. James J. Martin, *American Liberalism and World Politics, 1931–1941* (New York, 1964), v.2, pp. 1032–7; *New Republic*, 17 July 1935, pp. 267–9; ibid., 26 June 1935, p. 177; *Nation*, 3 July 1935, p. 224; ibid., 29 August 1936, pp. 226–7.

22. The attitudes of upper midwesterners toward foreign affairs are examined in detail by Robert P. Wilkins in two articles, 'The Non-Ethnic Roots of North Dakota Isolationism,' *Nebraska History* 44 (September 1963): 205–21, and 'The Non-Partisan League and Upper Midwest Isolationism,' *Agricultural History* 39 (April 1965): 102–9; see also Cole, *Gerald P. Nye*, and Edward C. Blackorby, *Prairie Rebel: The Public Life of William Lemke* (Lincoln, NE, 1963).

23. Quincy Howe, *England Expects Every American to Do His Duty* (New York, 1937), pp. 48, 60; Richard Arnold Harrison, 'Appeasement and Isolation: The Relationship of British and American Foreign Policies, 1935-1938' (Ph.D. diss., Princeton University, 1974), pp. 65–6.

24.   Dallek, *Franklin D. Roosevelt*, p. 71; Johnson to Hiram Johnson, Jr., January 6, 1935, in Burke (ed.), *Diary Letters*, v.6.
25.   Harrison, 'Appeasement and Isolation,' p. 175; Bennett, *Demagogues in the Depression*, pp. 75–6; Alan Brinkley, *Voices of Protest: Huey Long, Father Coughlin and the Great Depression* (New York, 1982), pp. 151–3; Johnson to Hiram Johnson, Jr., 31 January 1935, in Burke (ed.), *Diary Letters*, v.6.
26.   Bennett, *Demagogues in the Depression*, pp. 75–6; A. F. Minisi to Borah, 14 December 1935, Box 412, Borah MSS; Divine, *Illusion of Neutrality*, pp. 150–2; Radio Address by Sweeney, 29 December 1935, Sweeney MSS, Western Reserve Historical Library, Cleveland, Ohio; Martin, *American Liberalism and World Politics*, pp. 418–20; V. K. Krishna-Menon, 'Labor Militancy Spreads in India,' *Nation* (12 September 1934): 293; T. A. Bisson, 'Britain Tightens Control in India,' *Nation* (21 August 1935): 210–212.
27.   'American Neutrality in British Eyes,' *Living Age* 350 (April 1936): 167–9; Borchard to Borah, 25 August 1935, Box 412, Borah MSS; Breckenridge Long to Hull, 17 September 1935, *FRUS*, 1935, v.1, pp. 752–61.
28.   *Congressional Record*, 74th Cong., 1st Sess., 79 (29 July 1935): 12028; Borchard to Borah, 22 February 1936, Box 439, Borah MSS.
29.   William Clark, *Less than Kin: A Study of Anglo-American Relations* (Boston, 1957), pp. 57–8; Allen, *Great Britain and the United States*, p. 774; Edwards, *Col. MCormick's Tribune*, pp. 101–2; *Chicago Tribune*, 1 January 1937; Howe, *England Expects*, p. 169.
30.   One who pointedly did not mourn Long's passing was Ambassador Lindsay, who compared the populist senator to the bluebottle fly. Both, he wrote, shared 'the same frantic, relentless activity, the same intolerable, strident note, the same maddening elusiveness, the same origin in corruption, the same affront to the decencies and the same menace to health.' Rhodes, 'Sir Ronald Lindsay,' p. 75.
31.   Borchard to Borah, 22 February 1936, Box 439, Borah MSS; Bennett, *Demagogues in the Depression*, pp. 245–7; Wendt and Kogan, *Big Bill of Chicago*, pp. 341–5. Big Bill thereupon faded into obscurity, though it was reported in 1939 that Thompson had admitted having 'no real dislike' toward the British, but simply needed 'a catchword of some sort' for his election campaigns. Thomas E. Hachey (ed.), 'Profiles in Politics: British Embassy Views of Prominent Americans in 1939,' *Wisconsin Magazine of History* 54 (Autumn 1970): 3–22.
32.   Bennett, *Demagogues in the Depression*, pp. 269–71. Certainly, the British themselves did not by any means consider Roosevelt the 'pro-English' or 'internationalist' candidate in 1936. Neville Chamberlain, at this time Chancellor of the Exchequer, had already reached the conclusion that FDR was wholly unreliable in foreign affairs. Nor was he the only one: Roosevelt received reports from his embassies abroad that a group of prominent Englishmen headed by Lord Beaverbrook was paying William Randolph Hearst to conduct a press campaign against the president's reelection. Richard A.

Harrison, 'The United States and Great Britain: Presidential
Diplomacy and Alternatives to Appeasement in the 1930s,' in David
F. Schmitz and Richard D. Challener (eds.), *Appeasement in Europe: A
Reassessment of U.S. Policies* (New York, 1990): 51–74; William E.
Kinsella, Jr., *Leadership in Isolation: FDR and the Origins of the Second
World War* (Cambridge, 1978).

CHAPTER 5 'WHOM HE LOVETH HE CHASTISETH'

1. Thomas E. Hachey (ed.), 'Winning Friends and Influencing Policy:
   British Strategy to Woo America in 1937,' *Wisconsin Magazine of
   History* 55 (Winter 1971/2): 120–9.
2. *Ibid.*; see also Nicholas John Cull, *Selling War: The British Campaign
   Against American 'Neutrality' in World War II* (New York, 1995), pp.
   6–10.
3. Harrison, 'Appeasement and Isolation,' p. 463; 'Anti-British
   Hysteria,' *Nation* 145 (11 September 1937): 253.
4. Divine, *Illusion of Neutrality*, pp. 185–6; Jonas, *Isolationism in America*,
   pp. 195–7; Lower, *Bloc of One*, pp. 313–14; Borchard to Borah, 1
   March 1937, Box 468, Borah MSS; Ronald L. Feinman, *Twilight of
   Progressivism: The Western Republican Senators and the New Deal*
   (Baltimore, 1981), pp. 167–8.
5. Divine, *Illusion of Neutrality*, pp. 313–14; Jonas, *Isolationism in
   America*, pp. 195–7; Lower, *Bloc of One*, pp. 313–14; James M.
   Weinberger, 'The British on Borah: Foreign Office and Embassy
   Attitudes toward Idaho's Senior Senator, 1935–1940,' *Idaho
   Yesterdays* 25 (Fall 1981): 2–14.
6. Dallek, *Franklin D. Roosevelt*, pp. 148–50.
7. *Congressional Record*, 75th Cong., 2d Sess., 82 (17 November 1937):
   91; ibid., (18 November 1937): 146; *Chicago Tribune*, 6 October 1937,
   15 January 1938, 30 January 1938; Martin, *American Liberalism*, p.
   548. The Amritsar massacre took place on April 13, 1919, in the
   Punjab province. British troops opened fire on a crowd of between
   ten and twenty thousand protesters assembled in an enclosed area.
   According to official estimates, 379 were killed and over 1200
   wounded. Percival Spear, *A History of India* (Middlesex, 1965), p. 191.
8. Johnson (Charge to the United Kingdom) to Hull, 13 December,
   FRUS, 1937, v.4, pp. 494–5; Leutze, *Bargaining for Supremacy*, pp. 18,
   25; *Congressional Record*, 75th Cong., 2d Sess., 82 (13 December
   1937): 1357; The concept of a national referendum remained
   popular among the American public, however – a Gallup poll taken
   in March 1939 showed that 58 percent of those surveyed still supported a constitutional amendment providing for such a
   referendum. George H. Gallup, *The Gallup Poll: Public Opinion,
   1935–1971*, v.1, 1935–1971 (New York, 1972), p. 144.
9. A. Whitney Griswold, *Far Eastern Policy of the United States* (New
   Haven, 1938); Hull to Straus, 24 May 1934, *FRUS*, 1934, v.1., pp.
   238–9; Hull to Bingham, 14 May 1937, ibid., 1937, v.3, pp. 95–6;

Davis to Hull, 2 November 1937, ibid., v.4, pp. 145–7; Johnson to
FDR, 27 February 1939, ibid., 1939, v.3, pp. 512–4.

10. Radio address by Lemke, 31 May 1938, Box 26, Lemke MSS,
University of North Dakota Department of Special Collections,
Grand Forks, North Dakota; Anderson, 'Senator Burton K.
Wheeler,' p. 103; *Congressional Record*, 75th Cong., 3rd Sess., 83 (2
May 1938): 6027; ibid., (3 May 1938): 6111; 'T.R.B. from
Washington,' *New Republic* (2 March 1938): 99–100.

11. *Congressional Record*, 75th Cong., 3rd Sess., 83 (8 February 1938):
1622; Johnson to Hiram Johnson, Jr., 29 January 1938, in Burke
(ed.), *Diary Letters*, v.6.

12. Bingham to Hull, 27 April 1936, *FRUS*, 1936, v.1, pp. 296–8;
Harrison, 'Appeasement and Isolation,' p. 564; Bruce Bliven,
'England Woos the Fascists,' *New Republic* (24 November 1937): 60–1.

13. Memorandum of Conversation by Welles with Lindsay, 8 March
1938, *FRUS*, 1938, v.1, pp. 126–30; Roosevelt to Chamberlain, 17
January 1938, ibid., pp. 120–2; *Congressional Record*, 75th Cong., 3rd
Sess., 83 (11 March 1938): 3246; ibid., (26 April 1938): 5780; Oswald
Garrison Villard, 'England Shows Her Colors,' *New Republic* (2
March 1938): 87–8.

14. Kinsella, *Leadership in Isolation*, pp. 60–1; FDR to E. Cudahy, 9
March 1938, in Elliott Roosevelt (ed.), *F.D.R.: His Personal Letters*
(New York, 1970), vol. 3, pp. 233–4.

15. Frederick W. Marks III, 'Six Between Roosevelt and Hitler:
America's Role in the Appeasement of Nazi Germany,' *Historical
Journal* 28 (December 1985): 971–2; C. A. MacDonald, *The United
States, Britain and Appeasement, 1936–1939* (New York, 1981), p. 88;
George H. Gallup, *Gallup Poll*, p. 84. There is considerable disagreement among historians as to why Roosevelt followed such an
erratic course. Most support the contention of Robert Dallek, who
claim that the president was far too hemmed in by 'isolationist'
public opinion to offer more than words of encouragement to
Britain and France. Frederick Marks, on the other hand, maintains
that Roosevelt himself was one of the guiding forces behind
American anti-interventionist sentiment. Regardless of which interpretation is closer to the truth, it is difficult to imagine how the
president's policy – that of attacking British appeasement while simultaneously refusing to take any action that might encourage an
alternative approach – could have had any other effect than to alienate Chamberlain's government and to gain for Roosevelt an
international reputation for untrustworthiness.

16. Martin, *American Liberalism*, p. 1040; Robert Briffault, *The Decline and
Fall of the British Empire* (New York, 1938), pp. 251, 254; for the
American Communist position in 1938–1939, see Earl Browder's
pamphlet, 'Concerted Action or Isolation: Which Is the Road to
Peace?' (New York, 1938), as well as his book, *Fighting for Peace* (New
York, 1939).

17. *Chicago Tribune*, 22 August 1937, 19 November 1937; Edwards, *Col.
McCormick's Tribune*. McCormick's deep dislike for the British

Empire was believed by many to have originated in the canings he received while a schoolboy at Eton, though he himself denied this. Frank C. Waldrop, *McCormick of Chicago: An unconventional portrait of a controversial figure* (Englewood Cliffs, NJ, 1966), p. 33; Hachey (ed.), 'Profiles in Politics,' p. 20; Gies, *Colonel of Chicago*, pp. 4–5.

18. *Congressional Record*, 75th Cong., 3rd Sess., 83 (14 March 1938): 3351; Randoph Leigh, *Conscript Europe* (New York, 1938), p. 71; Jerome Frank, *Save America First: How to Make our Democracy Work* (New York, 1938), p. 156.

19. Wayne S. Cole, *Roosevelt and the Isolationists, 1932–1945* (Lincoln, NE, 1983), p. 237; Radio Address by Nye, 20 May 1938, Nye MSS; Cole, *Gerald P. Nye*, pp. 111–14; Maddox, *William E. Borah*, p. 230.

20. Rhodes, 'Sir Ronald Lindsay,' p. 78; MacDonald, *U.S., Britain and Appeasement*, pp. 96–8; Jane Karoline Vieth, 'Munich and American Appeasement,' in David F. Schmitz and Richard D. Challener (eds.), *Appeasement in Europe: A Reassessment of U.S. Policies* (New York, 1990): 66–7; Marks, 'Six Between Roosevelt and Hitler,' pp. 975–6.

21. Gallup, *Gallup Poll*, v.1, p. 121; Arnold A. Offner, *American Appeasement: United States Foreign Policy and Germany, 1933–1938* (New York, 1969), pp. 268–9; James MacGregor Burns, *Roosevelt: The Lion and the Fox* (New York, 1956), pp. 387–8; William E. Leuchtenburg, *Franklin D. Roosevelt and the New Deal* (New York, 1963), p. 285; FDR to Mackenzie King, 11 October 1938, in Roosevelt (ed.), *F.D.R*, v.2 (New York, 1970), p. 816; *Chicago Tribune*, 2, 12 October 1938; Richard Kay Hanks, 'Hamilton Fish and American Isolationism, 1920–1944,' Ph.D. dissertation, University of California at Riverside, 1971, p. 140.

22. Messersmith to Hull, 29 September 1938, *FRUS*, 1938, v.1, pp. 704–7; Offner, *American Appeasement*, p. 272; Adolf A. Berle, *Navigating the Rapids, 1918–1971* (New York, 1973), p. 201; Harrison, 'Appeasement and Isolation,' p. 698.

23. Offner, *American Appeasement*, pp. 272–3; MacDonald, *The United States, Great Britain and Appeasement*, p. 106; Gallup, *Gallup Poll*, v.1, p. 121; McKenna, *Borah*, p. 356; Maddox, *William E. Borah*, p. 237; Borah to Lippmann, 18 October 1938, Box 765, Borah MSS; J. Samuel Walker, *Henry A. Wallace and American Foreign Policy* (Westport, CT, 1976), p. 67; Briffault, *Decline and Fall of the British Empire*, p. 260.

24. FDR to Herbert C. Pell, 12 November 1938, in Roosevelt (ed.), *F.D.R.*, v.2, p. 819; Dallek, *Franklin D. Roosevelt*, p. 171; Reynolds, *Creation of the Anglo-American Alliance*, pp. 42–3; Harrison, 'Appeasement and Isolation,' pp. 725–6.

25. Memorandum by Hull, 18 July 1937, *FRUS*, 1937, v.2, pp. 1–3; Bingham to Hull, 28 October 1937, ibid., v.4, pp. 114–16; Hull to Kennedy, 25 July 1938, ibid., 1938, v.2, pp. 39–42; Lindsay to Hull, November 17, 1938, ibid., pp. 70–76. Hull himself considered the German threat 'a lever against British Empire preference systems.' Warren F. Kimball, 'Lend-Lease and the Open Door: the Temptation of British Opulence, 1937–1942,' in Kimball, *The*

Juggler: Franklin Roosevelt as Wartime Statesman (Princeton, 1991), p. 46.

26. Lowell T. Young, 'Franklin D. Roosevelt and America's Islets,' *Historian* 35 (February 1973): 205–20; Francis X. Holbrook, 'The Canton Island Controversy: Compromise or American Victory,' *Journal of the Royal Australian Historical Society* 59 (June 1973): 128–47; Lindsay to Hull, 22 July 1937, *FRUS*, 1937, v.2, pp. 125–35; Roosevelt to Hull, 26 July 1937, ibid.; Mallet to Hull, 20 October 1937, ibid.; Memorandum by Moffat of Conversation with Roosevelt, R. Walton Moore, and Ernest H. Gruening, 16 February 1938, ibid., 1938, v.2, pp. 77–80; Memorandum by Moffat of Conversation with Lindsay and Moore, 6 April 1938, ibid., pp. 86–8.

27. Memorandum by J. P. Moffat of Conversation with Lindsay and Hugh Wilson, 29 December 1937, ibid., 1937, v.2, pp. 125–35; Aide-Memoire from the British Embassy to the State Department, 23 May 1938, ibid., 1938, v.2, pp. 106–9; Memorandum by Moffat of Conversation with Lindsay, 23 May 1938, ibid., pp. 101–3.

28. See, for example, Mark L. Chadwin, *The Warhawks: American Interventionists before Pearl Harbor* (New York, 1970); for more on the makeup of the Seventy-Sixth Congress, see David L. Porter, *The Seventy-Sixth Congress and World War II, 1939–1940* (Columbia, MO, 1979).

29. Vernon Van Dyke and Edward Lane Davis, 'Senator Taft and American Security,' *Journal of Politics* 14 (May 1952), p. 177; for more on the ideological basis for Taft's foreign policy, see Geoffrey Matthews, 'Robert A. Taft, the Constitution, and American Foreign Policy, 1939–53,' *Journal of Contemporary History* 17 (July 1982), and especially James T. Patterson's biography, *Mr. Republican: A Biography of Robert A. Taft* (Boston, 1972).

30. Justus D. Doenecke, 'Non-interventionism of the Left: The Keep America Out of War Congress, 1938–1941,' *Journal of Contemporary History* 12 (April 1977): 221–36.

31. Cull, *Selling War*, pp. 26–7; Thomas E. Hachey (ed.), *Confidential Dispatches: Analyses of America by the British Ambassador, 1939–1945* (Evanston, IL, 1974), pp. 5–6.

32. David Reynolds, 'FDR's Foreign Policy and the British Royal Visit to the U.S.A., 1939,' *Historian* 45 (August 1983), pp. 462–3; *Washington Times-Herald*, 25 May 1939; *Chicago Tribune*, 18 May 1939; Freda Kirchwey, 'Royalty Is Not Enough,' *Nation* 148 (10 June 1939): 661.

33. Benjamin D. Rhodes, 'The British Royal Visit of 1939 and the "Psychological Approach" to the United States,' *Diplomatic History* 2 (Spring 1978), p. 208; *Washington Times-Herald*, 8 June 1939; *Congressional Record*, 76th Cong., 1st Sess., 84 (8 June 1939): 6846; Dimbleby and Reynolds, *An Ocean Apart*, p. 132; Johnson to Hiram Johnson, Jr., 3 June 1939, in Burke (ed.), *Diary Letters*, v.7; Reynolds, 'FDR's Foreign Policy,' pp. 464–5.

34. Dallek, *Franklin D. Roosevelt and American Foreign Policy*, pp. 180–5, 187–92; *Congressional Record*, 76th Cong., 1st Sess., 84 (27 June 1939): 7984, 8168; McKenna, *Borah*, p. 360.

CHAPTER 6 'TIES OF BLOOD AND LANGUAGE'

1. 'The *Fortune* Survey: XXVI,' *Fortune* 21 (January 1940): 88; Bayor, *Neighbors in Conflict*, p. 201, n.1; Francis Sill Wickware, 'What We Think About Foreign Affairs,' *Harper's* 179 (September 1939): 397–406.
2. Dallek, *FDR and American Foreign Policy*, pp. 200–1; Norris to William Allen White, 30 October 1939, Box 112, Norris MSS; Hoover to William Castle, 14 September 1939, Castle MSS.
3. It would also be his last congressional battle; Borah died of a stroke in January, 1940.
4. Dallek, *FDR and American Foreign Policy*, pp. 200–3; Wayne S. Cole, *Charles A. Lindbergh and the Battle Against American Intervention in World War II* (New York, 1974), pp. 91–2; *Congressional Record*, 76th Cong., 2d Sess., 85 (2 October 1939): 69; ibid., (16 October 1939): 446-7; ibid., (9 October 1939): 183.
5. *Congressional Record*, 76th Cong., 2d Sess., 85 (27 October 1939): 1024; ibid., (2 November 1939): 1344; Dallek, *FDR and American Foreign Policy*, pp. 204–5; Chamberlain to FDR, November 8, 1939, *FRUS*, 1939, v.1, pp. 680–1.
6. Hachey (ed.), *Confidential Dispatches*, pp. 5–6; Maddox, *William E. Borah*, pp. 241–2; *New York Times*, 19 September 1939; Notes by Borah [n.d.], Box 794, Borah MSS.
7. *Congressional Record*, 76th Cong., 3rd Sess., 86 (4 April 1940): 4007; Hull to Kennedy, 24 November 1939, *FRUS*, 1939, v.2, pp. 231–3; McKellar to Everett R. Cook, 31 May 1940, McKellar MSS; Hachey (ed.), *Confidential Dispatches*, p. 18; Various correspondence between Kennedy and Hull, 2 September – 2 October 1939, *FRUS*, 1939, v.2, pp. 213–17; Hull to Kennedy, 14 October 1939, ibid., p. 221; Kennedy to Hull, 1 November 1939, ibid., p. 225; Memorandum of Conversation by Hull with Lothian, 20 March 1940, ibid., pp. 112–13.
8. Kennedy to Hull, 7 October 1939, ibid., pp. 266–9; Edwards, *Col. McCormick's Tribune*, p. 150; *Congressional Record*, 76th Cong., 3rd Sess., 86 (23 January 1940): 548–51; ibid., (15 February 1940): 1475, 1499; Berle, *Navigating the Rapids*, pp. 295–6; Fred L. Israel (ed.), *The War Diary of Breckenridge Long: Selections from the Years 1939–1944* (Lincoln, NE, 1966), pp. 59–61.
9. Oswald Garrison Villard, 'England, America, and the War,' *Nation* 149 (30 September 1939): 349; Norman Thomas and Bertram D. Wolfe, *Keep America Out of War: A Program* (New York, 1939), p. 145; Louis Bromfield, *England: A Dying Oligarchy* (New York, 1939), p. 3; *Detroit News*, 3 March 1941, Box 3, Gerald L.K. Smith MSS, Bentley Historical Library, University of Michigan, Ann Arbor, MI; Radio address, 5 October 1939, La Follette MSS; Patrick J. Maney, *'Young Bob' La Follette: A Biography of Robert M. La Follette, Jr., 1895–1953* (Columbia, MO, 1978), p. 231.
10. Lemke to A. V. Overn, 22 October 1939, Box 17, Lemke MSS; Jonas, *Isolationism in America*, pp. 227–9; Hugh S. Johnson, *Hell-Bent for War*

(Indianapolis, 1941), pp. 45–9; Thomas and Wolfe, *Keep America Out of War*, p. 149; H. L. Mencken, 'Notes on a Moral War,' Baltimore *Sun*, 8 October 1939.

11. K. R. M. Short, '"The White Cliffs of Dover": Promoting the Anglo-American Alliance in World War II,' *Historical Journal of Film, Radio and Television* 2 (March 1982): 3; Alistair Cooke, 'British Propaganda in the United States,' *Fortnightly* 153 (June 1940): 606; J. R. M. Butler, *Lord Lothian, 1882–1940* (London, 1960), pp. 265–6; Sidney Rogerson, *Propaganda in the Next War* (London, 1938), pp. 146–8.

12. H. C. Peterson, *Propaganda for War: The Campaign against American Neutrality, 1914–1917* (Norman, OK, 1939), p. 4.

13. C. Hartley Grattan, *The Deadly Parallel* (New York, 1939), p. 65; *Congressional Record*, 76th Cong., 3rd Sess., 86 (6 June 1940): 7702; ibid., (12 June 1940): 8055.

14. Theodore Dreiser, *America is Worth Saving* (New York, 1941), p. 70; Albert Jay Nock, '"Unfinished Victory" – A Review,' *Scribner's Commentator* 9 (April 1941), p. 20; Porter Sargent, *Getting US into War* (Boston, 1941), p. 44; Cull, *Selling War*, p. 35; Cooke, 'British Propaganda,' p. 608.

15. Reynolds, *Creation of the Anglo-American Alliance*, p. 92; Berle, *Navigating the Rapids*, pp. 308–9; Martin, *American Liberalism and World Politics*, p. 1047.

16. Marks, *Wind Over Sand*, p. 194; Martin, *American Liberalism and World Politics*, pp. 1049–52. American liberals also applauded the British government's crackdown on anti-war organizations in the summer of 1940, expressing admiration for the willingness of Britons to accept 'a suspension of their rights' to support the war effort. *Nation*, June 1, 1940, p. 665.

17. Reynolds, *Creation of the Anglo-American Alliance*, pp. 109, 112, 119–20; Kennedy to Hull, 27 September 1940, *FRUS*, 1940, v.3, pp. 48–9.

18. Notes by Borah, 1939, Box 794, Borah MSS; 'All-Out-Aid-For-Britain,' *Catholic World* 152 (March 1941), pp. 641–3; *Congressional Record*, 76th Cong., 3rd Sess., 86 (27 August 1940): 11039; Cole, *Gerald P. Nye and American Foreign Relations*, p. 194; Press clippings [n.d.], Box 1, Nye MSS.

19. Gerhard L. Weinberg, *A World at Arms: A Global History of World War II* (Cambridge, 1994), pp. 154–5; Lemke to Walter White, 5 September 1940, Lemke MSS; *Congressional Record*, 76th Cong., 3rd Sess., 86 (9 August 1940): 10105; Dallek, *FDR and American Foreign Policy*, pp. 248–50.

20. Reynolds, *Creation of the Anglo-American Alliance*, p. 132; Sir Robin Renwick, *Fighting with Allies: America and Britain in Peace and at War* (New York, 1996), p. 35; Philip Goodhart, *Fifty Ships that Saved the World: The Foundation of the Anglo-American Alliance* (New York, 1965), pp. 96–8.

21. Leutze, *Bargaining for Supremacy*, p. 121; Goodhart, *Fifty Ships that Saved the World*, pp. 178–9; *Congressional Record*, 76th Cong., 3rd Sess., 86 (3 September 1940): 11354–7.

22. Goodhart, *Fifty Ships that Saved the World*, pp. 186–7; *Congressional Record*, 76th Cong., 3rd Sess., 86 (15 August 1940): 10406; ibid., (23 August 1940): 10825; ibid., (3 September 1940): 11399; Edwards, *Col. McCormick's Tribune*, p. 158; Robert A. Divine, *Foreign Policy and U.S. Presidential Elections. Volume One: 1940–1948* (New York, 1974), p. 46.

23. Cole, *Roosevelt and the Isolationists*, p. 395; Divine, *Foreign Policy and U.S. Presidential Elections*, pp. 56–7; Dallek, *FDR and American Foreign Policy*, pp. 249–50; Guinsberg, *Pursuit of Isolationism*, p. 246.

24. Adler, *Isolationist Impulse*, pp. 271–2; Martin, *American Liberalism and World Politics*, pp. 1056–63.

25. Oswald Garrison Villard, 'If This Be Treason – ' *Nation* 150 (February 3, 1940): 130. Some liberals, of course, continued to oppose entry into the war; men such as John T. Flynn and Charles Beard turned instead to *Uncensored*, a newsletter published by the KAOWC. Michele Flynn Stenehjem, *An American First: John T. Flynn and the America First Committee* (New Rochelle, NY, 1976), p. 60.

26. Alfred O. Hero, *The Southerner and World Affairs* (Baton Rouge, LA, 1965), pp. 73–5, 91–103; Paul Seabury, *The Waning of Southern 'Internationalism'* (Princeton, 1957).

27. Raymond James Raymond, 'American Public Opinion and Irish Neutrality, 1939–1945,' *Eire-Ireland* 18 (Spring 1983), pp. 38–41; Porter, *Seventy-sixth Congress*, pp. 18, 72, 85.

28. Adler, *Isolationist Impulse*, pp. 271–2; Memorandum of meeting between Hoover and Lord Halifax, 8 January 1943, Post-Presidential Individual File, Herbert Hoover Presidential Library. A glaring exception to noninterventionism's shift to the right were the communists, who from August 1939 to June 1941 (the period corresponding exactly to the duration of the Nazi-Soviet Pact) were vehement advocates of American neutrality. Earl Browder, general secretary of the CPUSA, accused Roosevelt of joining with American capitalists 'to aid the British ruling class to retain control of a slave empire in half of Africa, [and] to continue to rule three hundred and fifty million Indians against their will.' The United States, he claimed, was being groomed for the part of 'catspaw for the British Empire,…that role which the Soviet Union refused.' Earl Browder, *The Second Imperialist War* (New York, 1940), p. 125; Browder, *The Way Out* (New York, 1941), p. 200.

29. Adler, *Isolationist Impulse*, p. 273; Wayne S. Cole, *America First: The Battle Against Intervention, 1940–1941* (Madison, WI, 1953), pp. 35–9; Justus D. Doenecke (ed.), *In Danger Undaunted: The Anti-Interventionist Movement of 1940–1941 as Revealed in the Papers of the America First Committee* (Stanford, CA, 1990), pp. 25–6, 50–1; Robert L. Bliss to chapter heads, 11 February 1941, Box 1, America First Committee MSS. Smith in particular believed that there was 'a definite conspiracy' within the AFC to embarrass his group. Smith to Bernard A. Doman, 26 March 1941, Box 11, Smith MSS.

30. Doenecke, *In Danger Undaunted*, pp. 50–1; Edwin S. Webster to Nye, 23 October 1941, Nye MSS; Cole, *America First*, p. 191.

31. Johnson, *George Sylvester Viereck*, pp. 197–9, 217–20.
32. Ibid., pp. 199–200, 215–17; William Ellis Coffey, 'Rush Dew Holt: The Boy Senator, 1905–1942,' (Ph.D. diss., West Virginia University, 1970), p. 377. Flanders Hall's releases included George W. Booker (pseudonym of Conrad Oerich), *The Slave Business* (1941); Giselher Wirsing, *One Hundred Families that Rule the Empire* (1941); Nathaniel Greene, *Doublecross in Palestine* (1941); Sayid Halassie (pseudonym of Paul Schmitz), *Democracy on the Nile: How Britain Has 'Protected' Egypt* (1940); Shaemas O'Sheel, *Seven Periods of Irish History* (1940); Stephen A. Day, *We Must Save the Republic* (1941), and Viereck's own (under the pseudonym James Burr Hamilton) *Lord Lothian against Lord Lothian* (1941).
33. Johnson, *Viereck*, pp. 217–20; Chadwin, *Hawks of World War II*, p. 213.
34. Warren F. Kimball, *The Most Unsordid Act: Lend-Lease, 1939–1941* (Baltimore, 1969), p. 33; Kimball, 'Lend-Lease and the Open Door,' p. 48.
35. Hull to Johnson, 20 December 1940, *FRUS*, 1940, v.3, pp. 26–9; Kimball, 'Lend-Lease and the Open Door,' p. 49. Leon Martel, *Lend-Lease, Loans, and the Coming of the Cold War: A Study of the Implementation of Foreign Policy* (Boulder, CO, 1979), p. 4.
36. Kimball, *Most Unsordid Act*, p. 193; *Congressional Record*, 77th Cong., 1st Sess., 87 (13 January 1941): 135; ibid., (23 January 1941): 258; Guinsberg, *Pursuit of Isolationism*, pp. 252–3; Press release by Taft, 26 February 1941, Box 710, Taft MSS; Doenecke, *In Danger Undaunted*, pp. 50–1.
37. Kimball, *Most Unsordid Act*, pp. 185–7; *Congressional Record*, 77th Cong., 1st Sess., 87 (4 February 1941): 535–6, 543, 560; ibid., (5 February 1941): 580, 622; ibid., (14 February 1941): 1017; Anderson, 'Senator Burton K. Wheeler,' p. 173; Julian McIver Pleasant, 'The Senatorial Career of Robert Rice Reynolds,' (Ph.D. diss., UNC Chapel Hill, 1971), pp. 574–5; *Congressional Record*, 77th Cong., 1st Sess., 87 (20 February 1941): 1213; ibid., (4 March 1941): 1722; Cole, *Gerald P. Nye*, p. 180; Speech by Nye, 4 March 1941, Nye MSS.
38. Press clippings [n.d., 1941], Box 1, Nye MSS; Gray (Minister to Ireland) to Hull, 7 January, *FRUS,* 1941, v.3, pp. 215–16; *Congressional Record*, 77th Cong., 1st Sess., 87 (8 March 1941): 2097; Johnson to Hiram Johnson, Jr., in Burke (ed.), *Diary Letters*, v.7.
39. AFC Bulletin #464, 4 August 1941, AFC MSS; Gallup, *Gallup Poll*, vol. 1, pp. 157, 279. Halifax succeeded Lord Lothian after the latter's untimely death in December 1940. The response attributed to the new ambassador to the egg-throwing incident – to the effect that Americans were quite lucky to have eggs to throw around, given that Britons were only receiving one egg a month – was applauded in most segments of American public opinion. Earl of Birkenhead, *Halifax: The Life of Lord Halifax* (Boston, 1966), p. 508.
40. *Congressional Record*, 77th Cong., 1st Sess., 87 (19 May 1941): A2378–81; Radio address by Nye, 1 August 1941, Nye MSS; Cole, *Gerald P. Nye*, p. 186.

41. Richard W. Steele, 'The Great Debate: Roosevelt, the Media, and the Coming of War, 1940–1941,' *Journal of American History* 71 (June 1984), pp. 79–80; Short, '"The White Cliffs of Dover"', pp. 13–14.
42. Steele, 'The Great Debate,' pp. 81–2; Cole, *Gerald P. Nye*, pp. 188–9; Anderson, 'Senator Burton K. Wheeler,' pp. 230–2.
43. *Pittsburgh Post-Gazette*, 8 December 1941; Cole, *Gerald P. Nye*, pp. 198–9; Stenehjem, *An American First*, p. 115.
44. Frank C. Hanighen, 'What England and France Think About Us,' *Harper's* 179 (September 1939), pp. 377–8; Margaret Halsey, *With Malice Toward Some* (New York, 1938), p. 170.
45. Doenecke, 'Non-interventionism of the Left,' p. 230.
46. This view was especially prevalent in the State Department, embodied in such men as Under-Secretary of State Sumner Welles, Assistant Secretary of State for European Affairs Jay Pierrepont Moffat, and especially Adolf Berle, who in October 1940 compared the current global situation with that of 1917. While Britain was the leader of the Allies during World War I, '[t]his time,' he wrote, '...the thing should be the other way around. We have the ultimate strength. We also have the ultimate consistency of principle; we are the inevitable economic center of the regime which will emerge.' Berle, *Navigating the Rapids*, p. 342; see also Kathleen Burk, 'American Foreign Economic Policy and Lend-Lease,' in Ann Lane and Howard Temperley (eds.), *The Rise and Fall of the Grand Alliance, 1941–45* (London, 1995), pp. 43–68.
47. Martin, *American Liberalism and World Politics*, p. 1068.

CHAPTER 7 'INDIA AND THE BOER WAR' AND ALL THAT'

1. Dallek, *FDR and American Foreign Policy*, p. 324; Mikhail N. Narinsky, Lydia V. Pozdeeva, et al., 'Mutual Perceptions: Images, Ideals, and Illusions,' in David Reynolds, Warren F. Kimball, and A.O. Chubarian (eds.), *Allies at War: The Soviet, American and British Experience, 1939–1945* (New York, 1994), pp. 324–6.
2. Halifax, First Quarter Report for 1942, in Hachey (ed.), *Confidential Dispatches*, pp. 60–5; John Baylis, *Anglo-American Defence Relations, 1939–1980: The Special Relationship* (New York, 1981), p. 9; Johnson to Hiram Johnson, Jr., 13 December 1941, in Burke (ed.) *Diary Letters*, v.7.
3. Halifax to Eden, 4 February 1942, in H. G. Nicholas (ed.), *Washington Despatches, 1941–1945: Weekly Political Reports from the British Embassy* (Chicago, 1981), pp. 17–18; Halifax, First Quarter Report for 1942, in Hachey (ed.), *Confidential Dispatches*, pp. 60–5.
4. Ibid.; Short, '"The White Cliffs of Dover"', p. 15; Christopher Thorne, *Allies of a Kind: The United States, Britain and the war against Japan, 1941–1945* (New York, 1978), pp. 133, 392.
5. J. E. Williams, 'The Joint Declaration on the colonies: an issue in Anglo-American relations, 1942–1944,' *British Journal of International Studies* 2 (1976): 267–92; Amos Perlmutter, *FDR & Stalin: A Not So*

Grand Alliance, 1943–1945 (Columbia, MO: University of Missouri Press, 1993), pp. 195–6; Thomas A. Bailey, *The Man in the Street: The Impact of American Public Opinion on Foreign Policy* (New York, 1948), p. 216n.; 'We're not Perfect Ourselves,' *Collier's* 109 (4 April 1942): 66; Francis McCullagh, *Catholic World* 155 (May 1942): 202–10; Bruce Bliven, 'Deadwood at the Top,' *New Republic* 106 (2 March 1942): 285–6; 'Britain's Problem of Leadership,' *New Republic* 107 (6 July 1942): 6–7. Even Churchill's image was beginning to tarnish in liberal eyes. Writing in *Christian Century*, Charles Clayton Morrison accused the prime minister of seeing the world 'with the eyes of a Tory Imperialist. He represents the hope of a post-war order imposed from London.' Bruce Bliven agreed, claiming that Churchill was conducting 'a white British Tories' war.' Charles Clayton Morrison, 'Mr. Churchill and the Future,' *Christian Century* 59 (7 January 1942): 3–4; Bruce Bliven, 'Mr. Churchill's Untotal War,' *New Republic* 107 (28 September 1942): 370–2.

6. Memorandum by Hull of Conversation with Halifax, 7 May 1941, *FRUS*, 1941, v.3, p. 178; Memorandum by Berle, 5 May 1941, ibid., p. 176; Berle, *Navigating the Rapids*, p. 404; FDR to Winant, 25 February 1942, *FRUS*, 1942, v.1, p. 604; Gary R. Hess, *America Encounters India, 1941–1947* (Baltimore, 1971), p. 36; FDR to Churchill, 11 April 1942, *FRUS*, 1942, v.1, pp. 633–4; Fred E. Pollock and Warren F. Kimball, '"In Search of Monsters to Destroy": Roosevelt and Colonialism,' in Kimball, *The Juggler*, p. 135; Memorandum by Calvin H. Oakes of Conversation with Johnson, 26 May 1942, *FRUS*, 1942, v.1, pp. 657–9.

7. Hess, *America Encounters India*, p. 84; Charles Clayton Morrison, 'No Victory Without India,' *Christian Century* 59 (21 October 1942): 1278–9; Michael Straight, 'Is It a People's War?' *New Republic* 107 (16 November 1942): 633–5.

8. Terry H. Anderson, *The United States, Great Britain, and the Cold War, 1944–1947* (Columbia, MO, 1981), pp. 3–5; Wendell L. Willkie, *One World* (New York, 1943), pp. 14–15. Willkie went on to emphasize the great commercial opportunities which would exist for Americans in a post-imperial world, prompting one of Churchill's aides to comment bitterly, 'Political tutelage of backward peoples is wicked, but commercial exploitation without responsibility is to be encouraged.' Henry Butterfield Ryan, *The Vision of Anglo-America: The US–UK Alliance and the Emerging Cold War, 1943–1946* (Cambridge, 1987), p. 32; Wm. Roger Louis, *Imperialism at Bay: The United States and the Decolonization of the British Empire* (Oxford, 1977), p. 226; Foster Rhea Dulles and Gerald E. Ridinger, 'The Anti-Colonial Policies of Franklin D. Roosevelt,' *Political Science Quarterly* 70 (March 1955), pp. 5–17.

9. *Congressional Record*, 77th Cong., 2nd Sess., v.88 (25 June 1942): 5537; ibid. (23 February 1942): 1528; ibid. (20 August 1942): 6888–95; Hess, *American Encounters India*, p. 86.

10. Press Statement by Nye, 23 May 1941, Box 1, Folder 24, Nye MSS, Elwyn B. Robinson Depart of Special Collections, University of

North Dakota, Grand Forks, North Dakota; 'An Open Letter to the People of England,' *Life* (12 October 1942): 13; *Congressional Record*, 77th Cong., 2nd Sess., v.88 (23 October 1942): 8571–4. In a confidential study written for the Foreign Office in 1943, Professor Isaiah Berlin explained that Nye's apparent defense of Britain was designed more as an attack on Willkie, 'whom he hates even more than the British Empire.' Nye, he continued, 'evidently regards any stick as good enough to beat Willkie with.' Thomas E. Hachey (ed.), 'American Profiles on Capitol Hill: A Confidential Study for the British Foreign Office in 1943,' *Wisconsin Magazine of History* 57 (Winter 1973/74): 141–54.

11. Hanks, 'Hamilton Fish and American Isolationism,' p. 147; 'A Congress to Win the War,' (supplement) *New Republic* 106 (18 May 1942): 684–710; Press Statement by Justice Department, 4 January 1943, Nye MSS. In the course of the subsequent hearings, it emerged that a certain George Hill, a member of Hamilton Fish's staff, had been stealing the envelopes and passing them on to pro-Nazi groups such as William Dudley Pelley's Silver Shirts. Hanks, 'Hamilton Fish,' p. 175. Among the isolationist voices silenced in 1942 was that of Father Coughlin, whose newsletter *Social Justice* was prevented by the Espionage Act from being distributed through the U.S. Mail. The radio priest himself soon left the airwaves after being threatened with defrockment by Archbishop Mooney of Detroit. Charles J. Tull, *Father Coughlin and the New Deal*. (Syracuse: Syracuse University Press, 1965), pp. 234–5. See also Kenneth O'Reilly, 'A New Deal for the FBI: The Roosevelt Administration, Crime Control, and National Security,' *Journal of American History* 69 (December 1982): 638–58, and Richard W. Steele, 'Franklin D. Roosevelt and His Foreign Policy Critics,' *Political Science Quarterly* 94 (Spring 1979): 15–32.

12. Nicholas (ed.), *Washington Despatches*, pp. 116–17. The editors of the *New Republic* were even more pessimistic, predicting a 'return to Hardingism' after the war. *New Republic* 107 (November 16, 1942): 623–8.

13. Mark A. Stoler, *The Politics of the Second Front: American Military Planning and Diplomacy in Coalition Warfare, 1941–1943* (Westport, CT, 1977), pp. 58–9; Stephen E. Ambrose, *Rise to Globalism: American Foreign Policy Since 1938*, 4th edition (New York, 1985), p. 17; David Reynolds, Warren F. Kimball, and A. O. Chubarian, 'Legacies: Allies, Enemies, and Posterity,' in Reynolds, Kimball, and Chubarian (eds.), *Allies at War*, p. 418; see also Correlli Barnett, 'Anglo-American Strategy in Europe,' in Lane and Temperley (ed.), *Rise and Fall*, pp. 174–89.

14. Baylis, *Anglo-American Defence Relations*, p. 13; Mark A. Stoler, 'The "Pacific-First" Alternative in American World War II Strategy,' *International History Review* 2 (July 1980), pp. 432–4; idem., 'The United States: The Global Strategy,' in Reynolds, et al., *Allies at War*, p. 67; Thorne, *Allies of a Kind*, p. 288; Stilwell quoted in William B. Breuer, *Feuding Allies: The Private Wars of the High Command* (New York, 1995), p. 6.

15. *Congressional Record*, 78th Cong., 1st Sess., v.89 (17 May 1943): 4503–10; Roland Young, *Congressional Politics in the Second World War* (New York, 1956), pp. 149–50; Anderson, 'Senator Burton K.Wheeler,' p. 245; Churchill, quoted in Dimbleby and Reynolds, *An Ocean Apart*, p. 157; Baylis, *Anglo-American Defence Relations*, pp. 13–14. Despite his tendency to complain about this later on, Churchill himself bears some responsibility for the shift of forces to the Pacific. In early 1942, at the height of the Japanese advance, the Australian government sought to recall all of its armed forces to assist in home defense. But since this would have denied two crucial divisions to the embattled British Eighth Army in North Africa, Churchill instead sought and obtained assurances from the United States that its army and navy would take responsibility for the defense of Australia. Weinberg, *A World at Arms*, pp. 321, 331.

16. Robert M. Hathaway, *Ambiguous Partnership: Britain and America, 1944–1947* (New York: Columbia University Press, 1981), p. 47; Baylis, *Anglo-American Defense Relations*, pp. 14–15; Thorne, *Allies of a Kind*, p. 292; John J. Sbrega, *Anglo-American Relations and Colonialism in East Asia, 1941–1945* (New York, 1983), pp. 15–16; idem., 'Anglo-American Relations and the Selection of Mountbatten as Supreme Allied Commander, South East Asia,' *Military Affairs* 46 (October 1982), p. 139; Glen C. H. Perry (ed.), *'Dear Bart': Washington Views of World War II* (Westport, CT, 1982), pp. 257–8, 264–5; Dimbleby and Reynolds, *An Ocean Apart*, pp. 159–61; Dallek, *FDR and American Foreign Policy*, p. 385; Merrill Bartlett and Robert William Love, Jr., 'Anglo-American Naval Diplomacy and the British Pacific Fleet, 1942–1945,' *American Neptune* 42 (July 1982), pp. 204–5.

17. *Congressional Record*, 78th Cong., 1st Sess., v.89 (17 May 1943): 4503–10; ibid., 78th Cong., 2nd Sess., v.90 (21 September 1944): 8113; Young, *Congressional Politics*, p. 151.

18. Ryan, *Vision of Anglo-America*, pp. 43–4.

19. Halifax to Eden, 9 October 1943, Nicholas, *Washington Despatches*, pp. 257–9; Sbrega, *Colonialism in East Asia*, pp. 38–9; *Congressional Record*, 78th Cong., 1st Sess., v.89 (28 October 1943): 8863–6.

20. Lemke maintained that, since 'the lives of American soldiers, sailors, and marines are at stake,' Congress continued to vote extensions of Lend-Lease 'with all its stench.' News Release, 17 March 1943, Lemke MSS; *Congressional Record*, 78th Cong., 1st Sess., v.89 (8 March 1943): 1641; ibid. (28 October 1943): 8863–6. In the same speech, Ellender claimed that the British were allowing the U.S. to provide 70 percent of the oil for the war effort, while Britain's 'vast oil reserves in Iran' were being hoarded for after the war. ibid. (October 12, 1943): 8252–4; Halifax to Eden, 18 October and 22 November 1943, in Nicholas (ed.), *Washington Despatches*, p. 260, 274.

21. *Congressional Record*, 78th Cong., 1st Sess., v.89 (28 October 1943): 8863–6; ibid. (11 March 1943): 1849; ibid., 78th Cong., 2nd Sess., v.90 (7 March 1944): 2309; ibid., 78th Cong., 1st Sess., v.89 (11 February 1943): 834; Charles Smith, 'Lend-Lease to Great Britain, 1941–1945,' *Southern Quarterly* 10 (January 1972), p. 203; Pope,

'Senatorial Baron,' pp. 385–6; Eden to Halifax, 26 April 1944, Nicholas (ed.), *Washington Despatches*, pp. 351–2; *Congressional Record*, 78th Cong., 2nd Sess., v.90 (26 April 1944): 3718.

22. Robert A. Divine, *Second Chance: The Triumph of Internationalism in America During World War II* (New York: Atheneum, 1967), pp. 143–5; Halifax, Political Report for Third Quarter 1943, in Hachey (ed.), *Confidential Dispatches*, pp. 127–8.

23. *Congressional Record*, 78th Cong., 1st Sess., v.89 (24 June 1943): 6429; ibid. (20 September 1943): 7660.

24. Ryan, *Vision of Anglo-America*, pp. 43–4; Halifax to Eden, 9 October 1943, in Nicholas (ed.), *Washington Despatches*, pp. 257–9; Halifax, Political Report for Third Quarter, 1943, in Hachey (ed.), *Confidential Dispatches*, pp. 127–8.

25. Halifax to Eden, 25 September 1943, in Nicholas (ed.), *Washington Despatches*, p. 252, 257–9; Young, *Congressional Politics*, p. 154.

26. *Congressional Record*, 78th Cong., 1st Sess., v.79 (14 October 1943): 8330; ibid., 78th Cong., 2nd Sess., v.80 (18 February 1944): A842; ibid. (23 February 1944): 1963. Actually, British politicians and newspapers, recognizing that Anglophobia remained a potent force in the U.S., studiously avoided commenting on the elections, though Churchill made no attempt to conceal his relief at the results. Hathaway, *Ambiguous Partnership*, p. 71.

27. *Congressional Record*, 78th Cong., 2nd Sess., v.80 (19 June 1944): 6176; James Leutze, 'The Secret of the Churchill-Roosevelt Correspondence, September 1939–May 1940,' *Journal of Contemporary History* 10 (July 1975), p. 467. The Tyler Kent case would flare up again briefly in 1946, as part of a congressional inquiry into the Pearl Harbor disaster. See Ray Bearse and Anthony Read, *Conspirator: The Untold Story of Tyler Kent* (New York: Doubleday, 1991).

28. Divine, *Second Chance*, p. 241.

29. Halifax to Eden, 18 April 1943, in Nicholas (ed.), *Washington Despatches*, p. 177; Emery Reeves, 'Should the British Empire be Broken Up?' *American Mercury* 56 (May 1943), p. 553; Forrest Davis, 'The British Get Out of the Doghouse,' *Saturday Evening Post* 216 (18 September 1943), p. 18; 'American-British Alliance,' *Collier's* 112 (30 October 1943), p. 78; Ralph B. Levering, *The Public and American Foreign Policy, 1918–1978* (New York: Foreign Policy Association, 1978), pp. 83–4; Robert E. Wood to Arthur Vandenberg, 21 April 1944, Wood MSS.

30. Hachey (ed.), *Confidential Dispatches*, pp. 162–3; Halifax to Eden, 2 July, 28 October 1944, in Nicholas (ed.), *Washington Despatches*, pp. 379, 439; Stimson to Taft, 10 October 1944, Taft MSS; Divine, *Presidential Elections*, pp. 105–8.

31. Phillips to FDR, 14 May 1943, *FRUS*, 1943, v.4, pp. 220–2; Memorandum by Hull to FDR, 15 August 1944, ibid., 1944, v.5, pp. 241–2; Pollock and Kimball, 'In Search of Monsters to Destroy,' p. 136. Phillips resigned soon afterward, prompting charges from Sen. Chandler that he had been declared *persona non grata* by the British. This was not the case, although the British viceroy had asked

London to do so. *Congressional Record*, 78th Cong., 2d Sess., 90 (28 August 1944): 7336; Hess, *America Encounters India*, pp. 144–5; Kenton J. Clymer, 'The Education of William Phillips: Self-Determination and American Policy Toward India, 1942–45,' *Diplomatic History* 8 (Winter 1984), p. 33.

32. Perry (ed.), *'Dear Bart'*, pp. 305–6; James Lansdale Hodson, 'No Hard Feelings,' *Atlantic* 174 (July 1944), p. 84; Memorandum by Hull to FDR, 8 September 1944, *FRUS*, 1944, v.3, pp. 53–6. Few Americans realized, however, that the British had repeatedly suggested greater involvement in the Pacific war, but the opposition of high-ranking American officers such as Ernest King and Douglas MacArthur to any combined use of British and American troops precluded this. Ryan, *Vision of Anglo-America*, p. 25.

33. Halifax, Political Report for Fourth Quarter 1944, in Hachey (ed.), *Confidential Dispatches*, pp. 237–9.

34. Hathaway, *Ambiguous Partnership*, p. 90; Halifax to Eden, 2 December 1944, in Nicholas (ed.), *Washington Despatches*, p. 467; *Congressional Record*, 78th Cong., 2nd Sess., v.80 (21 September 1944): A4364.

35. Hathaway, *Ambiguous Partnership*, p. 91; Halifax, Political Report for Fourth Quarter 1944, in Hachey (ed.), *Confidential Dispatches*, p. 513; *Congressional Record*, 78th Cong., 2nd Sess., v.90 (7 December 1944): 8976; Halifax to Eden, 17 December 1944, in Nicholas (ed.), *Washington Despatches*, pp. 476–7.

36. Halifax to Eden, 24 December 1944, ibid., pp. 481–6; Hathaway, *Ambiguous Partnership*, p. 96; Charles Clayton Morrison, 'Unhappy Europe,' *Christian Century* 61 (20 December 1944), p. 1470; *Congressional Record*, 78th Cong., 2nd Sess., v.90 (5 December 1944): 8864; ibid. (8 December 1944): 9063; Joan Lee Bryniarski, 'Against the Tide: Senate Opposition to the Internationalist Foreign Policy of Presidents Franklin D. Roosevelt and Harry S. Truman, 1943–1949.' Ph.D. diss., University of Maryland, 1972; see also John Charmley, *Churchill's Grand Alliance: The Anglo-American Special Relationship, 1940–57* (New York, 1995), pp. 54–5.

37. Halifax, Political Report for Fourth Quarter 1944, in Hachey, *Confidential Dispatches*, pp. 237–9; *Congressional Record*, 78th Cong., 2nd Sess., v.90 (13 December 1944): 9308; Hathaway, *Ambiguous Partnership*, p. 96; Halifax to Eden, 24 December 1944, in Nicholas (ed.), *Washington Despatches*, pp. 481–6.

38. John Lewis Gaddis, *The United States and the Origins of the Cold War, 1941–1947* (New York: Columbia University Press, 1972), pp. 154–5. Hathaway, *Ambiguous Partnership*, p. 98.

39. 'Noble Negatives,' *The Economist*, 30 December 1944. Reaction to the article in Congress was predictably fierce: Emanuel Celler claimed that it was now not enough to 'twist the lion's tail.' Now we had 'to pull its whiskers.' He called British policy 'imperialism run riot': 'We are now bearing the brunt of the fighting on the Western Front while Churchill masses British tommies to kill Greek patriots.' Hathaway, *Ambiguous Partnership*, p. 104.

40. Elliott Roosevelt, *As He Saw It* (New York, 1946), p. 222; Lawrence S. Wittner, 'American Policy Toward Greece during World War II,' *Diplomatic History* 3 (Spring 1979), p. 138; Thorne, *Allies of a Kind*, p. 513; Emanuel Celler praised Stettinius for refusing 'to be a lickspittle for either Mr. Eden or Mr. Churchill.' *Congressional Record*, 78th Cong., 2nd Sess., v.90 (8 December 1944): 9063.

41. Halifax, Political Report for Fourth Quarter 1944, in Hachey, *Confidential Dispatches*, p. 247; Hathaway, *Ambiguous Partnership*, pp. 104–7; Halifax to Eden, 21 April 1945, in Nicholas (ed.), *Washington Despatches*, p. 544.

42. The only dissenters were Johnson (R-CA), Shipstead (R-MN), Reynolds (D-NC), Wheeler (D-MT), and William Langer (R-ND). Even Nye, Brooks, and Bennett Champ Clark (D-MO) voted in favor of the resolution. Divine, *Second Chance*, p. 153.

43. Owen Brewster, 'Let's Not be Suckers Again,' *American Magazine* 139 (January 1945): 24–5; among Brewster's warnings was of the existence of 'about 8000 Englishmen in the United States, working to advance the interests of the United Kingdom,' and that the British were hoarding oil for the postwar period.

CHAPTER 8 'WHO SHALL LEAD THE WORLD?'

1. James M. Gillis, 'Who Shall Lead the World?' *Catholic World* 162 (December 1945): 193–201; Halifax, Political Report for Fourth Quarter, 1945, in Hachey (ed.), *Confidential Dispatches*, pp. 259–60.

2. Strout, *American Image of the Old World*, pp. 230–1.

3. Hathaway, *Ambiguous Partnership*, p. 136; Bradford Perkins, 'Unequal Partners: The Truman Administration and Great Britain,' in Wm. Roger Louis and Hedley Bull (eds.), *The 'Special Relationship': Anglo-American Relations since 1945* (Oxford, 1986), pp. 43–5. Truman was, to be sure, far less susceptible than most American elites to the charms of the British court. Before leaving for the Potsdam Conference in the summer of 1945, he wrote his wife Bess that 'George VI…sent *me* a personal letter today….Not much impressed.' He later referred to his 'lunch with the limey King' at Plymouth. Roy Jenkins, *Truman* (New York, 1986), pp. 72–3.

4. Martin J. Sherwin, *A World Destroyed: The Atomic Bomb and the Grand Alliance* (New York, 1975), pp. 68–72; Dimbleby and Reynolds, *An Ocean Apart*, pp. 167–8; Barton J. Bernstein, 'The Uneasy Alliance: Roosevelt, Churchill, and the Atomic Bomb, 1940–1945,' *Western Political Quarterly* 29 (July 1976), pp. 208–10. Part of Stimson's attitude was determined by wartime strategy. As Brian Loring Villa suggests, Stimson was interested in using continued access to atomic technology as an incentive for Churchill's consent to a second front in France. Brian Loring Villa, 'The Atomic Bomb and the Normandy Invasion,' *Perspectives in American History* 11 (1977–1978): 461–502.

5. Sherwin, *A World Destroyed*, pp. 78–88; Bernstein, 'The Uneasy

Alliance,' p. 214; Dimbleby and Reynolds, *An Ocean Apart*, pp. 167–8.

6.   Gregg Herken, *The Winning Weapon: The Atomic Bomb in the Cold War, 1945–1950* (New York, 1980), pp. 61–2; Groves would later boast that he had been 'leaning over backwards' to keep information about the atomic bomb from passing into British hands. Bernstein, 'The Uneasy Alliance,' p. 221.

7.   Herken, *The Winning Weapon*, pp. 144–7; Groves to Sen. Bourke Hickenlooper, 12 March 1946, Hickenlooper MSS, Herbert Hoover Presidential Library, West Branch, IA; Memorandum by Groves to Dean Acheson, 29 April 1946, *Foreign Relations of the United States, 1946*, v.1, pp. 1240–1; *Congressional Record*, 79th Cong., 2d Sess., 92 (1 June 1946): 6076–98; Baylis, *Anglo-American Defence Relations*, pp. 24–6. The American atomic monopoly was particularly distressing to the British insofar as England became the main U.S. base for atomic bombers, thus making that country, as Churchill complained, 'the bull's eye of a Soviet attack.' David Reynolds, *Britannia Overruled: British Policy and World Power in the Twentieth Century* (London, 1991), pp. 180–1.

8.   Halifax to Eden, 13 May 1945, in Nicholas (ed.), *Washington Despatches*, pp. 559–62.

9.   Thorne, *Allies of a Kind*, pp. 664–5; Department of State to British Embassy, 6 November 1945, *FRUS*, 1945, v.6, pp. 206–11; Byrnes to Ernest Bevin, 10 December 1945, ibid., pp. 222–4.

10.   Memorandum by Byrnes of conversation with Peter Fraser, February 26, 1946, ibid., 1946, v.5, pp. 6–8; Byrnes to Halifax, 19 April 1946, ibid., pp. 28–30.

11.   Justus D. Doenecke, *Not to the Swift: The Old Isolationists in the Cold War Era* (Cranbury, NJ, 1979), pp. 60–1; Caroline Anstey, 'The Projection of British Socialism: Foreign Office Publicity and Public Opinion, 1945–1950,' *Journal of Contemporary History* 19 (July 1984), pp. 428–9, 440. It certainly did not help matters, however, when private British citizens such as Professor Harold Laski and Rev. Hewlett Johnson, Dean of Canterbury, insisted on visiting the U.S. in late 1946 and publicly attacking the American free enterprise system as '100 years behind the rest of the world.' *Congressional Record*, 79th Cong., 2d Sess., 92 (7 December 1945): 11612; ibid., (22 January 1946): A152.

12.   Joseph Grew to Winant, 17 May 1945, *FRUS*, 1945, v.6, p. 251; Robert J. McMahon, 'Toward a post-colonial order: Truman administration policies toward South and Southeast Asia,' in Michael J. Lacey (ed.), *The Truman presidency* (Cambridge, 1989), p. 342; Anderson, *The U.S., Great Britain, and the Cold War*, pp. 152–3; Speech by La Follette, 31 May 1945, Box C565, La Follette MSS; Francis McCullagh, 'England, Ireland and India,' *Catholic World* 161 (September 1945), pp. 495–6.

13.   H. Newman to Ernest Bevin, 12 June 1946, F.O. 371/51628 AN 1848/5/45; *Congressional Record*, 79th Cong., 2d Sess., 92 (8 May 1945): A1257; Press Release by Bender, 12 July 1946, Box 735, Taft MSS; *Congressional Record*, 79th Cong., 2d Sess., 92 (18 July 1946):

Notes 229

A4217; Speech by La Follette before Toledo Zionist District, 14 April 1946, Box C565, La Follette MSS.

14. Watt, *Succeeding John Bull*, pp. 108–9; Anderson, *The U.S., Great Britain, and the Cold War*, pp. 152–3. Truman himself admitted the political motivations behind his support for the lifting of immigration restrictions; as he said in 1947, 'I have to answer to hundreds of thousands who are anxious for the success of Zionism; I do not have hundreds of thousands of Arabs among my constituents.' Hathaway, *Ambiguous Partnership*, p. 291.

15. Dimbleby and Reynolds, *An Ocean Apart*, p. 182; There was actually some justification for this charge – former congressman John H. Hoeppel wrote to Sen. William Langer (R-ND) that a Jewish state in Palestine could provide a convenient dumping ground for 'such Jews as [Bernard] Baruch, [Henry] Morgenthau,…Sidney Hillman and others of the Red, Communistic stripe.' Hoeppel to Langer, 2 May 1946, Box 176, Langer MSS.

16. Contrary to legend, Churchill did not coin the term 'iron curtain' – it was first used by Lady Snowden during a visit to the Soviet Union. Nazi propaganda minister Joseph Goebbels also used the phrase in an attempt to warn the West of the consequences of a Soviet conquest of eastern Europe. See Henry B. Ryan, 'A New Look at Churchill's "Iron Curtain" Speech,' *Historical Journal* 22 (December 1979): 895–920.

17. Anderson, *The U.S., Great Britain, and the Cold War*, pp. 114–15; 'Churchill's "Union Now"', *Nation* 162 (16 March 1946): 303–4; Gaddis, *Origins of Cold War*, p. 309; *Congressional Record*, 79th Cong., 2d Sess., 92 (4 April 1946): 3087–8; Hathaway, *Ambiguous Partnership*, pp. 240–1; Alonzo L. Hamby, *Beyond the New Deal: Harry S. Truman and American Liberalism* (New York, 1973), pp. 102–5.

18. *Chicago Tribune*, 12 March 1946; American Press Summary, F.O. 371/5/624 AN 649/4/45; *Congressional Record*, 79th Cong., 2d Sess., 92 19 March 1946): A1487; Doenecke, *Not to the Swift*, pp. 62–3; Anderson, *The U.S., Great Britain, and the Cold War*, pp. 114–15.

19. Anderson, *The U.S., Great Britain, and the Cold War*, pp. 114–15; Hathaway, *Ambiguous Partnership*, pp. 240–1; Gaddis, *Origins of Cold War*, p. 309; Dimbleby and Reynolds, *An Ocean Apart*, pp. 184–5. Interestingly, however, the Foreign Office saw a silver lining to all this, as seen in a March 8 report by Halifax. Though allowing that '[t]he only out-and-out support of the speech appears to come from extreme-Right-wing anti-Soviet opinion,' he pointed out that, 'there has been virtually no reaction along the lines of 'How dare this Briton come to America and take it upon himself to give us advice?'….[B]efore the war any Briton…who made a speech of this kind would have been subjected to violent criticism of this sort. Indeed there would almost certainly have been a Resolution presented to Congress calling for the immediate expulsion from the United States of the offending speaker.' Far from viewing the response to the Fulton speech as a sign of renewed 'isolationism,' Halifax believed that it pointed toward 'a new and infinitely more

promising phase' in Anglo-American relations. Halifax to Bevin, 8 March 1946, F.O. 371/51624 AN 649/4/45.

20. Raymond P. Baldwin, 'British Trade and American Policy,' *Atlantic* 175 (February 1945): 50–5; *Congressional Record*, 79th Cong., 2d Sess., 92 (18 May 1945): A2386; ibid., (19 March 1946): A1487; ibid., (11 October 1945): 9571; Doenecke, *Not to the Swift*, pp. 61–2.

21. White House Press Release, 21 August 1945, *FRUS*, 1945, v.6, p. 109; Robin Edmonds, *Setting the Mould: The United States and Britain, 1945–1950* (New York, 1986), pp. 98–101; Martel, *Lend-Lease*, pp. 211–13. The condition regarding imperial preference apparently came in response to a House Resolution introduced by Rep. Emanuel Celler on September 13, which demanded that U.S. negotiators pledge no loan unless Britain agreed to 'dissolve the so-called sterling area bloc pool' and 'abrogate the so-called imperial preference trade barriers.' Text of H. Res. 341, Emanuel Celler MSS, Library of Congress Manuscript Division, Washington, D.C.

22. Earl of Birkenhead, *Halifax*, p. 558; Anderson, *The U.S., Great Britain, and the Cold War*, pp. 130–1; *Congressional Record*, 79th Cong., 2d Sess., 92 (4 February 1946): A450; ibid., (11 July 1946): 8701; *Chicago Tribune*, 20 December 1945; Hathaway, *Ambiguous Partnership*, pp. 234–5.

23. Doenecke, *Not to the Swift*, pp. 60–1; *Congressional Record*, 79th Cong., 2d Sess., 92 (11 September 1945): 8512; ibid., (13 July 1946): 8939; ibid., (7 February 1946): A556; ibid., (8 July 1946): A3954; Doenecke, *Not to the Swift*, pp. 61–2. One of those who charged that the British would use loan money to build a worldwide supremacy in trade was a young Wisconsin judge named Joseph R. McCarthy, who was at the time campaigning for the Republican nomination for Senate. Hathaway, *Ambiguous Partnership*, pp. 234–5.

24. Strout, *American Image of the Old World*, pp. 233–4; Anderson, *The U.S., Great Britain, and the Cold War*, pp. 130–1; Hathaway, *Ambiguous Partnership*, pp. 234–5; Doenecke, *Not to the Swift*, pp. 60–1.

25. Edmonds, *Setting the Mould*, pp. 101–2; Earl of Birkenhead, *Halifax*, p. 558; Martel, *Lend-Lease*, pp. 213–17; 'Arguments Against Britain,' *New Republic* 143 (1 October 1945): 424–5; 'Aid to Britain,' *Nation* 161 (15 December 1945): 649; 'The British Loan,' *Nation* 162 (9 February 1946): 155–6; 'Facts on the British Loan,' *New Republic* 114 (21 January 1946): 331–2.

26. 'The British Loan and Isolation,' *New Republic* 115 (15 July 1946): 46; 'Letter to Congressional Liberals,' *Nation* 163 (6 July 1946): 3–4.

27. 'We Can't Turn Down the British Loan,' *Saturday Evening Post* 218 (13 April 1946): 136; Taft to Herbert Hoover, 2 January 1946, Box 874, Taft MSS; Arthur Vandenberg, Jr. (ed.), *The Private Papers of Senator Vandenberg* (Boston, 1952), p. 231; Edmonds, *Setting the Mould*, p. 102. Taft's and Vandenberg's support for the loan was bitterly resented by many of their former allies in the prewar anti-interventionist movement. Robert E. Wood, former president of the AFC, claimed in a letter to Vandenberg that it was 'pure hypocrisy to call it a "loan" as they [the British] cannot and will not

be able to repay the amount proposed.' He went on to chastise the Michigan Republican for attempting to prop up 'a sick and worn-out system.' Wood to Vandenberg, 24 April 1946, Wood MSS.

28. Hathaway, *Ambiguous Partnership*, pp. 246–7; Strout, *American Image of the Old World*, pp. 233–4. One interesting trend evidenced in the vote on the British loan was the decline of 'anglophilia' in the South. Of the fifteen Democratic senators who opposed the agreement, no fewer than eight came from southern or border states. Paul Seabury suggests that southern sympathy for Great Britain was really nothing more than cultural solidarity with the sort of British conservatism which had apparently been repudiated in the 1945 Parliamentary elections. I. F. Stone, 'Line-up on the British Loan,' *Nation* 162 (May 18, 1946): 590–591; Paul Seabury, *Waning of Southern 'Internationalism'*, p. 9.

29. Raymond, 'American Public Opinion and Irish Neutrality,' p. 45; Memo by John D. Hickerson to Byrnes, 8 August 1946, *FRUS*, 1946, v.5, pp. 118–19; Chancery to Commonwealth Liaison, 26 December 1948, F.O. 371/68045E AN 0120/120/45; *Congressional Record*, 80th Cong., 1st Sess., 93 (24 February 1947): 1358.

30. Elizabeth Kimball MacLean, *Joseph E. Davies: Envoy to the Soviets* (Westport, CT, 1992), pp. 99, 106, 141; Henry Kissinger, *Diplomacy* (New York, 1994), pp. 430–1; J. Samuel Walker, *Henry A. Wallace and American Foreign Policy* (Westport, CT, 1976), p. 135; Karl M. Schmidt, *Henry A. Wallace: Quixotic Crusade, 1948* (Syracuse, 1960), pp. 19–20.

31. It is perhaps unsurprising that many of those most closely associated with McCarthyism in the early 1950s – men such as Rep. Hugh Butler (R-NE) and Rep. William Jenner (R-IN), as well as Mundt, Wherry, and McCarthy himself – had gained reputations for anglophobia during the debate over the loan. For more on populism's shift to the right, see Michael Kazin, *The Populist Persuasion: An American History* (New York, 1994).

32. Doenecke, *Not to the Swift*, p. 27; Glenn H. Smith, *Langer of North Dakota: A Study in Isolationism, 1940–1949* (New York, 1979); *Congressional Record*, 79th Cong., 1st Sess., 91 (4 December 1945): A5264; Wynona H. Wilkins, 'Two If By Sea: William Langer's Private War Against Winston Churchill,' *North Dakota History* 41 (Spring 1974), pp. 23–4; Burton K. Wheeler to Langer, Box 250, Langer MSS.

33. McMahon, 'Toward a post-colonial order,' p. 347; *New York Times*, 29 January 1947; Waldrop, *McCormick of Chicago*, p. 269; Chicago Political Report, August 1947, F.O. 371/61050 AN 3113/28/45; New York Consulate to Foreign Office, August 1947, F.O. 371/61050 AN 3154/28/45; Anderson, *The U.S., Great Britain, and the Cold War*, p. 183.

34. C. J. Bartlett, *'The Special Relationship': A Political History of Anglo-American Relations since 1945* (London, 1992), pp. 20–1, 26–7; Randall Bennett Woods, *A Changing of the Guard: Anglo-American Relations, 1941–1946* (Chapel Hill, NC, 1990), p. 268.

35. Hathaway, *Ambiguous Partnership*, pp. 306–7; Schmidt, *Henry A. Wallace*, pp. 189–90. As John Charmley has written, 'if the Soviet menace had not existed, Churchill would have needed to invent it.' Charmley, 'Churchill's Roosevelt,' in Lane and Temperley (ed.), *Rise and Fall*, pp. 90–107.
36. Hickenlooper to Secretary of State Marshall, 29 August 1947; Memorandum of Discussion between Secretary of Defense Forrestal, Under Secretary of State Lovett, Vandenberg and Hickenlooper, 17 November 1947; Memorandum of Meeting Re Exchange of Information with United Kingdom, 12 August 1948, Memorandum by Hickenlooper, 12 August 1948, all in Joint Committee on Atomic Energy File, Hickenlooper MSS.
37. Wilkins, 'Two if By Sea,' pp. 20–2; Smith, *Langer of North Dakota*, pp. 112–13; Bartlett, 'The Special Relationship', pp. 34–7.
38. There was not even a true revival of American anglophobia during the Suez affair of 1956, no doubt the most serious Anglo-American conflict of the postwar era. Britain's actions in Egypt were supported by a significant sector of the population, including such leading Democrats as Lyndon Johnson. Moreover, most protests against the British seizure of the Suez Canal centered on how this act could be used by the Soviets for propaganda purposes. Edmonds, *Setting the Mould*, pp. 234–7; Bartlett, *The Special Relationship*, pp. 82–7.

CONCLUSION

1. Montague Burton lecture by Halifax, 20 February 1947, F.O. 371/61000 AN 717/1/45.
2. Anthony D. Smith, *Theories of Nationalism*, 2d edition (New York, 1983), p. 220; idem, *The Ethnic Origins of Nations* (Oxford, 1986), p. 140.
3. Smith, *Ethnic Origins of Nations*, p. 151.
4. Contrary to the popular mythology of the time, Washington never used the term 'entangling alliances,' but merely called upon his fellow citizens to 'steer clear of permanent alliances.' It was Jefferson who added the word 'entangling.' Gilbert, *To the Farewell Address*, pp. 144–7.
5. Henry Kissinger, *Diplomacy* (New York, 1994), p. 431; Bailey, *Man in the Street*, pp. 232–4. The British blamed this attitude on 'jealousy' born of the 'latent inferiority complex...of a base and inferior subject.' By 1947, however, this feeling was largely in decline; a public opinion poll taken during that year showed that 55 percent of those surveyed believed that U.S. diplomats usually held their own in negotiations with the British. Only 27 percent felt that they were usually outsmarted. Ronald Sinclair to Foreign Office, 14 February 1947, F.O. 371/61000 AN 714/1/45; Bailey, *Man in the Street*, p. 234.
6. Robert P. Wilkins, Edward C. Blackorby, Wayne S. Cole, and Glenn H. Smith all point out that the farmers of the upper midwest often compared the British exploitation of their empire with the exploita-

tion which they believed they suffered at the hands of the industri-
al, commercial, and financial interests of the Northeast. See Wilkins,
'Non-Ethnic Roots of North Dakota Isolationism,' and 'Non-Partisan
League and Upper Midwest Isolationism,' Blackorby, *Prairie Rebel*,
Cole, *Gerald P. Nye*, and Smith, *Langer of North Dakota*.

7. Charles Krauthammer, 'Beyond the Cold War,' *New Republic* 199 (19
December 1988): 14–19.

Bibliography

UNPUBLISHED PRIMARY SOURCES – MANUSCRIPT COLLECTIONS

America First Committee MSS, Elwyn B. Robinson Department of Special Collections, University of North Dakota, Grand Forks, ND.
John J. Blaine MSS, Wisconsin State Historical Society, Madison, WI.
William E. Borah MSS, Library of Congress Manuscript Division, Washington, DC.
William R. Castle MSS, Herbert Hoover Presidential Library, West Branch, IA.
Emanuel Celler MSS, Library of Congress Manuscript Division, Washington, DC.
Bourke Hickenlooper MSS, Herbert Hoover Presidential Library, West Branch, IA.
Herbert Hoover MSS, Special Collections, Herbert Hoover Presidential Library, West Branch, IA.
Herbert Hoover MSS, Post-Presidential Individual File, Herbert Hoover Presidential Library, West Branch, IA.
La Follette Family Papers, Library of Congress Manuscript Division, Washington, DC.
William Langer MSS, Elwyn B. Robinson Department of Special Collections, University of North Dakota, Grand Forks, ND.
William Lemke MSS, Elwyn B. Robinson Department of Special Collections, University of North Dakota, Grand Forks, ND.
Kenneth D. McKellar MSS, Memphis Public Library, Memphis, TN.
George Norris MSS, Library of Congress Manuscript Division, Washington, DC.
Gerald P. Nye MSS, Herbert Hoover Presidential Library, West Branch, IA.
Gerald P. Nye MSS, Elwyn B. Robinson Department of Special Collections, University of North Dakota, Grand Forks, ND.
Gerald L.K. Smith MSS, Bentley Historical Library, University of Michigan, Ann Arbor, MI.
Martin L. Sweeney MSS, Western Reserve Historical Library, Cleveland, OH.
Robert A. Taft MSS, Library of Congress Manuscript Division, Washington, DC.
Charles Callan Tansill MSS, Herbert Hoover Presidential Library, West Branch, IA.
Thomas J. Walsh MSS, American Historical Survey, University of Illinois Library, Urbana, IL.
Walsh-Erickson Papers, Library of Congress Manuscript Division, Washington, DC.
Robert E. Wood MSS, Herbert Hoover Presidential Library, West Branch, IA.

UNPUBLISHED PRIMARY SOURCES – GOVERNMENT DOCUMENTS

British Embassy Papers, Washington, DC, 1945–1948.

PUBLISHED PRIMARY SOURCES – COLLECTIONS

Berle, Adolf A. *Navigating the Rapids, 1918–1971*. New York, 1973.
Burke, Robert E., ed. *The Diary Letters of Hiram Johnson*, vols. 4–7. New York, 1983.
Coblenz, Edmond D., ed. *William Randolph Hearst: A Portrait in His Own Words*. New York, 1952.
Doenecke, Justus D., ed. *In Danger Undaunted: The Anti-Interventionist Movement of 1940–1941 as Revealed in the Papers of the America First Committee*. Stanford, CA, 1990.
Gallup, George H. *The Gallup Poll: Public Opinion, 1935–1971*. vol. 1. New York, 1972.
Hachey, Thomas E., ed. 'Profiles in Politics: British Embassy Views of Prominent Americans in 1939.' *Wisconsin Magazine of History* 54 (Autumn 1970): 3–22.
——, ed. 'American Profiles on Capitol Hill: A Confidential Study for the British Foreign Office in 1943.' *Wisconsin Magazine of History* 57 (Winter 1973/74): 141–54.
——, ed. *Confidential Dispatches: Analyses of America by the British Ambassador, 1939–1945*. Evanston, IL, 1974.
Israel, Fred L., ed. *The War Diary of Breckenridge Long: Selections from the Years 1939–1944*. Lincoln, NE, 1966.
Nicholas, H. G., ed. *Washington Despatches, 1941–1945: Weekly Political Reports from the British Embassy*. Chicago, 1981.
Perry, Glen C. H., ed. *'Dear Bart': Washington Views of World War II*. Westport, CT, 1982.
Roosevelt, Elliott, ed. *F.D.R.: His Personal Letters*. vol. 2. New York, 1970.
U.S. Congress, *Congressional Record*, 67th through 80th Congresses.
U.S. Department of State, *Foreign Relations of the United States*. Annual volumes, 1921–1948. Washington, DC, 1938–1970.
Vandenberg, Arthur, Jr. *The Private Papers of Senator Vandenberg*. Boston, 1952.

PUBLISHED PRIMARY SOURCES – NEWSPAPERS AND PERIODICALS

Chicago Tribune, 1921–1948.
New York Times, 1921–1948.
'Admiral Plunkett's War with England.' *Literary Digest* 96 (11 February 1928): 7–9.
'Aid to Britain.' *Nation* 161 (15 December 1945): 649.
'All-Out-Aid-For-Britain.' *Catholic World* 152 (March 1941): 641–50.
'American-British Alliance.' *Collier's* 112 (30 October 1943): 78.
'American Language.' *Collier's* (23 January 1926): 20.

'American Neutrality in British Eyes.' *Living Age* 350 (April 1936): 167–9.
'Anti-British Hysteria.' *Nation* 145 (11 September 1937): 253–4.
'Arguments Against Britain.' *New Republic* 143 (1 October 1945): 424–5.
'Beware the Flag Flappers.' *Collier's* (26 November 1927): 50.
'Borah Twists the Lion's Tail.' *Literary Digest* 89 (10 April 1926): 13.
'Britain's Colonial Broils.' *Literary Digest* 72 (14 January 1922): 12.
'Britain's Problem of Leadership.' *New Republic* 107 (6 July 1942): 6–7.
'The British-American Alliance.' *Nation* 124 (30 March 1927): 332.
'The British Empire at the Conference.' *New Republic* 29 (7 December 1921): 44–6.
'The British Loan.' *Nation* 162 (9 February 1946): 155–6.
'The British Loan and Isolation.' *New Republic* 115 (15 July 1946): 46.
'Churchill's "Union Now".' *Nation* 162 (16 March 1946): 303–4.
'A Congress to Win the War.' Supplement. *New Republic* 106 (18 May 1942): 684–710.
'Deadwood at the Top.' *New Republic* 106 (2 March 1942): 285–6.
'Does Cooperation with Britain Mean Intervention?' *New Republic* 35 (14 November 1923): 296–8.
'End of British Rubber Control.' *Literary Digest* 96 (21 April 1928): 10.
'England and America.' *New Republic* 60 (9 October 1929): 186–8.
'England Woos the Fascists.' *New Republic* (24 November 1937): 60–1.
'Facts on the British Loan.' *New Republic* 114 (21 January 1946): 331–2.
'The *Fortune* Survey: XXVI.' *Fortune* 21 (January 1940): 86–8.
'Great Britain's Plan to Keep her Naval Supremacy.' *Literary Digest* 97 (7 April 1928): 10.
'King George Defied by "Big Bill".' *Literary Digest* 95 (5 November 1927): 5–8.
'Language by Legislation.' *Nation* 116 (11 April 1923): 408.
'Letter to Congressional Liberals.' *Nation* 163 (6 July 1946): 3–4.
'The Menace of Anglo-American Naval Rivalry,' *Literary Digest* 100 (5 January 1929): 5–7.
'Mr. Churchill's Untotal War.' *New Republic* 107 (28 September 1942): 370–2.
'Net Result of the Lloyd George Visit.' *Literary Digest* 79 (17 November 1923): 12.
'Noble Negatives.' *Economist* (30 December 1944): 22.
'An Open Letter to the People of England.' *Life* (12 October 1942): 13.
'Those Neutral Rights.' *Nation* 124 (15 June 1927): 659.
'Reefing in Rubber,' *Saturday Evening Post* (5 June 1926): 150
'The Source of Anti-Britishism.' *New Republic* 52 (16 November 1927): 325–6.
'T.R.B. from Washington.' *New Republic* (2 March 1938): 99–100.
'The "Unthinkable" Thing.' *Nation* (2 January 1929): 4.
'War with Britain not "Unthinkable".' *Literary Digest* 100 (9 February 1929): 5–7.
'We Can't Turn Down the British Loan.' *Saturday Evening Post* 218 (13 April 1946): 136.
'We're Not Perfect Ourselves.' *Collier's* 109 (4 April 1942): 66.
Baldwin, Raymond P. 'British Trade and American Policy.' *Atlantic* 175 (February 1945): 50–5.

Bausman, Frederick. 'Under Which Flag?' *American Mercury* 12 (October 1927): 195–203.

Bisson, T. A. 'Britain Tightens Control In India.' *Nation* 143 (21 August 1935): 210–12.

Borah, William E. 'Freedom of the Seas.' *Current History* 29 (March 1929): 922–7.

Brewster, Owen. 'Let's Not be Suckers Again.' *American Magazine* 139 (January 1945): 24–5.

Butler, Hamilton. 'The Anglo-American Love Affair.' *American Mercury* 29 (July 1933): 257–68.

Canby, Henry Seidel. 'Anglomania.' *Harper's* (21 November 1921): 713.

Cooke, Alistair. 'British Propaganda in the United States.' *Fortnightly* 153 (June 1940): 606–13.

Davis, Forrest. 'The British Get Out of the Doghouse.' *Saturday Evening Post* 216 (18 September 1943): 16–21.

Fullerton, Hugh. 'The Coming Naval Disarmament Conference and What We Won't Get Out of It.' *Liberty* (30 April 1927): 39.

Gardiner, A. G. 'England and America: Their Misunderstandings and Their Opportunity.' *Harper's* 149 (July 1924): 145–52.

Gardiner, William Howard. 'Naval Parity? The Outlook after Geneva.' *Harper's* 156 (January 1928): 211–19.

Garrett, Garet. 'A Primer of Propaganda.' *Saturday Evening Post* (15 January 1927): 4.

Gillis, James M. 'Who Shall Lead the World?' *Catholic World* 162 (December 1945): 193–201.

Hanighen, Frank C. 'What England and France Think About Us.' *Harper's* 179 (September 1939): 376–85.

Hodson, James Lansdale. 'No Hard Feelings.' *Atlantic* 174 (July 1944): 81–6.

Hutchison, Keith. 'Churchill and the British Loan.' *Nation* 162 (16 March 1946): 316.

Kirchwey, Freda. 'Royalty Is Not Enough.' *Nation* 148 (10 June 1939): 661.

Krishna-Menon, V. K. 'Labor Militancy Spreads in India.' *Nation* 142 (12 September 1934): 293.

McCullagh, Francis. *Catholic World* 155 (May 1942): 202–10.

——. 'England, Ireland and India.' *Catholic World* 161 (September 1945): 493–500.

Mencken, H. L. 'Editorial.' *American Mercury* 8 (June 1926): 155–7.

——. 'Notes on a Moral War.' *Baltimore Sun*, 8 October 1939.

Morrison, Charles Clayton. 'Mr. Churchill and the Future.' *Christian Century* 59 (7 January 1942): 3–4.

——. 'No Victory Without India.' *Christian Century* 59 (21 October 1942): 1278–9.

——. 'Unhappy Europe.' *Christian Century* 61 (20 December 1944): 1470–1.

Nock, Albert J. '"Unfinished Victory" – A Review.' *Scribner's Commentator* 9 (April 1941): 17–20.

Reeves, Emery. 'Should the British Empire be Broken Up?' *American Mercury* 56 (May 1943): 553–61.

Stone, I. F. 'Line-up on the British Loan.' *Nation* 162 (May 18, 1946): 590–1.

Straight, Michael. 'Is It a People's War?' *New Republic* 107 (November 16, 1942): 633–5.

Thompson, William Hale. 'Patriots and Propagandists.' *Forum* 79 (April 1928): 503–15.

Viereck, George Sylvester. 'Shall Uncle Sam Commit National Suicide?' *American Monthly* (January 1925): 341.

Villard, Oswald Garrison. 'England Shows Her Colors.' *New Republic* (March 2, 1938): 87–8.

——. 'England, America, and the War.' *Nation* 149 (September 30, 1939): 349.

——. 'If This Be Treason –' *Nation* 150 (February 3, 1940): 130.

Wickware, Francis Sill. 'What We Think About Foreign Affairs.' *Harper's* 179 (September 1939): 397–406.

PUBLISHED PRIMARY SOURCES – BOOKS AND PAMPHLETS

Booker, George W. (pseudonym of Conrad Oerich). *The Slave Business*. Scotch Plains, NJ, 1941.

Borchard, Edwin, and William Potter Lage. *Neutrality for the United States*. New Haven, CT, 1937.

Briffault, Robert. *The Decline and Fall of the British Empire*. New York, 1938.

Bromfield, Louis. *England: A Dying Oligarchy*. New York, 1939.

Browder, Earl. 'Concerted Action or Isolation: Which Is the Road to Peace?' New York, 1938.

——. *Fighting for Peace*. New York, 1939.

——. *The Second Imperialist War*. New York, 1940.

——. *The Way Out*. New York, 1941.

Day, Stephen A. *We Must Save the Republic*. Scotch Plains, NJ, 1941.

Denny, Ludwell. *America Conquers Britain: A Record of Economic War*. New York, 1930.

Dreiser, Theodore. *America is Worth Saving*. New York, 1941.

Engelbrecht, H. C., and F. C. Hanighen. *Merchants of Death*. New York, 1934.

Frank, Jerome. *Save America First: How to Make Our Democracy Work*. New York, 1938.

Grattan, C. Hartley. *Why We Fought*. New York, 1929.

——. *The Deadly Parallel*. New York, 1939.

Greene, Nathaniel. *Doublecross in Palestine*. Scotch Plains, NJ, 1941.

Griswold, A. Whitney. *Far Eastern Policy of the United States*. New Haven, CT, 1938.

Halassie, Sayid (pseudonym of Paul Schmitz). *Democracy on the Nile: How Britain Has 'Protected' Egypt*. Scotch Plains, NJ, 1940.

Halsey, Margaret. *With Malice Toward Some*. New York, 1938.

Hamilton, James Burr (pseudonym of George Sylvester Viereck). *Lord Lothian against Lord Lothian*. Scotch Plains, NJ, 1941.

Hammill, John. *The Strange Career of Mr. Hoover Under Two Flags*. New York, 1931.

Howe, Quincy. *England Expects Every American to Do His Duty*. New York, 1937.
Johnson, Hugh S. *Hell-Bent for War*. Indianapolis, IN, 1941.
Leigh, Randolph. *Conscript Europe*. New York, 1938.
Moley, Raymond. *After Seven Years*. New York, 1939.
O'Sheel, Shaemas. *Seven Periods of Irish History*. Scotch Plains, NJ, 1940.
Peterson, H. C. *Propaganda for War: The Campaign against American Neutrality, 1914–1917*. Norman, OK, 1939.
Rogerson, Sidney. *Propaganda in the Next War*. London, 1938.
Sargent, Porter. *Getting US into War*. Boston, 1941.
Simonds, Frank. *The ABC's of War Debts, and the Seven Popular Delusions About Them*. New York, 1933.
———. *Can America Stay at Home?* New York, 1932.
Thomas, Norman, and Bertram D. Wolfe. *Keep America Out of War: A Program*. New York, 1939.
Willkie, Wendell L. *One World*. New York, 1943.
Wirsing, Giselher. *One Hundred Families that Rule the Empire*. Scotch Plains, NJ, 1941.

UNPUBLISHED SECONDARY SOURCES

Anderson, John Thomas. 'Senator Burton K. Wheeler and United States Foreign Relations.' Ph.D. dissertation, University of Virginia, 1982.
Bryniarski, Joan Lee. 'Against the Tide: Senate Opposition to the Internationalist Foreign Policy of Presidents Franklin D. Roosevelt and Harry S. Truman, 1943–1949.' Ph.D. dissertation, University of Maryland, 1972.
Chalk, Frank Robert. 'The United States and the International Struggle for Rubber, 1914–1941.' Ph.D. dissertation, University of Wisconsin, 1970.
Coffey, William Ellis. 'Rush Dew Holt: The Boy Senator, 1905–1942.' Ph.D. dissertation, West Virginia University, 1970.
Dressler, Thomas Herbert Bernhard. 'The Foreign Policies of American Individualism: Herbert Hoover, Reluctant Internationalist.' Ph.D. dissertation, Brown University, 1973.
Hanks, Richard Kay. 'Hamilton Fish and American Isolationism, 1920–1944.' Ph.D. dissertation, University of California at Riverside, 1971.
Harrison, Richard Arnold. 'Appeasement and Isolation: The Relationship of British and American Foreign Policies, 1935–1938.' Ph.D. dissertation, Princeton University, 1974.
Kent, Alan Edmond. 'Portrait in Isolationism: The La Follettes and Foreign Policy.' Ph.D. dissertation, University of Wisconsin, 1956.
Mannock, James Harold. 'Anglo-American Relations, 1921–1928.' Ph.D. dissertation, Princeton University, 1962.
Meaney, Neville K. 'The American Attitude Towards the British Empire from 1919 to 1922 – A Study in the Diplomatic Relations of the English-Speaking Nations.' Ph.D. dissertation, Duke University, 1958.

Newton, Christina. 'Anglo-American Relations and Bureaucratic Tensions, 1927–1930.' Ph.D. dissertation, University of Illinois, 1975.

Pleasant, Julian McIver. 'The Senatorial Career of Robert Rice Reynolds.' Ph.D. dissertation, University of North Carolina at Chapel Hill, 1971.

Pope, Robert Dean. 'Senatorial Baron: The Long Political Career of Kenneth D. McKellar.' Ph.D. dissertation, Yale University, 1976.

Pullen, William George. 'World War Debts and United States Foreign Policy.' Ph.D dissertation, Harvard University, 1972.

Richards, David Allen. 'The Abortive Entente: The American Popular Mind and the Idea of Anglo-American Cooperation to Keep the Peace, 1921–1931.' Ph.D. dissertation, Florida State University, 1976.

Tanner, Ralph M. 'James Thomas Heflin: United States Senator, 1920–1931.' Ph.D. dissertation, University of Alabama, 1967.

PUBLISHED SECONDARY SOURCES – BOOKS AND ARTICLES

Adler, Selig. 'War-Guilt and American Disillusionment.' *Journal of Modern History* 23 (March 1951): 14–15.

——. *The Isolationist Impulse: Its Twentieth Century Reaction*. New York, 1957.

Allen, H. C. *Great Britain and the United States: A History of Anglo-American Relations, 1783–1952*. London, 1954.

Ambrosius, Lloyd. *Woodrow Wilson and the American Diplomatic Tradition: The Treaty Fight in Perspective*. Cambridge, 1987.

Anderson, Terry H. *The United States, Great Britain, and the Cold War, 1944–1947*. Columbia, MO, 1981.

Andrade, Ernest R. 'The Cruiser Controversy in Naval Limitations Negotiations, 1922–1936.' *Military Affairs* 48 (July 1984): 113–20.

Anstey, Caroline. 'The Projection of British Socialism: Foreign Office Publicity and Public Opinion, 1945–1950.' *Journal of Contemporary History* 19 (July 1984): 417–51.

Ashby, LeRoy. *The Spearless Leader: Senator Borah and the Progressive Movement in the 1920s*. Urbana, IL, 1972.

Bailey, Thomas A. *The Man in the Street: The Impact of Public Opinion on Foreign Policy*. New York, 1948.

Barnett, Correlli. 'Anglo-American Strategy in Europe,' in Ann Lane and Howard Temperley (eds.), *The Rise and Fall of the Grand Alliance, 1941–45* (London, 1995): 174–89.

Bartlett, C. J. *'The Special Relationship': A Political History of Anglo-American Relations since 1945*. London, 1992.

Baylis, John. *Anglo-American Defence Relations, 1939–1980: The Special Relationship*. New York, 1981.

Bayor, Ronald H. *Neighbors in Conflict: The Irish, Germans, Jews, and Italians of New York City, 1929–1941*. Baltimore, MD, 1978.

Bearse, Ray, and Anthony Read. *Conspirator: The Untold Story of Tyler Kent*. New York, 1991.

Bennett, David H. *Demagogues in the Depression: American Radicals and the Union Party, 1932–1936*. New Brunswick, NJ, 1969.

Bernstein, Barton J. 'The Uneasy Alliance: Roosevelt, Churchill, and the

Atomic Bomb, 1940–1945.' *Western Political Quarterly* 29 (July 1976): 202–30.

Birkenhead, Earl of. *Halifax: The Life of Lord Halifax.* Boston, 1966.

Blackorby, Edward C. *Prairie Rebel: The Public Life of William Lemke.* Lincoln, NE, 1963.

Braisted, William R. 'On the American Red and Red-Orange Plans, 1919–1939,' in Gerald Jordan (ed.), *Naval Warfare in the Twentieth Century, 1900–1945: Essays in honour of Arthur Marder* (London, 1977): 167–85.

Brandes, Joseph. *Herbert Hoover and Economic Diplomacy: Department of Commerce Policy, 1921–1928.* Pittsburgh, PA, 1962.

Breuer, William B. *Feuding Allies: The Private Wars of the High Command.* New York, 1995.

Brinkley, Alan. *Voices of Protest: Huey Long, Father Coughlin and the Great Depression.* New York, 1982.

Buckley, Thomas H. *The United States and the Washington Conference, 1921–1922.* Knoxville, TN, 1970.

Burk, Kathleen. 'American Economic Foreign Policy and Lend-Lease,' in Ann Lane and Howard Temperley (eds.), *The Rise and Fall of the Grand Alliance, 1941–45* (London, 1995): 43–68.

Burns, James MacGregor. *Roosevelt: The Lion and the Fox.* New York, 1956.

Butler, J. R. M. *Lord Lothian, 1882–1940.* London, 1960.

Carlton, David. 'Great Britain and the Coolidge Naval Disarmament Conference of 1927.' *Political Science Quarterly* 83 (December 1968): 373–98.

Carroll, F. M. 'The American Committee for Relief in Ireland, 1920–1922.' *Irish Historical Studies* 23 (May 1982): 30–49.

Carroll, John M. 'Henry Cabot Lodge's Contributions to the Shaping of Republican European Diplomacy, 1920–1924.' *Capitol Studies* 3 (Fall 1975): 153–65.

Chadwin, Mark L. *The Warhawks: American Interventionists before Pearl Harbor.* New York, 1970.

Charmley, John. *Churchill's Grand Alliance: The Anglo-American Special Relationship, 1940–57.* New York, 1995.

——. 'Churchill's Roosevelt,' in Ann Lane and Howard Temperley (eds.), *The Rise and Fall of the Grand Alliance, 1941–45* (London, 1995): 90–107.

Clark, William. *Less than Kin: A Study of Anglo-American Relations.* Boston, 1957.

Clymer, Kenton J. 'The Education of William Phillips: Self-Determination and American Policy Toward India, 1942–45.' *Diplomatic History* (Winter 1988): 13–35.

Cohen, Warren I. *The American Revisionists: The Lessons of Intervention in World War I.* Chicago, 1967.

Cole, Wayne S. *America First: The Battle Against Intervention, 1940–1941.* Madison, WI, 1953.

——. *Gerald P. Nye and American Foreign Relations.* Minneapolis, MN, 1962.

——. *Charles A. Lindbergh and the Battle Against American Intervention in World War II.* New York, 1974.

——. *Roosevelt and the Isolationists, 1932–1945.* Lincoln, NE, 1983.

Costigliola, Frank. *Awkward Dominion: American Political, Economic, and*

Cultural Relations with Europe, 1919–1933. Ithaca, NY, 1984.

Cull, Nicholas John. *Selling War: The British Propaganda Campaign Against American 'Neurality' in World War II*. New York, 1995.

Dallek, Robert. *Franklin D. Roosevelt and American Foreign Policy*. Oxford, 1979.

Dayer, Roberta Allbert. 'The British War Debts and the Anglo-Japanese Alliance, 1920–1923.' *Pacific Historical Review* 45 (November 1976): 569–95.

DeWitt, Howard A. 'The "New" Harding and American Foreign Policy: Warren G. Harding, Hiram W. Johnson, and Pragmatic Diplomacy.' *Ohio History* 86 (Spring 1977): 96–114.

Dimbleby, David, and David Reynolds. *An Ocean Apart: The Relationship between Britain and America in the Twentieth Century*. New York, 1988.

Divine, Robert A. *The Illusion of Neutrality*. Chicago, 1962.

——. *Second Chance: The Triumph of Internationalism in America During World War II*. New York, 1967.

——. *Foreign Policy and U.S. Presidential Elections. Volume One: 1940–1948*. New York, 1974.

Doenecke, Justus D. 'Non-interventionism of the Left: The Keep America Out of War Congress, 1938–1941.' *Journal of Contemporary History* 12 (April 1977): 221–36.

——. *Not to the Swift: The Old Isolationists in the Cold War Era*. Cranbury, NJ, 1979.

Dubay, Robert William. 'The Geneva Naval Conference of 1927: A Study of Battleship Diplomacy.' *Southern Quarterly* 8 (January 1970): 177–99.

Dulles, Foster Rhea, and Gerald E. Ridinger. 'The Anti-Colonial Policies of Franklin D. Roosevelt.' *Political Science Quarterly* 70 (March 1955): 1–18.

Edmonds, Robin. *Setting the Mould: The United States and Britain, 1945–1950*. New York, 1986.

Edwards, Jerome E. *The Foreign Policy of Col. McCormick's Tribune, 1929–1941*. Reno, NV, 1971.

Feinman, Ronald L. *Twilight of Progressivism: The Western Republican Senators and the New Deal*. Baltimore, MD, 1981.

Ferrell, Robert H. *American Diplomacy in the Great Depression: Hoover-Stimson Foreign Policy, 1929–1933*. New Haven, 1957.

Gaddis, John Lewis. *The United States and the Origins of the Cold War, 1941–1947*. New York, 1972.

Galbraith, John S. 'The United States, Britain, and the Creation of the Irish Free State.' *South Atlantic Quarterly* 48 (October 1949): 566–74.

Gerson, Louis. *The Hyphenate in Recent American Politics and Diplomacy*. Lawrence, KS, 1964.

Gibbs, Norman. 'The Naval Conferences of the Interwar Years: A Study in Anglo-American Relations.' *Naval War College Review* 30 (Summer 1977): 50–63.

Gies, Joseph. *The Colonel of Chicago*. New York, 1979.

Gilbert, Felix. *To the Farewell Address: Ideas of Early American Foreign Policy*. Princeton, NJ, 1961.

Goodhart, Philip. *Fifty Ships that Saved the World: The Foundation of the Anglo-American Alliance*. New York, 1965.

Grassmuck, George L. *Sectional Biases in Congress on Foreign Policy*. Johns Hopkins University Studies in Historical and Political Science, Series LXVIII, No. 3, 1951.

Green, Paul M., and Melvin G. Holli. 'Big Bill Thompson: The "Model" Politician,' in Paul M. Green and Melvin G. Holli (eds), *The Mayors: The Chicago Political Tradition* (Carbondale, IL, 1987): 61–81.

Guinsberg, Thomas N. *The Pursuit of Isolationism in the United States Senate from Versailles to Pearl Harbor*. New York, 1982.

Hachey, Thomas E. 'Winning Friends and Influencing Policy: British Strategy to Woo America in 1937.' *Wisconsin Magazine of History* 55 (Winter 1971/2): 120–9.

Hall, Christopher. *Britain, America and Arms Control, 1921–37*. London, 1987.

Hamby, Alonzo L. *Beyond the New Deal: Harry S. Truman and American Liberalism*. New York, 1973.

Harrison, Richard A. 'The United States and Great Britain: Presidential Diplomacy and Alternatives to Appeasement in the 1930s,' in David F. Schmitz and Richard D. Challener (eds), *Appeasement in Europe: A Reassessment of U.S. Policies* (New York, 1990): 51–74.

Hathaway, Robert M. *Ambiguous Partnership: Britain and America, 1944–1947*. New York, 1981.

Herken, Gregg. *The Winning Weapon: The Atomic Bomb in the Cold War, 1945–1950*. New York, 1980.

Hero, Alfred O. *The Southerner and World Affairs*. Baton Rouge, LA, 1965.

Hess, Gary R. *America Encounters India, 1941–1947*. Baltimore, MD, 1971.

Hicks, John D. *Republican Ascendancy, 1921–1933*. New York, 1960.

Hogan, Michael J. *Informal Entente: The Private Structure of Cooperation in Anglo-American Economic Diplomacy, 1918–1928*. Columbia, MO, 1977.

Holbrook, Francis X. 'The Canton Island Controversy: Compromise or American Victory.' *Journal of the Royal Australian Historical Society* 59 (June 1973): 128–47.

Holcomb, Michael. 'Sir John Simon's War with Henry L. Stimson: A Footnote to Anglo-American Relations in the 1930s,' in Clifford L. Egan and Alexander W. Knott (eds), *Essays in Twentieth Century American Diplomatic History Dedicated to Professor Daniel M. Smith* (Washington, DC, 1982): 90–110.

Hunt, Michael H. *Ideology and U.S. Foreign Policy*. New Haven, CT, 1987.

Hurt, R. Douglas. 'The Settlement of Anglo-American Claims Resulting from World War I.' *American Neptune* 34 (July 1974): 155–73.

Jenkins, Roy. *Truman*. New York, 1986.

Jha, Manoranjan. 'Britain and Pro-India Activities in the U.S.A.' *Political Science Review* 12 (Spring 1973): 1–34.

Johnson, Robert David. *The Peace Progressives and American Foreign Relations*. Cambridge, 1995.

Johnson, Niel M. *George Sylvester Viereck: German-American Propagandist*. Urbana, IL, 1972.

Jonas, Manfred. *Isolationism in America, 1935–1941*. Ithaca, NY, 1966.

Kazin, Michael. *The Populist Persuasion: An American History*. New York, 1994.

Kimball, Warren F. *The Most Unsordid Act: Lend-Lease, 1939–1941*. Baltimore, MD, 1969.

——. 'Lend-Lease and the Open Door: The Temptation of British Opulence, 1937–1942,' in Kimball, *The Juggler: Franklin Roosevelt as Wartime Statesman* (Princeton, 1991): 43–61.

Kinsella, William E., Jr. *Leadership in Isolation: FDR and the Origins of the Second World War*. Cambridge, 1978.

Kissinger, Henry. *Diplomacy*. New York, 1994.

Knock, Thomas J. *To End All Wars: Woodrow Wilson and the Quest for a New World Order*. New York, 1992.

Krauthammer, Charles. 'Beyond the Cold War.' *New Republic* 199 (December 19, 1988): 14–19.

LaFeber, Walter. *The New Empire: An Interpretation of American Expansion, 1860–1898*. Ithaca, NY, 1963.

Leffler, Melvyn. 'The Origins of Republican War Debt Policy, 1921–1923: A Case Study in the Applicability of the Open Door Interpretation.' *Journal of American History* 59 (December 1972): 585–601.

Leuchtenburg, William E. *Franklin D. Roosevelt and the New Deal*. New York, 1963.

Leutze, James R. 'The Secret of the Churchill-Roosevelt Correspondence, September 1939–May 1940.' *Journal of Contemporary History* 10 (July 1975): 465–91.

——. *Bargaining for Supremacy: Anglo-American Naval Cooperation, 1937–1941*. Chapel Hill, NC, 1977.

Levering, Ralph B. *The Public and American Foreign Policy, 1918–1978*. New York, 1978.

Levine, Robert H. *The Politics of American Naval Rearmament, 1930–1938*. New York, 1988.

Louis, Wm. Roger. *Imperialism at Bay: The United States and the Decolonization of the British Empire*. Oxford, 1977.

Love, Robert William, Jr. 'Anglo-American Naval Diplomacy and the British Pacific Fleet, 1942–1945.' *American Neptune* 42 (July 1982): 203–16.

Lower, Richard Coke. *A Bloc of One: The Political Career of Hiram W. Johnson*. Stanford, 1993.

Lubell, Samuel. *The Future of American Politics*. New York, 1948.

Lukacs, John. *Outgrowing Democracy*. New York, 1984.

McCoy, Donald. *Calvin Coolidge: The Quiet President*. New York, 1967.

MacDonald, C.A. *The United States, Britain and Appeasement, 1936–1939*. New York, 1981.

McKenna, Marian C. *Borah*. Ann Arbor, MI, 1961.

McKercher, B. J. C. *The Second Baldwin Government and the United States, 1924–1929: Attitudes and Diplomacy*. Cambridge, 1984.

——. *Esme Howard: A Diplomatic Biography*. Cambridge, 1989.

MacLean, Elizabeth Kimball. *Joseph E. Davies: Envoy to the Soviets*. Westport, CT, 1992.

McMahon, Robert J. 'Toward a post-colonial order: Truman administration policies toward South and Southeast Asia,' in Michael J. Lacey (ed.), *The Truman presidency* (Cambridge, 1989): 339–65.

Maddox, Robert James. 'Borah and the Battleships.' *Idaho Yesterdays* 9 (Summer 1965): 20–7.

——. *William E. Borah and American Foreign Policy*. Baton Rouge, LA, 1969.

Maney, Patrick J. *'Young Bob' La Follette: A Biography of Robert M. La Follette, Jr., 1895–1953* (Columbia, MO, 1978).

Marks, Frederick W., III. 'Franklin Roosevelt's Diplomatic Debut: The Myth of the Hundred Days.' *South Atlantic Quarterly* 84 (Summer 1985): 245–63.

——. 'Six Between Roosevelt and Hitler: America's Role in the Appeasement of Nazi Germany.' *Historical Journal* 28 (December 1985): 969–82.

——. *Wind Over Sand: The Diplomacy of Franklin Roosevelt*. Athens, GA, 1988.

Martel, Leon. *Lend-Lease, Loans, and the Coming of the Cold War: A Study of the Implementation of Foreign Policy*. Boulder, CO, 1979.

Martin, James J. *American Liberalism and World Politics, 1931–1941*. 2 vols. New York, 1964.

Matthews, Geoffrey. 'Robert A. Taft, the Constitution, and American Foreign Policy, 1939–53.' *Journal of Contemporary History* 17 (July 1982): 505–20.

Morison, Elting E. *Admiral Sims and the Modern American Navy*. Boston, 1942.

Narinsky, Mikhail N., Lydia V. Pozdeeva, et al., 'Mutual Perceptions: Images, Ideals, and Illusions,' in David Reynolds, Warren F. Kimball, and A. O. Chubarian (eds.), *Allies at War: The Soviet, American and British Experience* (New York, 1994): 307–32.

O'Brien, Patrick G. 'Senator John J. Blaine: An Independent Progressive During "Normalcy".' *Wisconsin Magazine of History* 60 (Autumn 1976): 25–41.

O'Connor, Raymond G. 'The "Yardstick" and Naval Disarmament in the 1920s.' *Mississippi Valley Historical Review* 45 (December 1958): 441–63.

——. *Perilous Equilibrium: The United States and the London Naval Conference of 1930*. Lawrence, KS, 1962.

O'Grady, Joseph, ed. *The Immigrants' Influence on Wilson's Peace Policies*. Lexington, KY, 1967.

O'Reilly, Kenneth. 'A New Deal for the FBI: The Roosevelt Administration, Crime Control, and National Security.' *Journal of American History* 69 (December 1982): 638–58.

Patterson, James T. *Mr. Republican: A Biography of Robert A. Taft*. Boston, 1972.

Perkins, Bradford. *The Great Rapprochement: England and the United States, 1895–1914*. New York, 1969.

——. 'Unequal Partners: The Truman Adminstration and Great Britain,' in Wm. Roger Louis and Hedley Bull (eds.), *The 'Special Relationship': Anglo-American Relations since 1945* (Oxford, 1986): 43–63.

Perlmutter, Amos. *FDR and Stalin: A Not So Grand Alliance, 1943–1945*. Columbia, MO, 1993.

Pollock, Fred T., and Warren F. Kimball. '"In Search of Monsters to Destroy": Roosevelt and Colonialism,' in Kimball (ed.), *The Juggler: Franklin Roosevelt as Wartime Statesman* (Princeton, 1991).

Porter, David L. *The Seventy-sixth Congress and World War II, 1939–1940.* Columbia, MO, 1979.

Rappaport, Armin. *The Navy League of the United States.* Detroit, 1962.

——. *Henry L. Stimson and Japan.* Chicago, 1963.

Raymond, Raymond James. 'American Public Opinion and Irish Neutrality, 1939–1945.' *Eire-Ireland* 18 (Spring 1983): 20–45.

Renwick, Sir Robin. *Fighting with Allies: America and Britain in Peace and at War.* New York, 1996.

Reynolds, David. *The Creation of the Anglo-American Alliance, 1937–1941: A Study in Competitive Co-operation.* London, 1981.

——. 'FDR's Foreign Policy and the British Royal Visit to the U.S.A., 1939.' *Historian* 45 (August 1983): 461–72.

——. *Britannia Overruled: British Policy and World Power in the Twentieth Century.* London, 1991.

——, Warren F. Kimball, and A. O. Chubarian. 'Legacies: Allies, Enemies, and Posterity,' in Reynolds, Kimball, and Chubarian (eds), *Allies at War: The Soviet, American and British Experience, 1939–1945* (New York, 1994): 417–40.

Rhodes, Benjamin D. 'Herbert Hoover and the War Debts, 1919–1933.' *Prologue* 6 (Summer 1974): 130–44.

——. 'Anglophobia in Chicago: Mayor William Hale Thompson's 1927 Campaign Against King George V.' *Illinois Quarterly* 39 (Summer 1977): 5–14.

——. 'The British Royal Visit of 1939 and the "Psychological Approach" to the United States.' *Diplomatic History* 2 (Spring 1978): 197–211.

——. 'British Diplomacy and the Silent Oracle of Vermont, 1923–1929,' *Vermont History* 50 (Spring 1982): 69–79.

——. 'Sir Ronald Lindsay and the British View from Washington, 1930–1939,' in Egan and Knott (eds), *Essays in Twentieth Century American Diplomatic History* (Washington, DC, 1982).

——. 'Harding v. Cox: The "Ohio" Election of 1920 as Viewed from the British Embassy at Washington.' *Northwest Ohio Quarterly* 55 (Winter 1982–83): 17–24.

——. 'British Diplomacy and the Congressional Circus, 1929–1939.' *South Atlantic Quarterly* 82 (Summer 1983): 300–13.

——. 'The Election of 1932 as Viewed from the British Embassy at Washington,' *Presidential Studies Quarterly* 13 (Summer 1983): 453–7.

Richards, David A. 'America Conquers Britain: Anglo-American Conflict in the Popular Media During the 1920s.' *Journal of American Culture* 3 (Spring 1980): 95–103.

Rippley, La Vern J. *The German-Americans.* Boston, 1976.

Roosevelt, Elliott. *As He Saw It.* New York, 1946.

Russett, Bruce. *Community and Contention: Britain and America in the Twentieth Century.* Cambridge, MA, 1963.

Ryan, Henry B. 'A New Look at Churchill's "Iron Curtain" Speech.' *Historical Journal* 22 (December 1979): 895–920.

Ryan, Henry Butterfield. *The Vision of Anglo-America: The US-UK Alliance and the Emerging Cold War, 1943–1946.* Cambridge, 1987.

Sbrega, John J. 'Anglo-American Relations and the Selection of

Mountbatten as Supreme Allied Commander, South East Asia.' *Military Affairs* 46 (October 1982): 139–45.

———. *Anglo-American Relations and Colonialism in East Asia, 1941–1945.* New York, 1983.

Schmidt, Karl M. *Henry A. Wallace: Quixotic Crusade, 1948.* Syracuse, NY, 1960.

Seabury, Paul. *The Waning of Southern 'Internationalism'.* Princeton, NJ, 1957.

Sherwin, Martin J. *A World Destroyed: The Atomic Bomb and the Grand Alliance.* New York, 1975.

Short, K.R.M. '"The White Cliffs of Dover": Promoting the Anglo-American Alliance in World War II.' *Historical Journal of Film, Radio, and Television* 2 (March 1982): 3–25.

Small, Melvin. *Democracy and Diplomacy: The Impact of Domestic Politics on U.S. Foreign Policy, 1789–1994.* Baltimore, 1996.

Smith, Anthony D. *Theories of Nationalism.* 2nd Edition. New York, 1983.

———. *The Ethnic Origins of Nations.* Oxford, 1986.

Smith, Charles. 'Lend-Lease to Great Britain, 1941–1945.' *Southern Quarterly* 10 (January 1972): 195–208.

Smith, Glenn H. *Langer of North Dakota: A Study in Isolationism, 1940–1949.* New York, 1979.

Spear, Percival. *A History of India.* Middlesex, 1965.

Spinelli, Lawrence. *Dry Diplomacy: The United States, Great Britain and Prohibition.* Wilmington, DE, 1989.

Sprout, Harold and Margaret. *Toward a New Order of Sea Power: American Naval Policy and the World Scene, 1918–1922.* Princeton, NJ, 1940.

Steele, Richard W. 'Franklin D. Roosevelt and His Foreign Policy Critics.' *Political Science Quarterly* 94 (Spring 1979): 15–32.

———. 'The Great Debate: Roosevelt, the Media, and the Coming of War, 1940–1941.' *Journal of American History* 71 (June 1984): 69–92.

Stenehjem, Michele Flynn. *An American First: John T. Flynn and the America First Committee.* New Rochelle, NY, 1976.

Stoler, Mark A. *The Politics of the Second Front: American Military Planning and Diplomacy in Coalition Warfare, 1941–1943.* Westport, CT, 1977.

———. 'The "Pacific-First" Alternative in American World War II Strategy.' *International History Review* 2 (July 1980): 432–52.

———. 'The United States: The Global Strategy,' in David Reynolds, Warren F. Kimball, and A. O. Chubarian (eds.), *Allies at War: The Soviet, American and British Experience, 1939–1945* (New York, 1994): 55–78.

Strout, Cushing. *The American Image of the Old World.* New York, 1963.

Thorne, Christopher. *The Limits of Foreign Policy: The West, the League and the Far Eastern Crisis of 1931–1933.* New York, 1972.

———. *Allies of a Kind: The United States, Britain and the war against Japan, 1941–1945.* New York, 1978.

Tull, Charles J. *Father Coughlin and the New Deal.* Syracuse, NY, 1965.

Van Dyke, Vernon, and Edward Lane Davis. 'Senator Taft and American Security.' *Journal of Politics* 14 (May 1952): 170–85.

Vieth, Jane Karoline. 'Munich and American Appeasement,' in David F. Schmitz and Richard D. Challener (eds), *Appeasement in Europe: A Reassessment of U.S. Policies* (New York, 1990): 51–74.

Villa, Brian Loring. 'The Atomic Bomb and the Normandy Invasion.' *Perspectives in American History* 11 (1978): 461–502.

Vinson, John Chalmers. *The Parchment Peace: The United States Senate and the Washington Conference, 1921–1922.* Athens, GA, 1955.

——. *William E. Borah and the Outlawry of War.* Athens, GA, 1957.

——. 'War Debts and Peace Legislation: The Johnson Act of 1934.' *Mid-America* 50 (July 1968): 206–22.

Waldrop, Frank C. *McCormick of Chicago: An unconventional portrait of a controversial figure.* Englewood Cliffs, NJ, 1966.

Walker, J. Samuel. *Henry A. Wallace and American Foreign Policy.* Westport, CT, 1976.

Watt, D. Cameron. *Succeeding John Bull: America in Britain's Place, 1900–1975.* Cambridge, 1984.

Weinberger, James M. 'The British on Borah: Foreign Office and Embassy Attitudes toward Idaho's Senior Senator, 1935–1940.' *Idaho Yesterdays* 25 (Fall 1981): 2–14.

Wendt, Lloyd, and Herman Kogan. *Big Bill of Chicago.* Indianapolis, IN, 1953.

Wheeler, Gerald E. *Prelude to Pearl Harbor: The United States Navy and the Far East, 1921–1931.* Columbia, MO.

Widenor, William C. *Henry Cabot Lodge and the Search for an American Foreign Policy.* Berkeley, CA, 1980.

Wilkins, Robert P. 'The Non-Ethnic Roots of North Dakota Isolationism.' *Nebraska History* 44 (September 1963): 205–21.

——. 'The Non-Partisan League and Upper Midwest Isolationism.' *Agricultural History* 39 (April 1965): 102–9.

Wilkins, Wynona H. 'Two If By Sea: William Langer's Private War Against Winston Churchill.' *North Dakota History* 41 (Spring 1974): 20–9.

Williams, J. E. 'The Joint Declaration on the colonies: an issue in Anglo-American relations, 1942–1944.' *British Journal of International Studies* 2 (1976): 267–92.

Witcover, Jules. *Sabotage at Black Tom: Imperial Germany's Secret War in America, 1914–1917.* Chapel Hill, NC, 1989.

Wittner, Lawrence S. 'American Policy Toward Greece during World War II.' *Diplomatic History* 3 (Spring 1979): 129–49.

Woods, Randall Bennett. *A Changing of the Guard: Anglo-American Relations, 1941–1946.* Chapel Hill, NC, 1990.

Young, Lowell T. 'Franklin D. Roosevelt and America's Islets.' *Historian* 35 (February 1973): 205–20.

Young, Roland. *Congressional Politics in the Second World War.* New York, 1956.

Index

Index 253